THE COURT OF FRANCE

IN THE SIXTEENTH CENTURY

VOLUME II.

The Court of France IN THE SIXTEENTH CENTURY. BY CATHERINE CHARLOTTE, LADY JACKSON

IN TWO VOLUMES
VOLUME II

WILDSIDE PRESS

Large Paper Edition

This edition is limited to one thousand copies, of which this is Number 139

CONTENTS OF VOL. II.

CHAPTER I.

The Court at Blois.—Thirty-six Years of Warfare.—Coronation of Queen Eleanor.—The Burgundian Heritage.—Woman Civilised France.—Eleanor's Mantle of State.—The Italian Carriages.—The Royal Procession.—The Queen's Public Entry.—A Long-standing Nuisance.—The Queen's State Reception.—The Wife and the Mistress.—Fans, Gloves, and High-heeled Shoes.—Denounced as a Heretic.—The Cordeliers of Orléans.—The Syndic of the Sorbonne.—Henri d' Albret.—The Heiress of Navarre 1

CHAPTER II.

The Protestant League.—The Heretics Defeat the Infidels.—Consternation at the Vatican.—The Tyranny of the Tiara.—The Dream of Francis's Life.—Seeking the Pope's Favour.—A Royal Marriage Annulled.—Marriage of Catherine de' Medici.—The Marriage Portion.—A Restless Mode of Life.—An Ambassador's Troubles.—Ever on the Move.—Scripture Quoted in Vain.—Would France Follow England?—Revolt of the Anabaptists.—The Prophet-King.—The Virgin of the Rue des Rosiers.—A Very Good Remedy.—Too Merciful.—Jacques Amyot.—Very Sound in the Faith.—Printing Prohibited.—A Set of Factious Rebels.—A Confession of Faith.—Calvin and Loyola.—The Society of Jesus . 18

CHAPTER III.

Death of Duprat.—A Privilege of Royalty.—Duprat's Lawful Heir.—An Interesting Fact.—The Purchase-money for the Tiara.—A Proof of Fidelity.—An Unforeseen Obstacle.—A New Holy War.—Freedom from War's Alarms.—Henri and Catherine.—Diane de Poitiers.—The Old King and His Mistress.—The Fall of Florence.—Infringing Court Etiquette.—The Mania for

Building. — Maître Roux. — The Mæcenas of France. — Expedition Against Tunis. — The Choice of Three Courses. — The Pope's Judgment Appealed to. — On Reflection. — A Modified Report Suggested. — War! . . 42

CHAPTER IV.

A War of Extermination. — The Stars in Their Courses. — A Propitious Date. — A Chivalric Example. — Unpatriotic Rebels. — Famine Looks Them in the Face. — A Fatal Game of Tennis. — Death of the Dauphin. — An Atrocious Decree and Its Victim. — A Daughter of the Medici. — Charles's Army in Full Retreat. — *Le Jeune Aventureux*. — Glory and Disaster. — A Change of Places at Court. — Diane and the Dauphiness. — The Intrigues of the Ladies. — James V. of Scotland. — Love at First Sight. — The Fair Madeleine. — A Flower Nipped in the Bud 63

CHAPTER V.

A Pleasant Change. — The Picturesque Turk. — Heart or Courage Fails Him. — Chivalric Souvenirs. — Summoned by the Sound of Trumpet. — The Merciless De Montmorency. — The Dauphin's First Command. — A Brilliant Feat of Arms. — Paul III. Desires Peace. — Conciliation of Differences. — "Once Again Your Prisoner." — The Reunion at Aigues-Mortes. — The Duchess and the Diamond. — The Victim of the Truce. — An Ardent Son of the Church. — A Project to Invade England. — His Righteous Soul Was Vexed. — The Mighty Constable. — Worshipping the Rising Star 81

CHAPTER VI.

The Good City of Ghent Revolts. — The Emperor's Difficulty. — Relieved from His Dilemma. — The Imperial Visitor. — Gracious Was His Mood. — An Imposing Cavalcade. — The Château de Chambord. — The Double Spiral Staircase. — "*Toute Femme Varie.*" — Charles's Entry into Paris. — A Very High Privilege. — Ambitious of Conquest. — A Silver Statue of Hercules. — "Now You Are My Prisoner." — The Courts of France and Madrid. — A Plot to Arrest the Emperor. — A Hint of a Very High Destiny. — When He Is at Leisure. — His Vengeance on His Birthplace. — Francis Enraged. — The Fall of an Enemy 98

CHAPTER VII.

Wider Becomes the Breach. — Improved in Health and Spirits. — Benvenuto Cellini. — Tramping the Country. — Now I Take My Leave of You. — Cellini's Pilgrimage. — Brought Back in Triumph. — Cellini an Abbot. — The Duchess's Hair-dresser. — The God of War, but No Venus. — The Gates of Fontainebleau. — Cellini Leaves France. — Expedition Against Algiers. — A Terrific Tempest. — Again the Storm Rages. — A Favourable Conjuncture 117

CHAPTER VIII.

A Formidable Host. — The Pope Reproves in Vain. — A False Rumour. — The Consequence of Delay. — The Rebels of La Rochelle. — Francis Shows Mercy. — A Satisfactory Conclusion. — Very Agreeable to God. — The Psalms of Marot. — The Inauguration of the Ruff. — A Marriage Annulled. — The Comte d'Enghien. — Blaise de Montluc. — "And Win We Will." — A Generous Offering. — The Victory of Cerisola. — The Hero and His Army Recalled. — The Siege of Montreuil. — Accused as a Traitress. — Marching on Paris. — Preparing to Defend the City. — The Treaty of Crépy. — French Pride Humiliated 131

CHAPTER IX.

A Pledge of Sincerity. — A Journey Heavenward. — Death of Martin Luther. — The Great French Fleet. — The Ship on Fire. — Cannonading the English. — The Baron Sinks the *Mary Rose*. — Powerful on the Ocean. — Death of the Duc d' Orléans. — Resentment towards His Heir. — An Eavesdropping Fool. — In a Furious Passion. — A Prayer for Pardon. — Étienne Dolet. — Vain Expectation. — "*Un Jeu de Mots*." — Weary of Warfare. — A Mass for Henry VIII. — The End Draws Nigh. — Beware of the Guises . 152

CHAPTER X.

Welcome News. — The King's Private Council. — Worshipping the Favourite. — François de Guise. — Henri II. — The Serious Business of Life. — In Swaddling Clothes. — Such is Our Good Pleasure. — Rapacious Favourites. — The Favourite's Favourite. — Cato, a Boudoir Knight. — The Double Funeral. — An Embarrassing Complaint. — A Peep into Purgatory. — The Tomb of Francis I. . . 170

CHAPTER XI.

Diane Takes the Helm. — The Queen and the Favourite. — Diane in Despair. — Catherine's Debts. — Reserved for Greater Deeds. — The *Procès* of Jean de Brosse. — A Guise to the Rescue! — Not Mercy, but Justice. — The Loss of a Triumph. — A Judicial Duel. — A Slanderous Report. — The Beau and the Athlete. — The *Coup de Jarnac.* — Anger and Resignation. — The Vanquished Foe. — A Crime to Be Expiated. — Excellent Servants of the Crown. — The Lady of Cental. — The Snares of the Heretics. — The Justice of Heaven 184

CHAPTER XII.

The Real Power in the State. — Summoning His Vassal. — Misty Visions of the Future. — Coronation of Henri II. — Insurrection in Angoumois. — The Common Cause of Guyenne. — A Wicked Gabeleur. — Festivity and Barbarity. — A Vain Appeal for Mercy. — "The Great Soldier." — A Striking Contrast. — Congenial Surroundings . 202

CHAPTER XIII.

A Delusive Dream Dispelled. — Marriage of Jeanne d'Albret. — The Ceremony at Moulins. — The Semi-royal Betrothal. — Marguerite's Last Years. — The Bride and Her Pages. — The Bride's Mother. — The Widow's Garb. — The King's Costume. — Antoine de Bourbon. — The Wedding Banquet and Ball. — La Balafré. — Ambroise Paré. — Journeying North. — An Excellent Bringing-up. — The King's Entry into Paris. — A Proof of His Orthodoxy. — The Wickedness of the Age 213

CHAPTER XIV.

The "Key of the Nation's Strong Box." — The New Coinage. — Too Many Counsellors. — Reform in Costume. — Ladies Exempted. — Henri II. a Reformer. — An Ungrateful People. — Defying the King's Decrees. — Catherine's Coronation. — The Court of Henri II. — The Heretical Tailor. — The Burning of the Heretic. — Death of Paul III. — Besieging Boulogne. — Public Entry into Boulogne. — Prince Débonnaire. — A Mass, a Ball, a Banquet . . 229

CHAPTER XV.

More Honours for the Guises. — Duc François de Guise. — Too Assiduously Attentive. — Claim of the Guises on

Naples. — The Council of Trent. — A Penitent Pope. — About to Meet His Conqueror. — Rejecting "The Interim." — Fears for His Soul's Salvation. — A Pact with the Lutherans. — Catherine Appointed Regent. — Catherine's Murmurings. — A Very Bold Champion. — Duke Maurice of Saxony. — Summoned to Innspruck. — A Declaration of War. — The Cap of Liberty. — The Fathers Take Flight. — The Capture of Metz. — A Perilous Position. — The Castle of Ehrenberg Taken. — Flight of the Emperor. — On the Banks of the Rhine. — The Treaty of Public Peace. — In Haste for Revenge. — A Terrible Disaster. — The "Courtoisie de Metz" 244

CHAPTER XVI.

Catherine's Indisposition. — The Rebuilding of Anet. — Diane's Boudoir Clock. — Bernard Palissy. — Chenonceaux and Chaumont. — Extremely Vexatious. — Progress of the Louvre, etc. — The Crescent Moon and Arrow. — Another Diane. — Premature Rejoicings. — Destruction of Terouenne. — Death of Maurice of Saxony. — Death of Edward VI. — An Offer of Marriage. — Worthily Celebrated. — Mary's Persecuting Zeal. — In the Event of Mary's Death. — An Apology for Mary's Cruelty. — No Decisive Results. — The Siege of Siena. — Starved into Surrender. — A New Model Republic 269

CHAPTER XVII.

Sumptuary Laws Disregarded. — Extravagance at Court. — Changes of Fashion in Dress. — Too Little Marital Vigilance. — A Severe Critic. — Fontainebleau in 1555. — Reading the Stars. — Mingled Emotions. — The Arrogant Paul IV. — De Montmorency Overruled. — Death of Joanna of Aragon. — Abdication of Charles V. — An Oversight of Early Years. — The Spains Resigned. — A Five-Years' Truce. — The Truce Is Broken. — The Soldier-Cardinal. — The Consecrated Sword. — A Pontiff of the Olden Time. — Philip's Pious Scruples. — Asking the Holy Father's Pardon. — A Humiliating Ceremony . . 288

CHAPTER XVIII.

Fortune's Favourites. — The Battle of St. Quentin. — Mary Declares War. — Philip's Transports of Joy. — Consternation in Paris. — Averting the Wrath of Heaven. — "Is my Son in Paris?" — The Guises Rule France. — Besieging Calais. — Surrender of Calais. — Hearty Enthusiasm.

— "The Chief Jewell of the Realme." — The Recovered Country. — Opposition Silenced. — The Scotch Refuse to Aid Henri. — Scotland Given to France. — Another Jewel in the Crown. — Mary's Regret for Calais. — The Great Scotch Marriage. — Interest on the Two Millions. — The Young Queen of Scotland 308

CHAPTER XIX.

Ready Again to Take the Field. — Sighing for His " Good Gossip." — Amicable Relations Renewed. — Unexpected Aid. — Contemplating Each Other. — A Terrible State of Things. — Not Quite Sound in the Faith. — Exceedingly Perplexed. — The King and the Heretic. — A Mutual Desire for Peace. — In Bondage to the Guises. — De Montmorency on Parole. — A Death-bed Reproach. — A Lamentable Ending. — Death of Mary of England. — Calais Must Be Given Up. — Mary Stuart Queen of England. — A Too Hasty Offer of Marriage. — Sparing England's Feelings. — The Unfortunate Peace. — Two Royal Marriages 327

CHAPTER XX.

Secret Reasons for the Peace. — A Crime to Be Punished — Heresy in the Parliament. — Reprimanding the President. — More Heterodox Than Orthodox. — A Great and Worthy Act. — A Strong Temptation. — D'Andelot Again a Prisoner. — The Counsellor Anne du Bourg. — The Counsellor Du Faur. — Arrest of Du Bourg and Du Faur. — Courtly Festivities. — Marriage of Madame Elisabeth. — Tilts and Tournaments. — The King's Promised Pleasure. — Yet One More Lance Must Be Broken. — A Mournful Wedding. — The Arm of the Lord. — Faithful unto Death 346

LIST OF ILLUSTRATIONS

VOL. II.

	PAGE
CATHERINE DE' MEDICI	*Frontispiece*
ANNE BOLEYN	24
PALACE OF FONTAINEBLEAU	106
CHARLES V.	148
FRANCIS I.	170
ANNE DE MONTMORENCY	210
QUEEN MARY OF ENGLAND	282
HENRI II.	344

THE COURT OF FRANCE

IN THE SIXTEENTH CENTURY

1514—1559

CHAPTER I.

The Court at Blois.—Thirty-six years of Warfare.—Coronation of Queen Eleanor.—The Burgundian Heritage.—Woman Civilised France.—Eleanor's Mantle of State.—The Italian Carriages.—The Royal Procession.—The Queen's Public Entry.—A Long-standing Nuisance.—The Queen's State Reception.—The Wife and the Mistress.—Fans, Gloves, and High-heeled Shoes.—Denounced as a Heretic.—The Cordeliers of Orléans.—The Syndic of the Sorbonne.—Henri d' Albret.—The Heiress of Navarre.

FRANCIS and his court were at Blois, and even gayer than usual — no war being on hand to interfere with their pleasures. He, however, had not yet thought fit, or may have not deemed it prudent, that his good people of Paris should see their new queen. She was the sister of his fortunate rival,— with the public, in itself, a disadvantage; the seal, too, and plèdge of a humiliating peace,—a peace which individually and collectively the French keenly felt to be a national disgrace. Doubtless Francis was also not wholly insensible to the fact of his diminished *prestige* in Europe as a consequence of it.

It was known that he was not quite resigned to the loss of "his heritage,"—that illusory claim of which France was the victim,— or to being so completely, as he now was, thrust out of Italy; *triste* result of thirty-six years of warfare;[*] of the expenditure of many millions of livres, and the sacrifice of tens of thousands of *livres*. No; Francis yet looked to be amply avenged.

Meanwhile, the soothing influence of time—no very long time, certainly (a twelvemonth)—had had its customary effect on exasperated feeling, and a grand state pageant in preparation seemed likely to raise the spirits of the Parisian people to that state of happy enthusiasm, or at least temporary forgetfulness of trouble, with which they ever were wont to greet public festivities.

Queen Eleanor was shortly to be crowned at St. Denis with wondrous pomp. Her marriage had been so private an affair that the splendour of the coronation was probably intended to atone for the absence of courtly ceremonial when the

---

[*] From the first invasion of Naples by Charles VIII. to the renunciation of all claims on Italy by Francis I., as stipulated by the Treaty of Cambrey.

former event took place. However, the people were now to have their part in the rejoicings, and those who cared for, and the many who needed, bread and wine — for, as was too frequently the case in those days, there was famine in the land — were to be regaled without stint.

The ceremony took place on the 5th of March. The solemn interior grandeur of the old abbey, as was usual on occasions of great rejoicing, was concealed from end to end by the festive hangings and velvet draperies of blue and gold. All the honours of the day were especially reserved for Queen Eleanor, the king attending in her retinue as first chevalier, the Queen of Navarre as first lady of honour.

This latter arrangement appears to have been an oversight of the grand master of the ceremonies. It was commented upon as suggestive of Navarre doing homage to Spain as its suzerain. So keenly sensitive and resentful was the public mind of any appearance of undue deference to the emperor, that it was ingeniously detected in this act of courtesy of the king's sister towards her brother's bride.

So much had been reported in disparagement of the emperor's personal appearance — "his greedy eyes, his projecting crocodile jaw, his inferior physique," as compared with those two stalwart royal Adonises, Henry of England and the King of France — that considerable curiosity was evinced by persons who were not of the court, to know whether Eleanor resembled her brother. Nature had indeed been niggardly towards Charles V. Of the four children of Joanna of Aragon and the Archduke Philip, surnamed "le Beau," he had the smallest claim to good looks; while that part of "his Burgundian heritage" he would probably have least coveted, the ugly projecting mouth of the House of Burgundy, was most conspicuous in him.

His brother Ferdinand bore a greater resemblance to his handsome father — who had nearly escaped this distinctive mark of his maternal Burgundian descent; and the two daughters, if not beauties, were not altogether without personal attractions. Eleanor had a rather pleasing countenance and a dignified carriage. Brought up at the dull, ceremonious Court of Spain, and married very early into the no less frigid and formal one of Portugal, it is not surprising that the fascinating *belles* of the Court of Francis I. should have pronounced her far too stiffly starched, and her cold, unbending stateliness not only unprepossessing, but chilling.

Yet etiquette and the most punctilious politeness were the rule of the French Court; doubtless covering a multitude of sins. But the genial character of the nation was evident in it, contrasting favourably with the haughty courtesy of the sombre Spaniard. France was then beginning to pique herself on being at the head of the nations in the superlativeness of her politeness. "Woman," says Michelet, "civilised France;" and from the time that woman took a prominent place at the French Court, and received from the lordly sex the honour and homage so justly her due, politeness naturally took root there. Thence it spread to the several classes of the community, descending to the general public, until, at the period in question, a want of courtesy was a punishable offence. "Politeness," says Paul Lacroix, "was the order of the day, and fines were imposed for incivility." *

But Queen Eleanor has arrived at St. Denis. She is arrayed in all the splendour of royal robes, and almost literally covered with jewels, exciting the admiration and envy of all the ladies and not a few of the gentlemen; for none could vie with her in this respect.† The crown jewels of France of course belonged to the *maîtresse-en-titre* for the time being, and were worn by Madame la

---

* "Vie Privée des Français XVIème Siècle."

† Many French ladies had valuable jewels; but diamonds were still but little worn. They were considered "dull stones," until towards the end of the fifteenth century, when Berghem, a jeweller of Bruges, discovered a method of cutting and polishing them, and bringing out all their fire and brilliancy. But even then, as his method entailed a loss of weight and size, besides much expense, many fine stones were long worn untouched by the new process. Eleanor's treasures from Golconda had evidently passed through the hands of the Flemish diamond-polisher.

Duchesse. But they appear to have been few in number, and comparatively of small value at that period; otherwise Francis, who was constantly in such pressing need, would not have scrupled to appropriate them.

Eleanor's jewels were her own private property, the gifts, almost wholly, of her first husband, Don Manuel, in whose reign the riches of the East were poured into Portugal, as into Spain, the wealth of the West.

Her dress of Venetian gold brocade was ornamented with a stomacher and tablier of diamond-work. The sleeves of gold tissue were similarly bordered, and looped up with bouquets of diamonds. Her violet velvet mantle of state was embroidered with *fleurs-de-lys* in seed-pearls, and bordered with jewels arranged in a sort of mosaic, rubies, emeralds, diamonds, etc.; the royal miniver, used as an inside facing, appearing only beyond the jewels as a narrow outer edge. A band of jewels with pendants of the same glittering gems encircled her throat. Her low, crown-shaped hat, or toque, was studded with the same costly gems, and edged with a string of alternate pearls and diamonds. It had also an aigrette of diamonds, and was placed rather jauntily, a little inclining towards the left side of the head.

The queen arrived in her carriage (*carrosse*)— the newest importation from Italy, for it was not till 1530 that carriages were used in France, and, at first, for the queen only. Others were now preparing. That intended for the favourite should have been ready for the coronation. Alas! it was not, and greatly irritated were both the monarch and the lady when the customary litter made its appearance instead of the carriage. These vehicles were round in form, had four wheels, were suspended by leathern straps, and drawn by two or four gaily caparisoned horses or mules. They were also curtained, cushioned, and carpeted, and contained seats for two persons only.*

The second seat in Queen Eleanor's carriage was occupied by the Queen of Navarre, who, if not so heavily laden with jewels, probably surpassed her sister queen in elegance. Her dress was of rich satin brocade of a deep lake or crimson colour (*laque-foncée*), long and training, open in front, showing the under dress of crimson and gold damask, hanging Venetian sleeves and square-cut bodice bordered with minever, jewelled cor-

* As they became more generally used their size was gradually increased, until found to be an intolerable nuisance in the narrow streets of Paris. Carriages so unwieldy in size were then prohibited except to travellers. But the boon was not great, for, owing to the terrible condition of the streets of the capital, these monster vehicles, swaying heavily from side to side, were continually being upset. The litters were not superseded by the carriages until very long after. Their motion was easier, less like the rolling of a ship in a heavy sea. But, whether in carriage or litter, the pedestrian in the streets of Paris could generally proceed at a quicker rate than the occupants of either. (Paul Lacroix.)

delière, and black and gold coiffe (afterwards called the Mary Stuart cap) edged with pearls, and with veil of gold tissue; mantle of crimson velvet bordered with minever.

When the royal ladies alighted, their long and heavy mantles of state were borne each by four pages of honour, the same number of ladies of honour following. Then came the ladies of the court; after them, Francis and his sons and attendant chevaliers, great officers of the household. The bishops and the Archbishop of Paris in gala vestments were there to receive them, and priests chanted the Magnificat as the procession moved slowly up the nave. The ceremony was the same in all respects as at the coronation of Queen Claude in 1517, followed by a similar harangue and the archbishop's benediction.

A few days after, Eleanor made her public entry into Paris with great *éclat*. The splendour of her dress and the glitter of her jewels appear to have astonished the people, though rich attire was no novel spectacle to them in those days of frequent state pageants and processions.* The

* It must have been on the occasion of her entry into Paris that Queen Eleanor wore those remarkable diamond earrings which "The Bourgeois" tells us were as large as walnuts. He says Bordeaux in his journal, but this may have been an error from haste or negligence, as it does not appear that he was at Bordeaux, though there is no doubt of his having seen her on her entry into Paris. Sometimes he forgets to date his entries, which is confusing.

new carriage, preceding the ladies on their ambling mules, was an attractive novelty. The young princes — the ransomed hostages — also excited much attention, and were received with great demonstrations of approval and favour.

The same unvaried round of festive pleasures followed the above event. Jousts and tiltings, banquets and balls, Te Deums, masques and illuminations, made, for awhile, old Paris and its inhabitants gay and happy. The visits of the court to the capital were always brief, the Palais des Tournelles being scarcely habitable, at any period of the year, beyond a few days. But royalty fled from it, abandoned it altogether when the misery of those frequent famines was succeeded by the plague, or the epidemic, so called, and mowed down the people by hundreds.

The command of the despotic "chevalier king" had availed as little as the request of the "Father of the people" to induce the municipality to remove, or even to cover up effectually, the loathsome sewer that still slowly wound its lingering course beneath the palace windows. Just as seventeen years before it offended both sight and smell when Louis XII., believing that the evil would be remedied during his absence, brought his young English bride to Paris, so it remained when the Spanish wife of Francis I. made her entry into the capital — having slain its thousands in the interval. Plans for the effectual removal of this terrible nuisance had many times been submitted to the king. But like the plans for building the College of France, no money could be spared for carrying them out during his reign.

Yet, in the course of the year 1531, the large sum hoarded by his mother came into his hands — an unexpected windfall. The debt, also, of Charles V. — for money advanced to him by Henry VIII., and which, by the treaty of Cambray, Francis had undertaken to pay — was wholly remitted by Henry. (By this act of apparent generosity he sought to secure the French king's support of his appeal to the universities of Europe for their opinion of his application to the Court of Rome for a divorce from Katharine — a course recommended by Cranmer.) But Francis, when he had any money, had other uses for it than the building of colleges, or improving the condition of pestiferous palaces.

Queen Eleanor, however, while at Des Tournelles, held there the formal state reception in the grand hall of St. Louis, which, from the time of Anne of Brittany, was the custom of the queens of France after their coronation. Then the foreign ambassadors, the great officers of the state and the household, and the ladies of the court were presented. Francis was present, but took no part in the ceremony. "He was seated at the further end of the hall, engaged in conversation with Madame d' Étampes, who was waiting to be presented.

When her turn came, she advanced with the air of an empress. The queen haughtily averted her head, and made some remark to Marguerite, who sat beside her, leaving the duchess, to whom she did not present her hand, to retire, much mortified and humiliated."

It was observed that the king, who looked on at a distance, viewed this little scene between the wife and the mistress with evident displeasure; and that he was careful, by his marked attentions to the latter, to let all present clearly understand that the duchess had lost by this treatment none of her favour with him. It is probable that it made no difference whatever in his relations with Eleanor. He behaved towards her as he had done towards her more youthful predecessor — with the utmost respect as the lady who presided at his court, but as a wife, with polite indifference; and Eleanor may have neither expected nor desired more from her political union with a man whose life was a continued course of depravity.

It is very likely that she returned him indifference for indifference, though she may not have chosen to countenance his mistress. But she soon became reconciled, if not so already, to the customs and manners of the French Court, so far as to tolerate the supremacy of Madame la Duchesse without any show of pique. The duchess had greatly the advantage of her in liveliness and *esprit*, as well as in education and talent; for Eleanor was not a learned lady. No Latinist, like Marguerite and the duchess — not even, as so many were, a poetess or rhymer.

She was exceedingly fond of dress, always appearing in great splendour on grand state occasions. Her chief influence was on the fashions, which, until her arrival, had undergone little change since the preceding reign. Slashed and puffed sleeves, called "*à l' espagnole*," were introduced by her; splendidly jewelled fans and embroidered Spanish gloves, rivalling those of Italy; also very high-heeled shoes with pointed toes. These, "giving height and dignity," as was at first supposed, were very generally adopted. But their reign was short; for although they added two or three inches to the height, they deprived the wearer of dignity and grace, rather than imparted them, when attempting to walk, besides torturing the foot out of its natural shape.

Sometimes she wore the national Spanish costume. But the court did not in that respect closely follow the queen. The duchess entirely refrained from doing so; "she would not awaken unpleasant memories in the king's mind, if the queen was so ill-advised as to do so." Her fancy, however, for wearing a hat with a plume, and bordered with feathers like that habitually worn by the king, was generally favoured by ladies when they rode abroad on their mules.

The friendship of Marguerite was doubtless a

great solace to Eleanor, especially in the first years of her transplantation from the sober Court of Charles V. at Madrid, where her stepdaughter reigned as queen, to the profligate one of Francis I. and his mistresses; though in their religious views there could have been little sympathy between them.

Eleanor was a rigid Catholic, while Marguerite, in her new home, had sheltered many who were suspected of a leaning towards "the new heresy." She had been denounced as a heretic herself in the sermons of fanatic monks. Her secret efforts, they said, to make her brother apostatise had been baffled only by his friend and her sworn enemy, the Maréchal Anne de Montmorency. "Why, then, was not this heretic sister of the king sewn up in a sack and thrown into the Seine?"

Marguerite's collection of religious poems, called "*Le Miroir de l'Âme pécheresse*," was published at about that time. It was condemned by the Sorbonne at the instance of their syndic. The furious, persecuting Béda — or Bedeus, according to the then prevalent custom of Latinising names — also prevailed on the principal of the College of Navarre to allow the students to perform an allegorical play (*moralité*) in which Marguerite figured as a woman leaving her spinning-wheel to accept from the hand of a Fury the Gospel translated into French.

Francis was then in Provence. When he returned, and was informed of the insults offered to his sister, he ordered the arrest of the principal of the college and his student actors. The censure of the Sorbonne was rejected by the doctors of the university, assembled by the rector, Nicolas Cop, for that purpose; he being rather in fear himself of the probable consequences of having preached on All Saints' Day a sermon written by Calvin — then a young man of twenty-four — who had just arrived in Paris from Orléans and Bourges, having given up the study of the law for theology.

The Cordelier monks denounced the rector to the Parliament as a preacher of the Lutheran heresy.* The greater part of the doctors of the university were prepared to defend their rector. He, however, neither caring to submit his opinions to

---

* The Cordeliers of Orléans had lately been accused themselves before the Parliament of that province of a sort of spirit-rapping fraud. The Provost of Orléans had recently lost his wife, who had died without leaving a legacy to the Cordeliers, who gave out that, in consequence of this omission, the soul of the deceased woman was suffering great torments in the other world, and further that she nightly wandered through their church wailing and lamenting her crime. Exorcism became necessary, and a young novice was chosen to represent the troubled spirit — replying to the questions put respecting the cause of her torment by rappings under the floor. The provost was unbelieving. He accused the monks of fraud, which, being proved, the Parliament sentenced them to imprisonment, and to a public avowal of the deception practised. But means were found to enable them to evade the public confession, and, probably, imprisonment also.

the consideration of a set of fanatics, nor to undergo imprisonment or burning at the stake at their decree, fled to Bâsle, then the headquarters of the emigrant French reformers. Calvin left Paris at the same time, but retired only to Saintonge. Finding that he could not remain there undisturbed, he rejoined his friend Cop at Bâsle. (Henri Martin.)

As for the restless persecutor Béda, as he began indirectly again to attack the Queen of Navarre, by qualifying as heresy the preaching of her almoner, Gerard Roussel, the king, who keenly resented the continual interruption of his pleasures by the denunciatory zeal of this ardent syndic of the Sorbonne, privately secured his dismissal from his office, and arrest for sedition. The Parliament condemned him, on retracting his accusation, to imprisonment for life at Mont St. Michel, where four years after he died.

Francis was then constantly wavering between toleration and persecution. To the former he was urged both by his sister and the Duchesse d'Étampes — to the latter by the counsels of the ferociously cruel Anne de Montmorency. He knew that Marguerite was considered "tainted with heresy," and that amongst the men of wit and learning, the scholars, poets, musicians, and painters who filled her *salons* at Bearn, many of those most graciously and royally received were far from being "sound in the faith."

Henri d'Albret, indeed, was believed to be a true son of the Church. He had not left his wife in doubt as to his dislike both of the doctrines and the person of the reformers, but had reproached her insultingly for her encouragement of them, and is said to have even raised his hand against her — the presence of Francis being necessary for her protection. Yet, when pressed to leave him, she refused "so greatly to fail in wifely duty." Henri appears to have been much struck by this reply. So marked, indeed, was its effect on him, that, although he may not at any time have been an ardent reformer, he afterwards took part approvingly in the religious services held in one of the vaults of the Château de Pau. From approving his wife's sentiments he had been brought to consider that the doctrines which suggested them must be good also.

But Francis thought it unsafe to trust Marguerite with the bringing up of her own daughter — Jeanne d'Albret, born at Fontainebleau in 1529, and who was now heiress-presumptive of the little kingdom of Navarre, Marguerite's son, born in 1531, having died in infancy. He therefore adopted the future Huguenot mother of Henri IV. in order to acquire such right in the direction of her education as would ensure her not being led astray from the true faith, of which he was himself so bright an ornament. The appointment of her lady of honour, her governess, or her preceptor, was therefore subject to his approval. Francis sought to separate the child from her mother at as early an age as possible, and to have her brought up at the gloomy old Château of Plessis les Tours. But Jeanne from her earliest years seems to have been devotedly fond of her mother; and, when taken from her, so pined away that Marguerite was summoned in all haste to save her daughter's life.

CHAPTER II.

The Protestant League. — The Heretics Defeat the Infidels. — Consternation at the Vatican. — The Tyranny of the Tiara. — The Dream of Francis's Life. — Seeking the Pope's Favour. — A Royal Marriage Annulled. — Marriage of Catherine de' Medici. — The Marriage Portion. — A Restless Mode of Life. — An Ambassador's Troubles. — Ever on the Move. — Scripture Quoted in Vain. — Would France Follow England? — Revolt of the Anabaptists. — The Prophet-King. — The Virgin of the Rue des Rosiers. — A Very Good Remedy. — Too Merciful. — Jacques Amyot. — Very Sound in the Faith. — Printing Prohibited. — A Set of Factious Rebels. A Confession of Faith. — Calvin and Loyola. — The Society of Jesus.

WHILE Francis, freed from the anxieties of war, returned with new zest to his pleasures, the emperor once more engaged in a vain contention with the Lutheran princes and Free States of Germany. To the Catholic League of Augsburg, which menaced them with persecution, they now opposed the Protestant League of Smalkalde — declaring their determination to resist by force of arms any attempt to interfere with their rights and liberties.

Henry VIII., greatly desirous of embarrassing both emperor and Pope, urged Francis I. to join him in this league with the German princes for the defence of their liberties. Rather unwillingly — for he could not with any consistency defend abroad the heresy he persecuted at home — Francis was prevailed on by his impetuous English ally and the representations of the agents of the princes, that "in all ancient treaties between France and the empire the French kings were considered the born defenders of the Germanic liberties," to sign this defensive treaty.

Fortunately, Francis was not called upon to fulfil this engagement, which, as was usual with him, he would doubtless have found a reason for evading, for Charles was compelled to yield to the heretics in order to defeat the infidels. Having driven the Austrians out of Hungary, Solyman II. was preparing for further conquests with a numerous army, to which the comparatively small force at the emperor's disposal could oppose very slight resistance. Money, of course, was wanting to raise an efficient army of mercenaries. Time, too, was pressing. But the Germanic States, if they chose, could release him from this dilemma.

The prudently politic emperor therefore signed at Nuremburg, on the 23d of July, a treaty — confirmed in the following month at the Diet of Ratisbon — according to the Protestant States "the continued free exercise of their religion until a council could be assembled to discuss the matter, or other means be determined on for appeasing the religious differences." This great victory, as it was considered, for the Lutherans, filled the Papal Court with consternation. But Charles was enabled by it to take the field against Solyman with an army 200,000 strong, to effectually repulse him, and to save Austria.

Francis was supposed to have sympathised but little with Eleanor in the satisfaction she expressed at her brother's release from the very critical position in which he was placed. He blamed him for making any terms with the Lutherans, oblivious, it would seem, that he was engaged by treaty, if necessary, to defend them. He is even said to have felt disappointment at being thus prevented from taking advantage of the troubles, political and religious, which then beset the emperor, and again to invade Italy.

He, however, did what was more advantageous both for himself and for France. He assembled at Vannes the States of Britanny, and with their full consent — the Bretons retaining their ancient rights and privileges — the duchy was declared to be an integral part of France. The union with that kingdom had hitherto rested only on the marriage contract of Anne of Brittany and the testament of Queen Claude, without the sanction of the Bretons and the constituted authorities.

The conduct of the three most powerful monarchs of Europe had latterly caused much uneasiness at Rome. The schism in England, and Henry's assumption of the title of supreme head of the

Anglican Church; the suspected alliance of France with the Turk; and lastly, the act of that zealous son of the Church, the emperor, in compounding with the heretics, naturally excited extreme anxiety and alarm at the Vatican. Further suspicion of mischief brewing was aroused by Francis, on leaving Brittany, proceeding at once to Boulogne, where Henry arrived soon after, to confer with him on the expediency, as it was given out, of forming a league to check the Sultan's inroads on Europe.

Henry's real motive — for it was he who sought the interview — "was to persuade the King of France to follow the example of the King of England, and free his crown from the tyranny of the Tiara" (H. Martin). Francis might indeed have been tempted to do so. The abolition of all uninvited interference of the "Bishop of Rome" in the internal affairs of his kingdom, the unreserved disposal of ecclesiastical property, the consummation of monarchical unity, made up a flattering picture for mental contemplation. But in opposition to it there was the dream of Francis's life, which even yet — even more than ever — he hoped to see realised — the possession of "his ultramontane heritage." Without the Pope's aid this dream of his life must prove but an empty vision. This chained him to the Vatican. But in no case, probably, would he have had the resolution to follow in the steps of his more energetic "royal brother."

The rupture between Henry and the Pope might then have been regarded as absolute; yet Francis made a feeble effort to lure back this erring son of the Church to the fold of the faithful; knowing that the welcome of the holy Father would be as warm as that vouchsafed to the returning and repentant prodigal son of the Gospel.

An interview between Francis I. and Clement VII. was shortly to take place, when the latter had decided on the spot most convenient for him, out of Italy, to meet the king. To induce Henry VIII. to be present at their conference, Francis promised to lead the Pope to give up his support of Katharine, despite the emperor's charge not to sacrifice her to Henry's ill-governed passions. Ultimately he was prevailed on to promise that, if unable to be present at this interview in person, he would at least send a representative; and further, Francis wrung from him a vague sort of engagement that in the interval "he would do nothing to render a reconciliation with his holiness impossible."

Both Francis I. and Charles V. were most anxious for the Pope's alliance. The latter, that he might count on his aid to keep the French out of Italy; the former, that he might help him to recover his lost possessions in it. To succeed in his object Charles had been so rigourous towards the Florentines, so determined to reimpose on them the hated despotism of the Medici; while further to flatter and, as he thought, honour Clement, he promised Alessandro de' Medici — the Pope's nephew or son — who was to reign in Florence, the hand of his illegitimate daughter, then a mere child.

Francis, however, determined to make a higher bid for the Pope's favour. As a French historian terms it, "he so abased the pride of the Capets as to offer the hand of his second son, Henry, Duc d'Orléans, to the great-granddaughter of a Florentine banker — to Clement's niece, in fact, Catherine de' Medici." And Clement really did consider himself and family much more honoured by an alliance with a legitimate scion of the royal House of France than with the natural daughter of Charles V. and a Flemish actress.

It was in consequence of this projected marriage that Francis believed his influence with the Pope to be paramount, and that he could venture to promise Henry VIII. that at his solicitation Clement would be favourable to his views respecting the divorce, and willing to forget the rebelliousness of his conduct towards him. But Henry, who had waited five years for the Pope's promised dispensation, soon after his return from Boulogne secretly married Anne Boleyn, having had his former marriage annulled by Cranmer, Archbishop of Canterbury.

At Easter, 1533, their marriage was publicly announced. In June, Anne was crowned; and in

September following her daughter Elizabeth was born. Of course the Pope annulled their marriage, Cranmer being invested with no power to declare Henry's previous one invalid. In terms as little irritating as possible, Henry and Anne were informed that they must separate, or sentence of excommunication would be passed on them. It was, however, added for their consolation, that their separation was to be provisional only, pending further investigation respecting Katharine's first marriage.

The Pope fancied that this cautiously worded decree — condemning while giving hope of a favourable result — would bring back Henry, and that ultimately some satisfactory compromise might be arrived at.

Buoyed up with the hope that England and the Defender of the Faith might even yet pause ere they threw off the shackles of Rome, Clement, accompanied by his niece, and escorted by the galleys of France, set out for Marseilles, where he had appointed to meet the king.

So incredulous was the emperor of any serious intention on the part of the King of France to take a wife for his son from the daughters of the Medici family; so certain that he would not condescend to sanction, much less propose such a misalliance, that he refrained, until it was too late, from taking such measures as it appears he might and would have done to prevent it. He,

Anne Boleyn.
Photo-etching from painting by Holbein.

perhaps, thought it derogatory to his sister to be even thus slightly brought into connection with the Medici. Otherwise he perfectly knew that with kings and popes, as he was himself an instance, the variations of external policy had more influence than family ties.

The Pope and his niece arrived at Marseilles towards the middle of October, and were received by Francis with every mark of distinction. On the 28th, the marriage of Henry d' Orléans — a fine, well-grown, handsome youth in his fifteenth year—and Catherine de' Medici—a short, thickset girl, two years his junior, with a large head, a round flat face, and restless eyes (Mèzeray) — took place almost privately, Clement VII. performing the ceremony.

Catherine was an orphan. Her father, Lorenzo de' Medici, titular Duke of Urbino, and her mother, a French lady of the family of Tour d'Auvergne, both died — poisoned, it was supposed — soon after her birth. Though but thirteen, "she was already very subtle-minded, reserved, full of ambition and artifice." Her dowry was small — not more, it was computed, than 200,000 silver crowns in money and lands. But Clement held out hopes, though he would bind himself by no formal promise, that Urbino, Parma, and Modena might probably, at some period in the uncertain future, be ceded to the young prince.

At the same time it was whispered to Francis,

not by the Pope — he artfully eluded all engagements, that he might return with a clear conscience to the emperor — but by those supposed to be in his confidence, that this alliance would put France into possession of "three gems of inestimable value;" in other words, would extend her dominion over Genoa, Milan and Naples. In return for these expected concessions — to which, though always deceived and always deceiving, Francis seemed confidently to look forward — he undertook to vigourously suppress heresy in France, and, if possible, to extirpate it.

The Venetian ambassador, Marino Giustiniani, who with other foreign envoys accompanied Francis to Marseilles, when some time after making his report to the Doge of Venice, refers to the marriage as displeasing to the French nation. The Pope, it was considered, in order to accomplish it, had deceived the king — with reference, of course, to his cherished views on Italy. He adds, however, that "Catherine was very submissive to the king — very quiet, very reserved."

Complaining of the expensiveness of his embassy, Giustiniani gives some curious particulars of the French king's restless mode of life. "During the forty-five months of my embassy," he says, "I was almost always travelling. Soon after my arrival in Paris, the king set out for Marseilles. We passed through the Bourbonnais, Lyonnais, Auvergne, and Languedoc, arriving in Provence at the hottest time of the year. It was then ascertained that the long-deferred visit of the Pope, which it was supposed would take place in summer, was again delayed until October or November.

"The ambassadors, who had provided themselves with summer clothing only, were, therefore, obliged to obtain a supply for the winter, having in consequence to pay for our furs half as much more than they were worth. During this journey I lost a horse and a mule. From Marseilles we went, *via* Provence, Dauphiny, the Lyonnais, Burgundy, and Champagne, to Lorraine, where the king had a private conference with the Landgrave of Hesse, and thence returned to Paris.

"I assure your serenity that this journey, occupying a whole year, cost me 600 crowns more than the salary I received from the states. Every one in fact was drawing bills on Venice, and the discount was raised to ten per cent. Pope Clement alone drew bills for 40,000 crowns.

"On my return to Paris I lost eleven horses and all their harness, owing to a fire that occurred in the stables. Only a mule was saved."

The king had scarcely arrived in Paris when he was off again on another expedition; and Giustiniani had to buy ten horses at any price that was asked for them, horses being in great demand, "the king having convoked the '*arrière ban*' to pass them in review, armed and on horseback;

his own retinue being so numerous that three thousand horses were required for them." No remittances arriving from Venice, the ambassador informs the Doge that, to meet this expense, he was compelled to sell part of his silver plate.

"Never," he adds, "during the entire period of my embassy, did the court remain a whole fortnight at the same place, but was ever on the move; first to Lorraine or to Poitou; then to various places in Belgium; then to Normandy; to the Isle of France; back again to Normandy, Picardy, Champagne or Burgundy, and so on. Of course these continual journeyings occasioned much outlay of money; and not I only" — complains the ambassador, "who, as every one knows, am but a poor gentleman, was inconvenienced by this lavish expenditure, but even the richest of the nobility."

He concludes his statement by begging that his serenity will confer on him some mark of his and the states' satisfaction with his services. They reimbursed him, it may be hoped, for all this extra expense; for, according to his account of the terrible condition of the roads, travelling, except by one or two royal (paved) roads, was rather a penance than a pleasure.

While the Pope and the bridal party were still at Marseilles, two envoys arrived from England to inform his holiness that the king proposed, at the next council, to appeal against his decree.

When Clement returned to Italy, Francis so far kept his word that he sent the Bishop of Paris, Jean du Bellay — who was accompanied by Rabelais as his medical attendant — to Rome to interpose and quote Scripture on Henry's behalf. But in spite of his newly acquired claim on the pontiff, the influence of the emperor in the Sacred College far outweighed that of the King of France. In full consistory, Henry's first marriage was pronounced good and valid. This was considered definite; and Henry was therefore peremptorily ordered, with the Pope's sanction (23d of March, 1534), again to receive Katharine, his lawful wife.

Before the month was out, priest-ridden England was emancipated from the humiliating bondage of the Church of Rome; and the Act by which the clergy recognised the sovereign as the head of the Anglican Church was confirmed by both Houses of Parliament as a fundamental law of the kingdom.

This event had a startling effect on the whole of Christendom. On Rome it fell like a thunderclap, though Henry's previous acts might well have prepared both Pope and cardinals for it. A large part of Europe, half of Germany and Switzerland, at least, Sweden and Denmark, and now England, with Scotland likely to follow, had been lost to Rome during the pontificate of Clement VII. It profoundly affected him; for all that he had done to crush reform had but imparted new vigour to it.

The anxious eyes of Europe were now fixed on France. Would she follow England? The time had arrived to settle the question of acceptance or rejection of reform. In their terror of what might happen, the clergy assembled and at once granted a contribution which Francis for two years past had vainly claimed from them — the Pope even authorising a larger grant than the king had named, which was immediately sent to him.

It is not surprising, then, that such a man should under such circumstances have hesitated to break with Rome, and at a time, too, when by papal influence he hoped to regain his footing in Italy.

Francis, indeed, knew not how to render himself and his kingdom independent. So the decisive moment for doing so was allowed to pass away, and France neither became Protestant nor constant in her adherence to Rome; she fluctuated, as it suited the caprice or good pleasure of her sovereign, between partial tolerance and atrocious persecution.

Six months after Henry VIII. had finally thrown off all allegiance to the Holy See, Clement VII. died. With him vanished all the brilliant hopes for which Francis I. had condescended to seek an alliance for his son with a daughter of the Medici — that fatal marriage with Catherine, destined to bring incalculable misery on France — years of religious strife, the horrors of civil war, persecution, and every species of crime.

But the scenes of horror and bloodshed, of which France was so long the theatre during the reign of Catherine and her sons, were preceded at intervals by persecution and cruelty, no less revolting, under that of their predecessors, Francis I. and Henri II.

The enemies of reform, at the time of the king's return from Marseilles, availed themselves of a revolt of the Anabaptists of Germany in order to inflame his persecuting zeal against the French Protestants, whom it was sought to confound with the Anabaptists. Those fanatics had joined in the Peasants' War of 1525 — burning and destroying, robbing and murdering in the towns and villages through which they passed on their way to Lorraine. They now rose in arms, attacked and took the city of Münster in Westphalia, proposing to make it the capital of a new kingdom — "New Israel" — under the "prophet-king," John of Leyden (a tailor of that city, named Jean Bokholt), who began his reign by establishing polygamy and community of property.

The German princes, Catholic and Protestant, united their forces to put down this rebellion, which for some time defied all their efforts, and was only quelled after much bloodshed, the capture and execution of the "prophet-king," and the imprisonment and punishment of the ringleaders of the revolt.

Unhappily this event served as a prelude to sad

atrocities in France. A bundle of papers, printed in Switzerland, inveighing in strong terms against the doctrine of the real presence in the Eucharist, was forwarded to Paris for dissemination, it appears, among the people. Some reformers, with more temerity than prudence, affixed a certain number of them on the Hôtel de Ville and other public buildings.

A chorister of the royal chapel of the Château de Blois contrived to fasten one on the door of the king's apartment. When discovered and handed to the king, his majesty gave way to one of those explosions of wrath in which he occasionally indulged, resembling the rage of an infuriated bull. His favourite, Anne de Montmorency (lately elevated to the office of Constable of France), was then with him, also the persecuting Cardinal de Tournon. "Both urged on him the necessity of speedily adopting the most rigourous measures for the extermination of the Anabaptists, who, they assured him, were very numerous in Paris, and fully determined, as had lately transpired, to set fire to all the churches and to pillage the Louvre.*"

* The old feudal fortress of the Louvre, or what then remained of it, could have contained nothing worth pillaging. For many years it had been wholly abandoned as a royal residence. But Francis I., who began to build, rebuild, and enlarge so many of the châteaux of France, but finished none of them, at the beginning of his reign proposed to entirely rebuild the Louvre, which was fast falling to ruin. The great tower

Many arrests were made; many barbarous executions followed, as in 1528, when sacrilegious but unknown hands threw down and mutilated an image of the Virgin affixed at the corner of the Rue des Rosiers and the Rue des Juifs. The Parisians, who are said to have cared very little for the Pope, but very much for images and the ceremonies of religion, were greatly enraged. The king was no less so. He immediately ordered a statue to be made of silver, and at the head of a very grand expiatory procession he placed it in the niche where the profaned image had previously stood. The popular agitation was kept up by the report that the broken image was a miracle-working one. ("*Bourgeois de Paris.*")

On the present occasion, when the festivities of the carnival were ended, the king, still greatly angered, came to Paris with Queen Eleanor and his children, and accompanied by many ladies, princes, and courtiers, for the purpose of appeasing the Divine wrath by a solemn, expiatory procession through the city, at which he personally assisted. On the return of the procession, he publicly addressed the people. His discourse was full of menace and denunciation against the ene-

---

built by Philippe Auguste in 1204 was removed in 1527. Little more was done until 1541, when the west wing was begun. When Francis died in 1547 the work had made but small progress; but under Henri II. it was actively continued. — Guilhermy, "Paris Archéologique."

mies of the holy sacrament, and of pious exhortation to all present to use their best efforts to root out this new heresy.

"The king then ordered six condemned heretics to be burnt that same day. A very good remedy, and a very opportune one, to check this rising evil. And would to God," continues the pious narrator,* "that it were applied with more constancy, that it might produce the effect which good Christians expect from it!"

It is asserted that Francis, in the course of his address to the people, declared that "if his own children were so unfortunate as to fall into such accursed and execrable opinions, he would himself give them up as a sacrifice to God." It was on this occasion that Montmorency, the declared enemy of Marguerite, ventured to say to the king, "Sire, you should begin with your sister." "Oh, as for her," he replied, "she is too much attached to me ever to believe anything I do not approve."

His pious harangue was delivered in January. The arrests and executions consequent on it continued till May, and with ever-increasing cruelty and refinement of torture. When these horrors began, the wretched victims of the profligate king's fanaticism were strangled before they were burnt. But this was soon thought too merciful,

* Marco Antonio Barbosa, "Reports of Venetian Ambassadors."

and that it would be more acceptable to God to follow the custom of the holy inquisition and burn them alive, or even to go beyond that infamous tribunal in cruelty, and invent a machine to prolong the sufferings of the unhappy people condemned to the stake. The burning pile must do its work more slowly.

They were therefore suspended above the flames by chains attached to a cross-beam, having a sort of see-saw motion, by which means the poor victims were plunged into the burning mass and raised up again, until it pleased the wretched creature who superintended this horrible exhibition (to which crowds flocked as to a festival) to remove the bolt or chain that held up the sufferers, when they dropped into the flames and their misery was ended. With them were burned the papers relating to what was termed their trial, in order that the reformers might not be able to collect any records of their martyrs.

Many young students of the University of Paris fled at this time to Neufchâtel in Geneva, alarmed by a royal edict condemning the "harbourers of heretics, Lutherans, and others, to the same punishment as the said heretics themselves, but promising to all denouncers of heretics a fourth part of whatever property these heretics might possess." Among those terrified youths was the future translator of Plutarch, Jacques Amyot, to whom has been assigned the palm for purity of language, then so rare, in his prose writings, placing him above all his contemporaries as the "father of French prose," as some have styled Clément Marot the "father of French poetry." *

The study of the classic languages had occasioned great neglect of the vernacular. Indeed, many of the learned philologists of that day scarcely considered a language spoken by the unlettered people in the ordinary affairs of life worthy of their attention.

Amyot was probably very slightly "tainted by the new heresy," and may have fled to avoid being included in the band of fellow students more inclined to reform. At all events, he was less attached to his heretical principles than poor Marot, as he afterwards entered the priesthood, became Bishop of Auxerre, and eventually almoner to Charles IX., which proves that he must have been, if only in appearance, as so many were, very "sound in the faith." To return to the "chevalier king."

While the zealous fit continued, his signature daily sent to the stake suspected heretics from whom torture had wrung the confession that condemned them. While more effectually to put a stop to an evil on which other modes of repres-

* Marot, during this persecution, though in favour with the king, yet deemed it prudent to seek refuge with Marguerite at Béarn, and afterwards with the Duchesse Renée at Ferrara.

sion had so little effect, the "father of letters" issued a decree "abolishing printing in France, it being a means of propagating heresy." Every one, "under pain of being hanged," was prohibited from printing any book.

Some historians of the Reformation (Sleidan, for instance, referred to by H. Martin) assert that Francis witnessed the public executions, when, as if in honour of his presence, horrors unspeakable were heaped on his hapless victims.* The very singular rumour was also current in Paris that "even the Pope" (Paul III., successor of Clement) had written to the king desiring him "to moderate those execrable and horrible punishments he was inflicting on the Lutherans, and begging that he would be merciful to them and spare their lives."† The fierceness of the king's anger did then actually begin to abate. The party of toleration had probably regained the ascendency. The edict against printing was suspended indefinitely, but a censorship, both parliamentary and clerical, replaced it.

*MM. Michelet and Martin are, however, of opinion that these were merely reports spread in Germany to render him more hateful to the Lutherans. No entry of the kind is found in the journal of the "*Bourgeois de Paris*," who sets down everything very impartially. If he does not censure the conduct of the king, neither does he praise it. He relates facts, but makes no comment on them. His silence on this head is therefore accepted by those inclined to give the king the benefit of the doubt, as in his favour.

† "*Journal d'un Bourgeois de Paris.*"

An ambassador from the Sultan arriving in Paris at this time, removed all doubt of the king's relations with the infidel — an alliance regarded with horror throughout Christendom, and for which Clement had excommunicated the King of Hungary. Francis therefore hastened to explain his proceeding to the princes and states of Germany, with whom, for his own purposes, he desired to remain on friendly terms.

The heretics he was supposed to have burnt were, he told them, "a set of factious rebels who, using religion for a cloak to their schemes, sought to unsettle the minds of his subjects, and to incite troubles and commotions in his kingdom. An anxious desire on his part," he also assured them, "to secure peace between the Turk and the Christian republic — from which he was far from wishing to separate himself — had alone led him into negotiations with Solyman." All Germans under arrest he at once liberated. A general amnesty — excluding Sacramentarians and Anabaptists — was granted, on condition that all abjured their errors within six months, and lived henceforth as good Catholics.

Francis, to convince the reformers how favourably he regarded them, even wrote to Melancthon, pressing him to visit France, as Marguerite had also some time previously done. Meanwhile, she requested him to send her some formulas for guidance in matters of religion. Calvin's stern doctrines, ever increasing in severity, were becoming repellent to natures kindly and sensitive as Marguerite's. Calvin's angry, arbitrary God might inspire terror, but scarcely love and trust in Him. Melancthon, though not induced to visit France, sent a confession of faith — very moderate in tone, very tolerant of mere error. It was submitted to the Sorbonne, and of course absolutely condemned.

Once more, then, persecution for awhile was materially abated, if not wholly at an end. The curiosity of the public, no longer gratified by the spectacle of burning heretics, was now more especially directed towards the proceedings of a new religious order that appeared in Paris towards the end of 1534, under the appellation of the "Society of Jesus." The founder and head, who took the title of "General," was the young Biscayan military officer, Ignatius Loyola,* who in 1521 distinguished himself by his gallant defence of the citadel of Pampeluna.

Having recovered from the injuries he then sustained, he began to prepare himself for the realisation of projects first inspired by much reading of an imaginative but pious kind — the lives of saints. He went to Jerusalem, begging his way there and back. Feeling his need of more learning, he studied for some years — being

---

* Or more correctly, Inigo Lopez de Recalde y Loyola.

then thirty-two years old — at the same college as
Calvin. But Loyola, except during his hours of
study, was wholly occupied in praying, fasting,
and inflicting severe penances on himself, which
induced a frequent state of catalepsis, more or
less prolonged, in which he beheld brilliant visions
of the Deity, or terrific ones of Satan.

At first his disciples were few — six only in
1534, when they assembled in the church of Notre
Dame de Montmartre; and having received the
communion together, made a solemn vow to
renounce henceforth worldly wealth and honours,
and to devote themselves to the salvation of their
fellow creatures. Their number had increased to
ten only when, in the following year, they renewed
their vow.

But it was not until 1537 that the general and
his lieutenants, being assembled at Venice, received
orders of priesthood, at the same time making a
solemn renunciation of all ecclesiastical dignities.
In 1540, the plan of their association being fully
and officially approved by Paul III., they added
to their three vows of poverty, chastity, and
obedience a fourth — viz., "to be at all times
ready to execute the orders and accept the com-
missions, whatever their nature, that the sovereign
pontiff should see fit to impose on them — un-
questioningly, unhesitatingly, and without delay."
From this small group sprang the numerous,
powerful, and wonderfully organised "Society of

Jesus." Rapidly it increased in numbers, and its teachers and confessors in reputation, until its influence, sometimes for good, more frequently for evil, was felt in every rank of life, — not only throughout Christendom, but even extending to China, Japan, and Paraguay.

CHAPTER III.

Death of Duprat. — A Privilege of Royalty. — Duprat's Lawful Heir. — An Interesting Fact. — The Purchase-money for the Tiara. — A Proof of Fidelity. — An Unforeseen Obstacle.— A New Holy War. — Freedom from War's Alarms. — Henry and Catherine. — Diane de Poitiers. — The Old King and His Mistress. —The Fall of Florence. —Infringing Court Etiquette. — The Mania for Building. — Maître Roux. — The Mæcenas of France. — Expedition Against Tunis. — The Choice of Three Courses. — The Pope's Judgment Appealed to. — On Reflection. — A Modified Report Suggested. — War!

HE Grand Chancellor of France, Duprat, after twenty years of office, during which he had freely availed himself of his immense facilities for heaping up wealth, and conferring honours on himself both civil and ecclesiastical, died on the 9th of July, 1535, at his Château of Nantouillet. This sumptuous residence — in the erection of which he had employed the first architects of that day — if not more elaborate in its exterior decorations, yet far surpassed any of the royal châteaux in the artistic elegance of the furniture.

Like Moulins, the former residence of the Constable Bourbon, as before mentioned, and many others belonging to the nobility, Nantouillet had the advantage of being permanently furnished. No long train of beasts of burden, of baggage-wagons, and army of retainers awaited the noble owners' departure, to follow with carpets, and curtains of cloth of gold; an ample supply of bedding, and at least two of the less ponderous couches for the queen and the king; gold and silver plate without stint, and heavy loads of fine dresses. This was the uncomfortable privilege reserved for royalty when, with its retinue of court favourites and court beauties, it rambled from place to place, a pompous pageant, in quest of pastures new, as scenes for gaiety and revelry.

The furniture of the Château of Nantouillet is said to have been of exceeding magnificence, each article a *chef-d'œuvre* of its kind. A miracle of early Italian sixteenth-century work; when, as we learn from Vasari, genius was nurtured in the workshop, and artists were artificers in the strictest sense of the word; when, as a writer on the subject remarks, machinery had not ruined art, and the tool grasped by man became a part of himself, and the hammer was pervaded by the vitality of the hand.

It would almost seem that the king — both a connoisseur and admirer of *objets d'art* — had long looked with covetous eyes on those marvels of artistic workmanship. For Duprat was not yet dead — though he then lay dying — when Francis ordered their seizure.

He well knew, having so often profited by his devices, how fertile was the chancellor's brain in schemes for obtaining money from the people; and as by the same honourable means he had so well filled his own purse also, the king probably thought that none with greater right than he could claim to be the worthy Duprat's lawful heir. For Francis was not content to take the furniture only, and to send it off for the adornment of his Château of Madrid — that enamel-faced palace of delights he had raised for himself, and thus named, in the Bois de Boulogne. There all that made life worth living to Francis I. surrounded him, deriving new zest from the gratifying contrast between this new French Madrid and the old Moorish Alcazar of the Spanish capital, where for a year or more he sighed and pined and prayed in vain, for the dissolute pleasures with which at his ease and at liberty he now solaced himself.

It had long been the ambition of Duprat to terminate his career on the papal throne, and from the time when, late in life, he entered the Church and obtained an archbishopric, with a cardinal's hat, as his first step in the priesthood, he had been laying aside money for the purchase of the triple crown.

Leo X. died; but it was not to have Duprat to reign over them that even those cardinals not above bribery thought it worth while to sell their votes. Adrian VI. soon succumbed (to the skill of his physician, as supposed). But Duprat was still no nearer the object of his wishes than was Wolsey, who, like the chancellor, was then aiming at the papacy. By and by Clement VII. also died, vexed at heart at the little heed given by the temporal princes to the spiritual authority of the pontiff.

When Clement's health began to fail, the chancellor's hopes rose high. He had in reserve, in his private coffers, 400,000 crowns, which, judiciously employed, he expected would secure his election when the chair of St. Peter became vacant. This interesting fact he in strict confidence revealed to the king, who seems to have carefully treasured it up in his memory. Clement died in September, 1534; but the mere suggestion of Duprat as his successor excited only derision. No member of the Sacred College could be found even to propose his name.

Whether this disappointment preyed on his mind or not — for it was, as age must have convinced him, his last chance — the stern fact was that the ambitious cardinal-chancellor, who flattered himself with reviving the dimmed glories of the Vatican and surpassing the fame of the pontificate of Leo X. by the overwhelming splendour of his own, took to indulging so excessively in the "pleasures of the table," that in less than a twelvemonth after Clement's death his hopes were also buried in the tomb.

Scarcely had Duprat drawn his last breath when his strong box was taken possession of in the king's name. The purchase-money for the tiara was found intact, and probably something more — as welcome an addition to the king's needy private purse as were his mother's large hoardings some two or three years before. He was then in want of large sums (at what period of his reign was he not in want of them?) to pay his army, which he was reconstructing — levying legions, after the manner of the ancient Romans, to form a national infantry — a plan which at first seems to have met with some approval even from the military men of that day; but ultimately, like most of the French king's projects, it was abandoned before the scheme was fully carried out.

Notwithstanding, a very considerable force had been raised and equipped, with which he purposed again to invade Lombardy, in order to chastise the perfidy of the Duke of Milan, who had ordered the imprisonment and assassination of a Milanese gentleman named Maraviglia — a secret diplomatic agent, privately accredited to him, in the service of Francis I. The emperor's suspicions had been aroused respecting this gentleman, and he at once accused Sforza of adding "knavery to mystery."

Fearing some ill consequences from the emperor's resentment, the duke immediately sent assurances of his unswerving fidelity to his suzerain, with a promise of certain and speedy proof of it. Maraviglia was arrested, conveyed to prison, and, after some summary proceedings in private, beheaded in his dungeon. The news was at once sent off to the emperor. So striking a proof of Sforza's readiness in divining and carrying into effect his imperial majesty's wishes seems to have met with his full approval, as he rewarded his vassal's zeal with the hand of one of his nieces.

Sforza, in making some excuses to Francis, threw the blame on Maraviglia's own imprudence. But, indignant at what he regarded as a personal insult, "the king denounced to all Europe this shameful infraction of the law of nations, and expressed his intention of avenging it by force of arms." The emperor declared that it in no way concerned him, and two years elapsed before the changes the king was making in the organisation of the army were sufficiently perfected to enable him to send into the field the large number of troops requisite for the object he had in view.

But when prepared to march, the Duke of Savoy, the king's uncle, refused to permit the passage of the French army through his dominions Francis therefore determined on occupying the States of Savoy, and even laid claim to them as his heritage, in right of his mother. The claim, of course, was not allowed.

The French troops, under the king's lieutenant-general, Admiral Chabot de Brion, then entered Piedmont, took Turin, and several other towns; the duke vainly expecting assistance from the emperor, with whom he was in alliance. Arrived at Mont Cenis, Brion received the news of the death of Sforza, an event which at once considerably modified the political situation.* The king, on being apprised of this unexpected turn in affairs, renewed his claims on Milan, which he was now prepared to waive in favour of his second son, the Duc d' Orléans; promising the renunciation of his pretensions in right of his wife, Catherine de' Medici, to the seigniory of Florence and duchy of Urbino.

The consideration of this proposal was deferred for awhile — the emperor being engaged in an expedition against the Turks, who had taken Tunis. All Christendom was deeply interested in it, and anxious for Charles's success. Francis was invited to join in this new holy war, and to add his forces to the emperor's. But he declined. He was, in fact, secretly in alliance with Solyman to

* To the admiral (suspected of heretical opinions) it was probably more satisfactory than to Francis, to know that the invasion of Savoy had greatly served the cause of reform — the assistance afforded by the French to Geneva, which for two years had been blockaded by the duke and the emperor, enabling that city to recover her liberty. Henceforth Geneva became the capital of the reformed religion, and headquarters of the reformers. Her population rapidly increased, and her manufactures and commerce were soon doubled.

drive Charles out of Italy, as soon as the former returned from his invasion of Persia; while during his absence, aided by Barbarossa's pirate fleet, he purposed to retake Genoa. But events had not fallen out quite in harmony with this programme; and Barbarossa and his corsairs were now fully occupied in defending Tunis.

Admiral de Brion, however, had taken possession of nearly the whole of Piedmont; the towns, by the advice of their duke, offering little or no resistance. He and his family took refuge in Milan, whither he had sent his artillery, his furniture, jewels, and other valuables.

The emperor was greatly irritated by the proceedings of the French in Piedmont. But as he was unable, until the war he was engaged in was off his hands, to turn his forces against France, he showed a disposition, though he had no intention of giving up Milan to either Francis or his sons, to enter into a negotiation on the subject; proposing to grant the investiture of the duchy to the king's third son, the Duc d' Angoulême, and to unite him to the House of Austria by marriage. As a preliminary, he required that hostilities should be wholly suspended in Piedmont.

This request was complied with; and Charles contrived to submit to the king a variety of flattering but impracticable proposals for his consideration, when he could snatch a moment from his pleasures. By many skilful subterfuges he also kept the ambassadors employed throughout the winter in fruitless negotiation.

Meanwhile the court, rejoicing in this freedom from war's alarms, passed a very gay winter — the carnival being unusually brilliant. The presence of the king, however, did not add to the gaiety of carnival festivities; for as years advanced he became morose and, if possible, more dissolute than ever. But the three young princes, who, with their pages or companions, now took part in the court revelry, dispelled, by their hearty enjoyment of it, much of the gloom which the fits of depression the king was so often subject to threw over courtiers and ladies generally.

The staid Queen Eleanor, too, did little towards enlivening the scene; yet, in the full splendour of court dress, she was doubtless its most dazzling ornament. Near her, as if to seek the protection which her position afforded, if not her influence — for of that she had none — the quiet, subtle girl-wife of the youthful Prince Henri was always to be found. Of all that passed around her, nothing escaped her vigilant, restless eyes. She was inwardly taking notes to serve for her guidance in the future — resigned to live, and learn, and bide her time; fully assured — for was it not written in the stars? — that, as time rolled on, her turn would come to sway the destinies of the kingdom.

No attentions did Catherine receive or look for from her boy husband. He was a fluttering captive in the chains of first love; and the most brilliant beauty of the court — the famed Diane de Poitiers — was the lady of his heart, then in the maturity of her charms, at the shrine of whose loveliness he bowed the knee. Youths of Prince Henry's age — he was seventeen — often are said to fancy themselves in love with women several years their seniors. In this instance the disparity was great, but the lady was exceedingly beautiful, as she might well be, though she had numbered thirty-seven summers. As to the winters, they glided o'er her smooth, fair brow, leaving no trace of their passage, or any snowy signs of age on her luxuriant raven hair. Nature had made her beautiful forever; and beautiful she remained — unaided by art, we are told — until the end of three score years and nine.*

At this early period of Henry's attachment to her, Diane derived from it no influence at court. The king disliked his second son, whose sentimental worship of an "aged siren," as envious ladies were pleased to call her, was a subject of jest among his companions, while Diane professed for the royal youth a tender but motherly affection, placid Catherine looking on unmoved.

The Duchesse d'Étampes still reigned supreme, as *maîtresse-en-titre*. Many attempts had been

---

* Her husband, the Comte de Dreux-Brézé, died in 1531, when she erected a very magnificent monument to his memory, and ever after wore the widow's dress.

vainly made to dethrone her. Her efforts, when possible, in favour of reform; her advocacy of toleration, had been privately urged against her when Francis was in a persecuting mood, but had met with no success. None had the same power of amusing the king, and with such apparent artlessness; of dispelling his gloom, and checking his violent bursts of anger — anger so vehement, so outrageous, that he was sometimes thoroughly exhausted by it and his health affected.

If it ever occurred to him that the *spirituelle* duchess might be "tainted with heresy," he thought it right to be tolerant of her errors, because of the frequent need he now had of her lively, playful conversation. For Francis was beginning to think himself what others named him — an old man, "the old king." Yet he was but forty-two.

The duchess had certainly availed herself of her great influence to provide handsomely for her numerous poor relations. But, except that one of her uncles had received a cardinal's hat at her suggestion, and one or two others bishoprics of some value, she had raised none of them to very prominent stations. Abbeys, priories, and some advantageous marriages were among the moderately good things she obtained for them; perhaps thinking it safer, both for herself and them, thus to secure them ease and comfort, than to elevate them to positions of greater distinction.

The fall of Florence and the expulsion of the French from Italy had occasioned a fresh influx of Italians into France — among them many distinguished men who sought refuge at the court of the monarch who had once more so cruelly abandoned his allies to the mercy of the relentless Charles and to the despotism of the Medici. Francis received them well — he could scarcely do otherwise — and conferred diplomatic and military rank on some refugees of high station, such as the Prince of Malfi (Caraccioli) and the Florentines, Pietro and Leo Strozzi, who were made marshals and admiral, respectively, in the service of France.

But besides these, there were men of letters, poets, musicians, sculptors, painters, and architects. The first of these repaid the king's hospitality by dedications of their works, flattering addresses, and panegyrics in verse. The court was all the gayer by this blending of French and Italian rank, high art, and learning, and new amusements were introduced, more varied, picturesque, and interesting. There was now more dancing than formerly, for dancing had hitherto been so much of a solemnity that it had found little favour at court, and was reserved for state occasions, until the Italians imparted an animation to it, which, though attempted before by Madame d'Étampes, was checked as an infringement of the stateliness of court etiquette.

All that was best in Italy seemed to have followed the French in their third expulsion from it; thus conferring immense advantages on the country to which the Italians owed nothing but their misfortunes. Florence, especially, could boast of every human talent and worldly gift in which are found the sources of power and prosperity, and these her citizens carried with them to the country of their adoption. Literature and the beaux-arts flourished with new vigour, and the improvements introduced by Florentine skill into the industrial arts resulted in largely increased commerce.

Italian was generally understood at court, and was a frequent medium of conversation. This led to many Italian words and phrases becoming, as it were, naturalised in the French tongue; also to a less rugged pronunciation, and eventually, as the language became more cultured, a considerable change in its orthography.

There were then so many royal châteaux in course of reconstruction or enlargement, and so many of the rich nobility vying with each other in following the example of the king in his mania for building, that there was ample employment in France both for French and Italian architects, sculptors, and painters. The talented Italian artists were most in request, at least for plans and designs. For it was the Italian palaces that first gave Francis the idea of Italian superiority over other nations, and inspired the desire of making France a second Italy — an abode of learning and the arts.

It was then that so many old feudal fortresses were razed to the ground to give place to those châteaux of the Renaissance, more suited in their arrangements to the changed habits of the court and nation, and which have in their turn disappeared, leaving scarce a trace of the site on which they stood.

Great works were in progress at Chambord, also at Fontainebleau, which, originally a hunting-seat of Saint Louis IX., had been for eight years past rising into a stately palace, under the direction first of the architect Sebastian Serlio, but afterwards conjointly, for a time, with Rosso, a Florentine, driven from Italy by the sack of Rome. Some pictures he painted on his arrival in France, and presented to the king, won the royal favour — the pictures being of great merit, and the painter a man of commanding presence and courtly manners, always a passport to Francis's good graces.

A house in Paris, and apartments at Fontainebleau, were soon after assigned him; for Battista di Jacopo — such was Rosso's real name * — was accustomed to live *en grand seigneur*. The king then named him " chief and superintendent over all the buildings, paintings, and other decorations

---

* The French called him Maître Roux, the Italians Rosso, because of his ruddy complexion.

of the palace," with a salary of 400 crowns a year. This probably was insufficient for the support of his numerous retinue of servants, his horses, the expenses of his banquets, and his profuse hospitality towards Italian friends; for Francis gave him a rich abbacy, and conferred on him other lucrative marks of his favour. He appears, indeed, to have merited this liberality. As a painter his industry was as great as his ability, and his wonderful exuberance of fancy was displayed in his designs for the decoration of the gallery (Galerie de François I.) which he constructed over the lower court.*

Francis had taken a great fancy to Fontainebleau and its forest, and was anxious to inhabit his palace. The diligence of Rosso and the host of modellers, painters, and sculptors he employed — all men of ability, who completed the master's designs — was therefore very gratifying to the king, and was rewarded accordingly. What remains of the palace of Francis I. gives no idea of the original plan of the building, so much has it been altered and added to in the various styles of different epochs. Francis greatly preferred it to other royal residences. Consequently, several fine châteaux were built in its vicinity by the nobility.

The king lived in greater familiarity with artists,

* Some of Rosso's paintings were discovered during the reign of Louis Phillippe under a coating of whitewash, and were restored by that king's order.

men of letters, and celebrities generally, both French and Italian, than with his courtiers. The homage of the former was especially agreeable to him; while no less gratifying to his *protégés* were the easy air and affable manner he assumed when conversing with them — the patron appearing to be entirely merged in the friend, whom they flattered by surnaming the "Mæcenas of France."

But spring was advancing, and the negotiation respecting Milan had made little or no progress. Charles declared that the Pope was opposed to the pretensions of the young Duc d' Orléans, and no solution of this difficulty was suggested. The king, indeed, in his eagerness to recover the duchy of Milan, which he never succeeded in retaining, was willing to make any sacrifices short of surrendering the kingdom of France.

He would have turned his arms against Solyman, as he indeed proposed to do, though he had just before asked a subsidy of him; would have joined Charles in "rooting out heresy;" have thrown up his alliance with the Germans and Henry VIII., and have come under an engagement to support the hereditary rights of Mary Tudor, the daughter of the repudiated Katharine, and have renounced his pretensions on Genoa. At the same time his troops were again marching on his other heritage — the duchy of Savoy.

The emperor, contrary to his custom, which was

to leave the command of his armies to his generals, headed in person the expedition against Tunis. His success was complete. Twice he beat the formidable corsair Barbarossa, whose name struck terror into the hearts of fathers and mothers who dwelt with their families on the shores of the Mediterranean, and even several miles inland. Charles had expelled the pirate hordes from Tunis. He had re-established its former king as a vassal of Spain; and so desperate had been the fighting which success had crowned, that to political fame, which hitherto had alone been allowed him, military renown was now added.

He had returned to Naples when he received the French king's proposals, and at the same time heard of the renewed invasion of Savoy. No reply was given to them — perhaps he despised the man who could condescend to make such proposals — but he pressed forward the completion of his armaments, and from Naples, accompanied by the French ambassador, he proceeded to Rome, making a solemn entry into that city.

Up to this time he appears to have been in a state of suppressed indignation. No longer able to restrain the expression of his feelings, he at length, in full consistory — Pope and cardinals, the French and other ambassadors, and many persons of distinction being assembled — launched forth in vehement reproaches against Francis I., entering into all the details of the king's frequent breaches of faith in the past, and pointing out the injustice of his present wanton attacks on Piedmont; desiring, he said, that all who heard him might judge whether he or the King of France had the greater cause for complaint.

Notwithstanding these provocations on the part of France, "he would yet give the king," he said, "the choice of three courses, in order to make evident his own upright intentions and earnest desire for the peace of Christendom. First, if it would really be the means of ensuring an honourable and durable peace, he would give the investiture of Milan to the king's third son, the Duc d'Angoulême. Secondly, in the event of the king failing to accept this offer within twenty days, he proposed that they should meet on bridge or boat in single combat, with sword or poniard, in their shirts only;* he deeming it but reasonable that they should encounter the dangers who had excited the troubles — blood enough, and more than enough, having been shed on their account." Milan and Burgundy were to be staked on the issue of this strange combat. "Thirdly, failing the duel, war."

"It would be with extreme regret," he said, "that he entered on a new war. But if constrained to do so, no power in the world should turn him from it until either he or the king was reduced

---

* "*En chemise*," in shirt or coat of mail, without other protecting armour beneath it, as was customary.

to the condition of the poorest gentleman in his country."

This long harangue was spoken in Spanish, and ended with an appeal to the Pope's judgment between him and his rival.

The emperor's impetuous address appears to have been listened to in mute astonishment. The Pope spoke a few conciliatory words in reply to the emperor's appeal to him, but declared his resolution, "as advised by his brothers, the cardinals, to remain neuter as the common father of the faithful." As to the French ambassadors, Charles relieved them from their embarrassment by refusing to listen to any reply from them. "No more words," he said, "but results."

On reflection, Charles perceived that for once he had allowed excitement to get the better of his usually cool head. In the morning he sent for the ambassadors, and, before the same assembly as on the preceding day, explained away much that in the heat of passion had then fallen from him. He had not intended, he told them, to blame or accuse their king, but simply to exonerate himself; that "he esteemed the said king," and "wished to succeed in arranging a solid peace with him, that together they might fight the infidel and bring back the Lutherans and other heretics into the bosom of the Church."

He did not recall his three propositions; but with reference to the alternative of the duel, it was not to be regarded, he said, in the sense of an ordinary challenge to the king. On the present occasion the emperor spoke in Italian, which appears to have been more familiar to his auditory than Spanish.

Paul III. was very anxious to be a peacemaker between emperor and king, but absolutely refused to be made a judge of their differences. At his earnest request the French ambassadors gave a very modified report of Charles's vehement recital of the wrongs he had sustained at the French king's hands. But in submitting the three propositions to the king's consideration, the challenge could not, of course, be altogether omitted. "It is singular," remarks M. Henri Martin, with reference to it, "that during the long contest for power between Charles V. and Francis I., it was the ' frigid politic emperor ' who twice threw down the gauntlet, and called on the ' chevalier king ' to settle the point in dispute between them by single combat ; and that it was owing to the failure of the latter that no encounter took place." *

* This would seem to confirm in some degree the assertion of Charles's biographer — Amadée Pichot — " that the emperor was a man of the most romantic heart," while it impresses one with the idea that there was much less chivalric feeling in Francis I. and more romance and passion in Charles V. than generally have been attributed to them. It is, however, certain that both were blindly bigoted and superstitious, and, as a natural consequence, cruel persecutors. It is, therefore, difficult to believe that true chivalry, noble, generous, and humane in its sentiments, could really belong to either.

While the scenes above described were occurring in Rome, an ambassador, the Cardinal Jean de Lorraine, was on his way thither, authorized by Francis to sign and seal a truce or peace on almost any terms, provided that Milan was promised to the Duc d' Orléans. The emperor having left the Holy City, an interview with him was arranged at Siena. Charles remained firm to the terms of his declaration. To Angoulême, not to Orléans, would he resign the coveted duchy — the investiture of the young duke to take place on the evacuation of the States of Savoy. The cardinal argued in vain. He could induce no change in his resolution. So, setting aside the emperor's challenge without remark, he announced in his master's name the acceptance of its alternative — war!

CHAPTER IV.

A War of Extermination.— The Stars in Their Courses.— A Propitious Date.— A Chivalric Example.— Unpatriotic Rebels.— Famine Looks Them in the Face.— A Fatal Game of Tennis.— Death of the Dauphin.— An Atrocious Decree and Its Victim.— A Daughter of the Medici.— Charles's Army in Full Retreat.— *Le Jeune Aventureux.*— Glory and Disaster.— A Change of Places at Court.— Diane and the Dauphiness.— The Intrigues of the Ladies. — James V. of Scotland.— Love at First Sight.— The Fair Madeleine.— A Flower Nipped in the Bud.

THE war about to be waged between emperor and king was to be a war of extermination. Such, at least, was the spirit with which on both sides it was entered upon. History scarcely records a more cruel war, or one of which it would be more difficult to determine whether the victorious king or the vanquished emperor was the greatest sufferer. The evils resulting from it were certainly longer felt by the former, or, more correctly, by the unhappy people on whom so much misery and ruin fell.

The vast army that had repulsed the invincible Solyman, and thoroughly beaten the terrible Barbarossa, now, flushed with conquest — the commander-in-chief and the distinguished generals who served under him being no less elated than their troops — was preparing to march on Provence. Large detachments were also assembling in the Netherlands and in Germany, to invade France on the side of Picardy and Champagne. Of victory they deemed themselves certain; for even the stars in their courses, it was supposed, would fight for Charles — a prophecy having gone forth, which was credited far and near, promising him universal monarchy.

It was modest, therefore, in the emperor to limit the prize of victory to Paris and the crown of France. The prophecy, however, gained him an ally — the Marquis de Saluzzo — who, like Pope Paul III., was a firm believer in astrology and the influence of the stars on human affairs. As soon, therefore, as the marquis was informed that the heavenly bodies were adverse to Francis, he, an old and hitherto faithful ally of France, transferred his allegiance to the emperor, and with it the body of troops of which the king had given him the command for the defence of a portion of Piedmont.

But the emperor himself apparently relied less on the aid of the stars than on his "big battalions," whose real or fancied superiority over those of his opponent he vaunted in rather bombastic terms. "Had the King of France," he said, "such an army as his, and he one like the king's, he would go to him with his hands tied behind his back and beg for mercy." Some advantage, gained by the emperor in a skirmish with a body of French troops, as he approached Provence, was magnified — according to French writers — as a "glorious prelude to the triumphs awaiting him."

He had arranged the movements of his army so as to cross the frontier of France on the 25th of July — a propitious date — being the day of the patron saint of Spain, Saint James, and the anniversary of the brilliant achievement of the preceding year — the taking of Tunis.

The plan adopted by De Montmorency for the defence of Provence and the defeat of the emperor was to avoid giving battle — "Fabian warfare," as it was termed — being the system pursued by the old Roman general, Fabius, to check the progress of Hannibal. Two camps, at Valence and Avignon, strongly intrenched, were occupied by the French army, and the whole of the fair province of Provence was laid waste, to deprive the enemy of the means of subsistence in the country abandoned to him. Three cities only were excepted — Marseilles, Arles, and Tarascon, which, being fortified and sufficiently garrisoned, were able to resist an attack.

All other towns and villages, even Aix, the capital, were burnt to the ground; the order of the inhuman De Montmorency being to storm the towns that resisted — an order carried out with most cruel rigour. "The spirit of chivalry" is said to have "led the nobility who possessed estates in Provence generously to set their humbler neighbours an example, by beginning the work of destruction." With their own hands they set fire to their barns and granaries, laid waste their fields, pulled down their mills, and broke the millstones. All the wine in their cellars which the soldiers could not drink was thrown into the brooks and rivulets. In a word, they sacked their own residences, lest anything should be left in them for the enemy.

But the poorer inhabitants of the towns and the peasantry of the surrounding country evinced no eagerness to do likewise. Instead of humbly submitting to the cruel order to burn and destroy, and reduce themselves to the most miserable poverty, they resisted it. The "great soldier," enraged at this opposition to his commands, sent a detachment of troops under General Bonneval, commissioned to accomplish by force what those "unpatriotic rebels" refused quietly to do themselves.

Terrible scenes are said to have ensued. Moans, sobs of despair, shrieks of rage, and curses on the man who had deliberately planned this outrage, rose in the air as farm after farm was burnt, and flames ascended from each cottage home. Animals were slaughtered; the ripened corn and the fodder were fired, and with them were consumed the fruits of past labour and the resources of the future. Many of these unhappy people were with difficulty restrained from rushing through the lines of soldiers in order to perish in the flames, or vainly to strive and snatch from the burning some remnant of the subsistence so cruelly torn from them.

The emperor meanwhile continued his march into the desolate country, once the garden of France, nowhere encountering resistance or meeting an enemy, except in the peasants, who, with their families, had taken refuge in the caves and recesses of the mountains, near which the path of the army lay. Made furious by the wrongs they had suffered, they assembled in bands, and vowed to put an end to the war by waylaying and killing the emperor. Several of his officers, also the poet Garcilasso de la Vega, whom, from the richness of his dress, they mistook for him, were slain in this way. Charles captured a party of fifty concealed in a ruined tower, and hanged the whole of them.

But provisions began to fail the imperialists, and famine to look them in the face. The emperor declared that he would seek his invisible enemy in his very intrenchments, and compel him to give battle. He, however, turned his arms on Marseilles and Arles, and was repulsed with considerable loss of both officers and men. Murmuring and dissensions were now rife amongst

Charles's troops. The fatigue of long marches beneath the glowing summer sun of the South; the utter disappointment of their hopes of conquest and plunder, together with the starvation rations to which they were reduced, had resulted in sickness, and pestilence threatened a rapid thinning of the ranks of the imperial army.

A supply of biscuit was, however, brought by Andrea Doria to Toulon, and all the available mules and horses were assembled to carry this relief to the famished camp. But a number of the Provençal peasantry — ever on the alert to harass the imperialists, though mercilessly burnt, hanged, or massacred whenever any were captured — contrived to lie in ambush, and, undetected, to cut the hamstrings of the mules, and to carry off a large part of this anxiously expected bread-supply.

The emperor assembled his officers — amongst them was the ferocious Duke of Alba, in cruelty rivalling De Montmorency. What course was it best to take in the midst of so many disasters? Should he immediately retreat, or announce an attack on the camp of Avignon? The latter course was determined on; and as money and provisions for eight days were fortunately received in safety from Spain, the menace, together with the information that the emperor had reviewed his army and given the order to march, was forwarded by spies to the camp as news to be relied on.

The king was at Lyons when the news reached him. He immediately left by the Rhône for Valence, to be nearer De Montmorency. The dauphin Francis desired to accompany him, and the king was willing that he should gather his first laurels in this expected battle, should the emperor carry out his threatened attack. They stopped on their way at Tournon, where, on one of the hottest days of what appears to have been an unusually hot summer, the young prince engaged in a game of tennis with some of his companions.

Being excessively heated, he called for a glass of iced water, and drank it off with avidity. Presently he was seized with shiverings, followed by fever and inflammation of the lungs. The king continued his journey. The prince was to follow in a few days, when it was expected that he would be well again. But on the fourth day of his attack (August 10th), he died.

The cause of his death was by no means doubtful; but Francis less than almost any one could bow to the decrees of Providence. His grief usually took the form of rage and anger, and misfortune inspired him only with a desire for revenge. He accused the emperor of conspiring to poison him and his three sons. To effect this he imagined that the Count Sebastiano Montecuculi de Ferrara was the agent employed; he, in his quality of the prince's cupbearer, having handed him the glass of iced water. He was immediately arrested, and it was pretended that a book on the use of poisons was found amongst his papers.

The unfortunate count was a man of nervous temperament and weak constitution. He was put to the torture, and so severely that, unable to support the torments inflicted on him, he acknowledged anything and everything suggested to him. He confessed that he had been induced by Generals de Leyva and Gonzaga, and indirectly by the emperor himself, to poison the king and his sons. The wretched man was condemned, by an atrocious decree of the grand council assembled at Lyons, to be "quartered"—torn asunder by four horses.

The king determined to be present at this horrible spectacle; to feast his eyes (*repaître ses yeux*) with the anguish of his victim. He was accompanied by the princes of the blood, two or three bishops, the foreign ambassadors, and all the courtiers then in attendance on him at Lyons. A vast throng also assembled to look on the terrible sight, which worked them up to such a pitch of frenzy that to the revolting horrors of the execution they added the further one of seizing the mangled remains, and tearing them in pieces.

The "horrible plot of Charles V." was widely circulated in France, and firmly believed in by the people. The king also sent information of this imaginary crime to the Protestant German princes, with particulars of the "just punishment" he had inflicted on the emperor's agent. But the emperor and his officers indignantly repelled the odious accusation; and the name of Catherine de' Medici was openly pronounced by their partisans, and whisperingly echoed in the French Court, as the most likely one to be connected with an attempt to poison — if poisoning there really had been — in order that the crown might devolve on Henri, and she become Queen of France.

Catherine was then but fifteen, and, though ambitious beyond her years, and full of dissimulation, had not then developed into the unscrupulous and cruel intriguer she became at a later period. Doubtless in that excellent school, the Court of Francis I., she was in forward training for it; yet evidence to connect her with the dauphin's death there was none — that calamity was so evidently due to his own imprudence. But that suspicion should even point towards so mere a girl as capable of so dark a deed, shows that, beside a love of the arts, of which she had already given strong indications, she had also evinced other less praiseworthy characteristics of the House of the Medici, of which she gave such early promise of becoming a worthy daughter.

The king, too, when, after gloating over the torture of an innocent victim, his raging grief subsided, began to judge the matter more sanely. He had not the magnanimity to publicly withdraw his accusations, but simply ordered all charges brought against the emperor and his two generals to be suppressed in the record of the proceedings against Montecuculi.

The death of his eldest son had for a time diverted the king's attention from the expected advance of the emperor; but in anticipation of it he had sent the Duc d'Orléans, now dauphin, to the camp at Avignon, where the soldiers, so long unwillingly active, received him with enthusiasm; a rumour having been spread that he, with the young nobility of the camp, was to lead them to battle. All the harsh harangues and rigourous punishments of De Montmorency scarcely availed to detain them prisoners in camp any longer.

Soon, however, came the news that, instead of advancing, Charles was in full retreat, taking the route by the sea. Famine and the plague compelled him to hesitate no longer. The sick were left in the camp at Aix; and with an army reduced from fifty to twenty-five thousand he began his march — the dead and dying that fell by the way filling the air with pestilence. Several of his officers died of the terrible epidemic, amongst them the distinguished General Antonio da Leyva. The peasants disarmed the dead, making use of their weapons to harass the army in its flight, to break down bridges, and otherwise impede their progress; the retreat thus proving as disastrous as the invasion.

"With the miserable remnant of his much-boasted army, Charles reached Genoa, where he embarked for Barcelona, to conceal his mortification from the Italians, and — as a *bon-mot* of the time expressed it — to bury in Spain the honour that had died in Provence "(Martin). To complete his misfortune, he lost eight of his vessels in a heavy storm.

The French did not take advantage of the emperor's utter discomfiture. De Montmorency, who was an admirer of Queen Eleanor, and really favoured, it appears, the Austrian alliance, was unwilling to reduce her majesty's brother to such extremities as must have ensued from the following up of his great defeat. The French troops, therefore, hastened to the relief of Peronne, besieged by imperialists under the Comte de Nassau. There, too, fever and pestilence prevailed, and there the fatal malady carried off the famous Maréchal de Fleuranges — the companion of Francis in his youth, and so well known by the chivalric name of "*Le jeune Aventureux*," as well as by his interesting yet frequently exaggerated memoirs.

While these calamitous events were taking place, two Spanish galleons, laden with the gold of Peru, were on their way to Spain. When almost within sight of port, they were captured by Normandy pirates. This was further misfortune for Charles, always, like his brother of France, in want of money — a portion of the precious metal with which they were so richly freighted, and which became the booty of the marauders of the sea, having been destined for the imperial treasury.

The year 1536, a year so truly disastrous to the emperor, was considered in France the most glorious year, after Marignan, of the reign of Francis I.; the expulsion of the imperialists being regarded as a very great triumph. "But how much more important, how much more praiseworthy to have prevented their entry than to entice them into the country and to make their retreat a subject for felicitation. For whatever misfortunes and hardships the emperor and his army may have endured, they fell far short of the immensity of suffering inflicted on the people of Provence, both personally and in the destruction of their property." *

It was long, very long, ere Provence, with its ruined and depopulated towns, and utterly devastated country, recovered a tithe of its former prosperity. When the Parliament of this unfortunate province, whose inhabitants were in the greatest distress, petitioned the king for a diminution of the taxes, he replied, while declaring how willingly he would have granted their request, that "the needs and the dangers of the state made it impossible to yield to their wishes — at present." They knew him too well to flatter themselves with so vain a hope that he would find it less impossible to yield in the future.

* Servan, "*Guerres des Français.*"

The death of the dauphin occasioned a considerable change in the respective positions of certain ladies of the court, and the degree of influence exercised by them. For the party of the Duc d' Orléans — whose younger brother, Angoulême, now took his title — had been hitherto but little considered, because of the indifference, if not exactly dislike, shown by the king towards his second son. Now, he and those on whom he looked with favour were surrounded by flatterers, in anticipation — from the king's state of health and mode of life — of his probable early accession.

His brother Francis, whom he succeeded as dauphin, had at one time, from his application to study and the apparent serious bent of his mind generally, given promise of becoming a great and wise ruler. But, released from the control of preceptors and governors at the too early age of sixteen, he gave up his studious habits, and showed himself well disposed to tread in the steps of his libertine father — having, like him, his *maîtress-en-titre*, though numbering but eighteen years when he died.

The political state of France had made it difficult to select from among the princesses of Europe an eligible bride for the young French prince. He is said to have been himself inclined to a renewal of the engagement with the Princess Mary of England, to whom he was betrothed with so much pomp and ceremony in infancy. But

Henry's secession from Rome, and his marriage with Anne Boleyn, put such a union out of the question. In the spring of this eventful 1536, Henry, after only three years of marriage, had beheaded the unfortunate Anne, for whom, in order to make her his wife, he for the previous five years may almost be said to have been literally moving heaven and earth, by his unceasing appeals to the spiritual and temporal rulers of the world.

With the elevation then of Prince Henri to the position of dauphin, the influence of Diane de Poitiers rose also, and in a far greater degree than that of the dauphiness Catherine, who was treated with much superciliousness by many ladies of the court, because not of royal birth. Having found friendliness in Diane, she, from gratitude or other feeling, apparently, was now content to be as much swayed by her as was Henry himself. The great rivalry, therefore, that ensued on this change of places was not between the dauphin's wife and his friend, but between Madame la Duchesse d'Étampes and Madame Diane de Brézé.

The intrigues of these ladies for supremacy greatly distracted the king, and fomented dissension between him and the dauphin. The queen was in no sort a party to them; her hopes and fears being wholly absorbed in her anxiety for the interests of her brother.

The desperate warfare and court intrigues of

this year were, however, destined to be followed by a romantic royal marriage. Romance, always unusual in such marriages, was especially absent from those of the sixteenth century. The king's fair daughter Madeleine was then sixteen, and had already rejected two or three suitors proposed by her father. Like her grandmother, Anne of Brittany, she declared she would marry none but a king — a reigning sovereign.

The reigning sovereigns at that period she might well have considered, personally, far from eligible, even had they been free to ask the hand of this self-willed daughter of France, whose absolute refusal to be disposed of otherwise than suited her own fancy proclaimed her Breton descent. War was then raging; but by and by some treaty of peace might bring on the scene at least an heir apparent, whose marriage should be the seal and pledge, according to custom, of everlasting unity.

However, a gallant youth — no other than James V. of Scotland — arrived in France at this time, for the purpose of offering the king his sword and the services of the small squadron that accompanied him. He was not yet married, but was betrothed to Mary of England, whose numerous betrothals to almost all the kings and princes of Europe had not hitherto resulted in a marriage. But Henry VIII., who as yet had no son, had set his heart on this alliance, hoping ultimately thus to unite Scotland to England. The young king, however, was not so anxious. He disapproved of the schism in England — of Henry's divorce and marriages — and cared not to fall under his influence. He was himself a fervent Catholic, though Scotland inclined to the reformed faith; while lastly, and 'this may have been chiefly, his affianced bride possessed no attractions for him.

James soon heard of Madame Madeleine's resolve, and prompted perhaps, at first, by curiosity, he went to the Vendôme, where the queen and princesses were then staying, and contrived to be introduced as a Scottish nobleman travelling in France, and desirous of paying his respects to her majesty. Queen Eleanor, accompanied by the Princesses Madeleine and Marguerite, received him graciously; the result being, that the young king, charmed by the beauty and grace of the fair Madeleine, left his heart at Vendôme; fortunately, however, carrying away with him that of the youthful princess. The attraction was mutual — love at first sight; though Madeleine knew not then that this handsome cavalier was Scotland's king.

Charles V. had then begun his disastrous flight; and Francis, having despatched troops to the relief of Peronne, was on his "triumphant return" to Paris. James, without delay, made his formal demand for the hand of Madeleine, which was willingly granted. Madame's "inclination for the Scottish king " is mentioned in Giustiniani's report, and the whole court seems to have been elated by the celebration of so almost unique an event as a royal love-match.

The marriage of Louis XII. and Anne of Brittany was supposed to be one of affection, though based on political expediency. But there was no romance connected with it like that of a young king visiting a young princess incognito, and each receiving in the heart, when their eyes first met, a shaft from Cupid's bow. The marriage festivities and the rejoicing at Charles's discomfiture made the court exceedingly gay. That Henry VIII. was deeply offended chiefly concerned Francis. As to Mary's betrothal to James, it was the usual fate of such arrangements to be unceremoniously set aside when they had served their purpose. What Henry VIII. most resented was the establishing in Scotland, by means of this marriage, a rival influence to his own. However, such considerations abated nothing of the *éclat* with which the carnival was celebrated at Blois.

But Madeleine must soon bid adieu to fair France. The royal vessel, with its escort, which is to convey the young bride to her northern home, awaits her at Dieppe. There, towards the end of January, James V. and his queen embarked.

The beauty of the fair Madeleine was, unhappily, that of a brilliant, fragile flower, destined early to droop and die. The discomforts of the voyage tried her greatly; yet she rallied a little on arrival. But Scotland's inclement climate was too surely to prove fatal to her. Gaiety gradually forsook her. Languor daily increased. Sometimes a deadly pallor would give place to a brilliant hectic flush, and a bright smile o'erspread her countenance, inspiring the young king with deceitful hopes. Thus Madeleine lingered on for awhile, until one morning in May — like a flower nipped in the bud — she drooped her head and died.*

* James is said to have been inconsolable — and for a time perhaps he was. But we find him in France again at the end of the year, and when he returned to Scotland in 1538 he was accompanied by another French bride, a daughter of Duc de Guise, whose beauty had greatly attracted him, it appears, on his former visit to France. She was the mother of the unfortunate Mary Stuart. This second marriage displeased Henry VIII. even more than the first. It appeared like a determination to oppose the French interest in Scotland to his.

CHAPTER V.

A Pleasant Change.— The Picturesque Turk. — **Heart or Courage Fails Him.** — Chivalric Souvenirs.— Summoned by the Sound of Trumpet.— The Merciless De Montmorency.— The Dauphin's First Command. — A Brilliant Feat of Arms.— Paul III. Desires Peace.— Conciliation of Differences.— "Once Again Your Prisoner."— The Reunion at Aigues-Mortes.— The Duchess and the Diamond.— The Victim of the Truce.— An Ardent Son of the Church.— A Project to Invade England. — His Righteous Soul Was Vexed.— The Mighty Constable. — Worshipping the Rising Star.

GREAT results for France were looked forward to from the campaign of 1537. After the episode of the royal marriage and accompanying festivities, followed by the usual boisterous mirth of the carnival, the prospects of a new war, and the preparations for it, were a pleasant change both for thought and occupation. For if war then formed a chief part of the serious business of life, it also supplied a want in the amusements of the period, and ladies of the court, as well as gentlemen, would have found the monotony of existence difficult to support without the hopes, and fears, and flutterings of heart those stimulating wars excited.

There was so little variety, if much depravity,

in their round of pleasure and whirlpool of dissipation, that some stirring excitement was now and then needed as a relief from other pleasures, and to prevent the mind from becoming palled by them, like the palate by too much mawkish sweetness.

In the present campaign, the picturesque Turk was to bear a prominent part. The magnificent Solyman had just returned from his conquests in Persia, where he had taken Bagdad, Tauris, and other cities, and carried off immense spoils of war. Hitherto, Francis had scarcely dared openly to avow the Franco-Turkish alliance, and was, indeed, constantly denying its existence. But it had made a great advance in the preceding year, when Baron La-Forest, the first French ambassador to the Porte, was officially recognised as such.

He had even signed with the Turkish plenipotentiary — the grand-vizier, Ibrahim Pasha — a treaty of commerce, in which other European sovereigns, including the Pope, were permitted to join, if so disposed, within a given time. But Paul III. — a believer in nothing at all — was horrified at the very idea of a treaty with the infidel, though simply one of commerce, and other potentates expressed no desire to be included in it. This treaty was, however, but a cover for a secret arrangement of a different nature, by which Solyman and Francis expected, not exactly, perhaps, to entirely crush the emperor, but certainly to lay him low for a considerable time by the shock of the double blow they proposed to deal him.

Solyman was all energy, and had the reputation of being the friend of justice and order, an excellent ruler, and faithful observer of his word. The "most Christian king" was the reverse of all this. Every year, too, brought with it increased disinclination to take any active part in those wars he could not resist the desire of fomenting. Therefore, when the time came to strike the meditated blow, he allowed the fact of his engagement with Solyman to transpire—heart or courage failing him—and was immediately assailed by urgent entreaties and tearful appeals from his ladies to refrain from entering on any enterprise in connection with the terrible infidel Turk.

Naturally, Queen Eleanor was anxious to prevent the menaced evil that was to overwhelm her brother. But had Francis been really bent on carrying out his part of the arrangement—that of marching on Milan while Solyman attacked the emperor by sea—the prayers of Eleanor would not have availed to dissuade him. Even now, when he desired to be dissuaded, it was the wily favourite's eloquence, supporting the wife's appeal, which seemed to shake his resolution, and to dispose him eventually to yield.

The exhortations of the pious Paul III. and the arguments of the Cardinals of Lorraine and Tournon, sent by the Pope to enforce his views, had Francis been in earnest, would have availed but little, had not the magic of the low, soft voice of the duchess assisted in awakening chivalric souvenirs of the past in the breast of the "chevalier king." It is she who now conquers, or seems to do so, and, at her bidding, he abandons the infidel Solyman, as, at his mother's, he before had abandoned his Christian allies, the Italians.

But this has not put an end to war. He proposes still to attack the emperor, but in the Netherlands instead of Italy; while, to show that want of courage in no way influenced his change of plan, he announces his valiant intention of heading his army in person. To invest the opening of the new campaign with further solemnity, Francis — in imitation of Charles's harangue and vehement conduct at Rome — assembled in the great hall of Des Tournelles the princes of the blood, peers of the realm, forty or more bishops, the Parliament of Paris, the knights of Saint Michael, and other persons of distinction.

When the king had taken his seat, having the King of Navarre on one side, the King of Scotland on the other,* "the king's advocate, or attorney-general, proceeded to lay before the illustrious assembly an account of the great rebellions and treasons perpetrated by Charles of Austria,

---

*This was the 15th of January, a few days before the departure of James V. and his bride.

Count of Flanders, Artois, and Charolais, and the wrongful holder of several other feudal dependencies of the crown of France, against his sovereign lord, the king." The above-named places were then declared confiscated and reunited to the crown. "The peers, after maturely deliberating on these matters, ordered that a herald be sent to the frontier to summon, by sound of trumpet, the aforesaid Charles of Austria, requiring him to send such person or persons as he should think fit to defend his cause."

As no one appeared on the part of the said Charles, the demand of the king's advocate was ratified in due form; the king announcing his determination to execute the sentence against the said Charles of Austria "by force of arms."

"If," as says the historian Henri Martin, "Francis I. had conquered Flanders, there might have been something imposing in this theatrical ceremony; but under then existing circumstances it was simply ridiculous."

However, Francis and Montmorency took the field towards the end of March. St. Venant was besieged and taken, and Montmorency, who revelled in slaughter, massacred the inhabitants and garrison with merciless cruelty. Some small open towns were laid waste, and St. Pol fortified as a convenient *place d'armes*. Francis having then had as much of the excitement of war as he cared for, disbanded a large part of his army, left a small garrison in St. Pol, sent off the rest of his troops to Piedmont, and hastened back to Paris.

He was anxious to see how the work of covering the façade of his retreat in the Bois with the coloured and enamelled baked earth — for which Girolamo and Luca della Robbia had introduced the taste into France — was progressing. The time, too, had come round for the hunting parties and summer rambles, in which Chénonceau, Fontainbleau, and Chambord were now included. Not that those two last-named royal residences at all approached completion; but the Italian colony employed at each of them — under the superintendence respectively of Rosso and Primaticcio (called by the French "*Le Primatice*") — had sufficiently advanced certain portions of those vast edifices to allow of the king and his court making an occasional brief sojourn in them.

Scarcely, however, had the king exchanged the camp for the court and the routine of life most congenial to him, than news was brought from the theatre of war of the assault and retaking of St. Pol by an army of 35,000 men from the Netherlands, just as its fortification was completed. The whole of the garrison had been massacred by way of reprisal for the barbarities of De Montmorency at St. Venant. A general battle was, therefore, expected; the king was obliged to re-form his army, and the dauphin received his first command, having De Montmorency for his adviser.

Yet both Charles and Francis desired peace. But both had publicly made bombastic declarations, which had resulted in such poor achievements that "neither was willing to compromise his oath and his glory by taking the first step towards conciliation."

In this dilemma the agency of the ladies — Charles's two sisters — was again employed. Mary of Austria, the Dowager-queen of Hungary, governing the Netherlands in her brother's name, proposed a truce as a preliminary to a conference for peace; and her sister, the Queen of France, aided by De Montmorency, once more brought to bear on Francis what little influence she possessed in furtherance of it. Terms of peace could not be agreed on, but a ten months' truce was signed between France and the Netherlands.

This truce enabled Charles to gain the upper hand in Piedmont, where war between the emperor and king was still carried on. The garrison of Turin, resolved to die rather than surrender, were suffering all the horrors of starvation. Relief, however, was afforded them by what was considered a brilliant feat of arms. Headed by the dauphin, under the guidance of De Montmorency, the French forced the Pass of Susa, and, overcoming all efforts of the Spanish general, Del Guasto, to prevent them, debouched in the plains of Piedmont, and once more France was successful in Italy.

This produced a three months' truce for Piedmont, at the instance of Paul III. — so anxious, in the interests of Catholicism, for the reconciliation of the two great Christian sovereigns of Europe. This old Roman cardinal was credited with considerable diplomatic ability and much decision of character. He possessed both *esprit* and learning; was distinguished for intelligence rather than for religion and morality, and in his desire to be a pacificator he assumed towards the emperor and the king a position of absolute impartiality.

The progress of Lutheranism and Calvinism in the different countries of Europe had determined Paul to convoke a general council at Trent, in order that religious differences might be discussed, and the heretics, if possible, be made to see their errors and be gathered into the bosom of the Church. Such an assembly of prelates could not take place while the armies of France and Spain were slaying each other, agitating men's minds, and devastating the country; or while the Turk — Ferdinand having broken faith with him — was again leading his victorious bands into Hungary and Austria, and Barbarossa, now aided by a few French galleys, was ravaging the coasts of Italy. Peace must first be restored.

The truce accordingly was prolonged, that a better understanding might be arrived at; and Charles V. and Francis I., at the pontiff's earnest request, promised to repair to Nice, whither he himself prepared to go — to hear their complaints and conciliate their differences. The Duke of Savoy was much alarmed at the choice of Nice for their rendezvous. It was the only place that the emperor and king between them had not despoiled him of. Believing that their proposed meeting concealed some plan to deprive him of his last refuge, he refused to receive them in Nice, thus giving great offence to the three persons whom it was his interest to propitiate.

The Pope, in consequence, was compelled to lodge in a Franciscan convent in the vicinity of Nice, the emperor in his galley off Villa Franca, and the king at Villeneuve, a quarter of a league distant from Nice on the French side. The rival monarchs declined to meet; the Pope, therefore, received them alternately in a tent set up in the grounds of the monastery. A good deal of intrigue was meanwhile carried on at the Court of France. Eleanor and De Montmorency were in constant correspondence with the pontiff; the duchess for some reason not joining them as before, but like Chabot de Brion — her friend and favourite, as well as the king's — holding entirely aloof.

The result of this conference was a ten years' truce; the two potentates, after some months of discussion, being unable to settle their differences by a peace. The truce was signed on the 18th of June. The next day the Pope took his departure for Rome; the emperor was supposed to have sailed for Spain, and the king was about to leave for Avignon.

According to French authors, Francis, when setting off, received an intimation from the emperor of a desire to communicate with him, naming Aigues-Mortes as the place where, if the king would repair thither, he would land to meet him. At once he assented. As soon as the imperial fleet came in sight, Francis, accompanied by the Cardinal de Lorraine and "five or six *grands seigneurs* of his suite," embarked in a small galley and went off to the emperor's vessel. As he set foot on the deck he exclaimed, "My brother, behold me once again your prisoner!"

Spanish authors, however, assert that it was Francis, not Charles, who sought this interview, and that, having consented to it, the emperor — knowing that he could trust to the honour of the chevalier, though he could place no confidence in the promises of the king — unhesitatingly landed, accompanied only by his chancellor, Granvelle, and the grand commander of Sant-Yago. At all events they met, and embraced each other with all the apparent cordiality of old and firm friends who had never had a difference in their lives, much less the furious struggles for conquest, the public accusations and challenges to single combat, that had occurred between them.

All went as smoothly and pleasantly as possible.

The monarchs exchanged the collars of their orders — the Golden Fleece and Saint Michael — and Francis made Charles a present of a diamond worth 50,000 crowns. It was set in a gold ring bearing the motto, "*Dilectionis testis et exemplum.*"* Charles not only landed, but dined and slept on shore as the king's guest. Queen Eleanor soon after arrived, and had the satisfaction of once more meeting her brother. With the Duchesse d'Étampes she assisted at the conferences between the emperor and the king, the *maîtresse-en-titre* being received by the former with extreme courtesy, notwithstanding the presence of the queen.

The emperor's amenities had doubtless for object the gaining over of a powerful ally to his interests. For when, as first lady of the court after the queen — for the dauphiness as yet had no influence, and apparently was not admitted to the reunion at Aigues-Mortes — the duchess, according to the custom of the time, presented the *aiguière*, or silver ewer and basin, to the imperial guest to wash his hands, he is said designedly to have let a large diamond fall on the floor, which, on being picked up by an attendant and handed to the duchess to return to the emperor, he begged that she "would retain it."

This anecdote, accepted by some French writers, is wholly rejected by Mézeray and others. It does indeed seem a singularly awkward and rather

* Henri Martin.

discourteous way of making a lady a present. It is doubted, too, whether a diamond would have bought her alliance. She cared less for jewels than for political influence, and since the death of the dauphin Francis, foreseeing that when the king also died her importance at court would cease, and that she would have everything to fear from Henri and Diane, she attached herself to the king's youngest son, and sought to promote his interests, in order to ensure herself a safe retreat and the prince's protection.

So complete was the reconciliation between emperor and king, that the latter gave a very gracious reception to Andrea Doria, commanding the imperial galleys, who had passed into the emperor's service from the king's — though certainly by the fault of the latter. What passed between the two monarchs, at the long conferences that were daily held, did not immediately transpire. But as besides the Cardinal de Lorraine, De Montmorency, and two members of Charles's suite, two ladies also were present, it oozed out that Francis, as usual, gave up his allies (the German princes), and consented to much that was more advantageous to Charles than to himself and France, for the sake of a vague promise of the cession of Milan.

On the 18th of July, a month after the departure of the Pope, the now fast friends separated — the parting being as cordial as the greeting — Francis, well satisfied with the arrangements entered into, and Charles, probably with greater reason, no less so. "Henceforth," exclaimed Francis, "my affairs and those of the emperor may be considered as one, having the same aim and object!" Eleanor was delighted; and the duchess? Had the emperor's great courtesy — assuming that no diamond had dazzled her — made her yet a traitor? It is supposed that she had not on this occasion quite made up her mind.

The victim of the truce and the interview was the unfortunate Duke of Savoy, who for years was deprived of all his domains, with the single exception of Nice. For the emperor and the king, though visiting and conferring together daily with so much show of friendliness and familiarity, were taking precautions against each other by clinging firmly to what they had secured of the duke's possessions : the king, that when it suited him he might make his way into Italy; the emperor, that his troops might be at hand to prevent him.

The interview ended, the king returned to the North. He was suffering greatly in his health, and, on arriving at the Château de Compiègne, the symptoms of his malady were so severe that doubts were for a time entertained of his recovery. Although he eventually regained health, yet a marked change came over him from this time.

De Montmorency meanwhile ruled France, and by no means to its advantage — persecuting and imprisoning the French reformers; treating the Protestant princes of Germany, whose alliance Francis had abandoned, with a sort of contumely that provoked resentment. This ardent son of the Church was also desirous — in support of a papal bull declaring Henry VIII. deposed, in favour of his daughter Mary — to induce Charles, conjointly with Francis, to invade England in defence of his cousin's rights, and for putting an end to the schism.

But the emperor had already more than enough on his hands in the way of suppressing heresy. The Protestant League gave him infinite trouble; and military revolts in Milan and Tunis induced him to seek the aid of Francis to obtain a truce with Solyman. He was also in absolute want of money — this great potentate, "on whose dominions the sun never set," being unable to pay his mercenary troops. He therefore turned a deaf ear to any project of invading England, though the French ambassador had suggested to De Montmorency that the moment was favourable, and that the country, once conquered, might be parcelled out between James of Scotland, Francis I., and Charles V.

The constable, however, did prevail on Charles to sign a treaty with Francis, by which each bound himself to contract no further alliance with Henry VIII. — political or matrimonial — without the full concurrence of the other. Though fiercely zealous for the true faith, De Montmorency was not unmindful of his private interests, which he did not disdain to serve at the expense of the state — heaping up wealth, and obtaining possession of estate upon estate by practices that threw the corruption of Duprat entirely into the shade.

In his superintendence of the various departments of the state he exercised extremest rigour, so far as concerned the subordinate *employés*. Their heads were not safe on their shoulders, if the rogues he employed to look after the rogues reported the smallest fraud or extortion in office. This, too, at a period when honesty was the exception, and corruption the rule, from the highest to the lowest official — of which De Montmorency himself was one of the most notorious examples. Of the financial reports of those whose opportunities for enriching themselves by plundering the state were most ample — governors of provinces, for instance — he himself took cognisance. Nothing escaped his vigilance, and the strictness of his enquiries struck terror into the breasts of defaulters.

How his righteous soul was vexed when he detected the evil practices that had flourished so long under Duprat's administration! The king must be informed of it. But, had the delinquent a fine estate or two, purchased with his ill-gotten wealth; had he in his strong box a good round sum that would buy one — the offer of either would by degrees subdue the "great soldier's" indignation; and by and by pity for his erring brother led him not only to suppress the accusation, but to report him as one of the most able and honest of the king's representatives. It was thus he gained ten fine estates in Brittany and Anjou, and built his palace of Écouen.*

His arrogance was great. The king might be approached with less humility than he exacted, and not only from persons of inferior station, but from equals, whose merits and importance, or perhaps their favour with the king, he considered less than his own. The Admiral Chabot de Brion, in whom the king permitted a greater familiarity of address than any other of his courtiers, came under the high displeasure of the mighty constable, for using the same freedom towards him.

Francis laid it down as a maxim that "all who were nobles were equals, and he the first gentleman of France." De Montmorency evidently thought otherwise; and ere long De Brion felt the full weight of his resentment.† De Montmorency

---

* See "Mémoires de Vieilleville."

† He was charged with corruption and extortion in the exercise of his office of Governor of Burgundy and as Admiral of France. The king threatened him with a criminal *procès*, and on his replying haughtily that he feared not the issue if the judges were not corrupted, he was immediately arrested and imprisoned in the fortress of Meudon. There he remained for a year before a commission was appointed to judge him — the king interfering to obtain a sentence of death on the companion and friend of his

was unable to displace the duchess, notwithstanding her heresy, which to so stern a moralist and good son of the Church must have been grievous indeed; but, looking anxiously towards the not-distant future (the king's death, which was then so generally expected), he devoted himself to Madame Diane, thus covertly worshipping the rising star — the king's suspicion and dislike of his heir rendering any open display of attachment to him perilous to those who would win or retain the monarch's favour.

boyhood and manhood. All the judges were not willing. A decree of banishment was therefore pronounced, with the confiscation of the whole of his property, and a fine of a million and a half of *francs*. Nothing being left him wherewith to pay the fine, the banishment became perpetual imprisonment. In prison he languished for upwards of another year, when the unceasing efforts of Madame d'Étampes in his favour at last obtained for him an interview with the king. Francis was so struck by the change he saw in his former light-hearted friend, that — passing from one extreme to another with, as has been observed, the caprice of an Eastern despot — he at once commanded his liberation; publicly declared him exonerated from all blame, and freed from all pain and penalty. In the following month he was reinstated in his governorship of Burgundy and post of Admiral of France. His estates, etc., were also restored. But Chabot de Brion's spirit was broken. He did not rally; grief and imprisonment had too deeply affected him, and within a year after his rehabilitation he died, June the 1st, 1543. Francis, whose conscience smote him probably for bringing him to an early grave, granted him the vain reparation of a splendid tomb — one of the finest works of the sixteenth century. Jean Cousin was its sculptor.

CHAPTER VI.

The Good City of Ghent Revolts.— The Emperor's Difficulty. — Relieved from His Dilemma. — The Imperial Visitor. — Gracious Was His Mood. — An Imposing Cavalcade. — The Château de Chambord. — The Double Spiral Staircase. — "*Toute Femme Varie.*"— Charles's Entry into Paris.— A Very High Privilege.— Ambitious of Conquest.— A Silver Statue of Hercules. —" Now You Are My Prisoner."— The Courts of France and Madrid.— A Plot to Arrest the Emperor. — A Hint of a Very High Destiny. — When He Is at Leisure. — His Vengeance on His Birthplace. — Francis Enraged. — The Fall of An Enemy.

N his return to Spain, the emperor was informed that "the good city of Ghent" had revolted, and that other cities were threatening to follow its example. The insurrection was of a very serious character, and the principal inhabitants secretly sent deputies to Francis I., claiming his aid and protection as the sovereign lord of Flanders.

Francis had now the opportunity of taking possession of the provinces over which so lately, in grandiloquent terms and with many formalities, he had claimed the suzerainty; declared them confiscated, reunited to France, and announced his intention of carrying out this sentence by force of arms. But a change had since come o'er the spirit of his dream. He and his delinquent vassal, "the aforesaid Charles of Austria," were now firm friends, and Milan, as he flattered himself, would be the immediate reward of his betrayal of the people who had offered themselves and their country to him as their lawful sovereign.

Charles had long imposed a heavy burden of taxation on his Flemish subjects for the support of his Spanish army and his hireling troops, in carrying on wars that in no way concerned them. He had obtained also large loans from the wealthy city of Ghent, and had promised that until they were fully repaid no further tax should be levied there. He had failed in his word. A heavy tax was imposed; the people refused to pay it, deposed the municipal authorities, elected others, and were now in open revolt.

The emperor's difficulty was how most readily to reach this remote part of his wide but scattered dominions. He was unwilling to risk an encounter with English ships by going by sea; besides, the ports of Flanders were now hostile to him; while, should he traverse Germany, trouble would be likely to ensue with the unfriendly Protestant states. He was relieved from this dilemma by Francis, who adopted the magnanimous part of informing him of the propositions of his rebellious subjects, and invited him to take the shortest route to Ghent, that which lay through France, to punish the seditious burgesses.

Charles gladly accepted the offer. He feared not to put his head, as more than one of his ministers hinted to him he was about to do, into the lion's mouth. He knew what a talisman he had in Milan. It was, indeed, partly promised at Aigues-Mortes to the young Duc d' Orléans, together with the hand of the emperor's eldest daughter, or that of one of the daughters of his brother Ferdinand. But Charles very wisely, before leaving Spain, enacted from Francis "an engagement not to require him, while journeying through his dominions, to sign any promises or treaty of marriage which had been discussed between them, lest it should be afterwards said he had signed them under constraint." He, however, declared that, on arriving at the first city within his own dominions, he would guarantee those promises so securely that the king would have reason "to be thoroughly satisfied." *

The king consented. He had surely forgotten how faithfully, how scrupulously he had kept a similar promise himself, for no doubts assailed him, and De Montmorency and the two young princes set off for Bayonne to receive the imperial visitor.

On the 20th of November, the emperor, with a retinue by no means numerous, crossed the Bidassoa. The king, to dissipate any possible disquietude his guest might feel respecting his

* Martin du Bellay; H. Martin.

personal safety on landing in France, ordered his two sons to be presented to the emperor by the constable as hostages. Charles, in replying to De Montmorency, said that he "accepted the young princes, his cousins, not as hostages to be sent to Spain, but as the companions of his journey."

Great preparations had been made for his entry into Bayonne, it being the good pleasure of the king that, from the time the emperor set foot in France till his departure, the same reception should be accorded to him in every city and town he passed through as was customarily given to the kings of France on their accession. The citizens accordingly spared no expense to impress Charles with the idea that France was a country overflowing with wealth and in a high state of commercial prosperity.

The municipal authorities, in their robes of office, met him at the city gates. The constable preceded him, bearing the sword of state unsheathed. The princes rode on either side, and the nobles who had assembled to form his *cortége* followed. The emperor, the object of whose journey, as Servan says, was to mercilessly hang, imprison, and reduce to poverty the unfortunate citizens of Ghent who had attempted to resist his exactions, now unbarred prison doors, pardoned the criminal, released the debtor, and so gracious was his mood that he would doubtless have even unbound heretics at the stake, had not De Montmorency burnt them all or driven them out of the country. Blessings, to which he was little accustomed, therefore attended Charles V. throughout his journey, cursings awaiting him at the end of it.

The prodigality and the extravagance in dress displayed by the *bourgeoisie* must have astonished the prudent Charles. "At Poitiers, he was received by near five hundred gentlemen, richly dressed, and two thousand of the citizens in robes of velvet and satin, bordered with gold and silver lace." From Orléans a still more imposing cavalcade rode out to meet him. The *bourgeoisie* of this royal city had certain privileges, which, like the citizens of Paris, they shared with the nobility. Ninety-two of these privileged merchants of the upper *bourgeoisie* accompanied the governor and persons of distinction, to greet the emperor and welcome him to their city.*

"All of them," says Paradin, "were mounted on excellent chargers, and all wore coats or casaques

---

* Orléans was then considered a large, handsome town. Charles V. said it was the finest city he saw in France. "Where, then," he was asked, "does your majesty place Paris?" "Oh, Paris," he replied, "is no city, but rather a little world." Yet Giustiniani thought it inferior to Venice, scarcely larger, and the population, given as 700,000, greatly over-estimated — the reason being, he fancied, that all the inhabitants had the habit of standing at their doors or in the streets; men and women, old people and children, masters and servants, were all visible, so that between 300,000 and 400,000 would be the more correct figure, he thought.

of black velvet, and doublets or vests of white satin fastened with gold buttons. Their boots were of white morocco, slashed, and their spurs either silver-gilt or gold. Their caps or toques were also of velvet, but elaborately ornamented with gold embroidery and precious stones. "One toque," he continues, "was valued at two thousand crowns, and not one of these merchants (all were young and wealthy, it appears) but had on him in jewels the value of at least two thousand *francs*."

What with the badness of the roads and these ever-recurring pageants, the imperial and royal progress was slow indeed. A whole month elapsed ere Charles arrived at Lorches, at whose famed château Francis, unable to proceed further, being scarcely convalescent, awaited him.

The monarchs cordially embraced and renewed their professions of friendship, and from Lorches travelled together, approaching Paris by very easy stages, the journey being diversified by hunting parties, grand *fêtes*, and banquets, in which the queen, the Duchesse d'Étampes, and ladies of the court participated on the emperor's arrival at Blois.

Both at Blois and Amboise the alterations and embellishments then in progress employed a host of Italian artists and skilled workmen. But Charles was most struck by that "marvel and *chef-d'œuvre* of the Renaissance," the Château de

Chambord, which, though not half of it was yet completed, excited the wonder and admiration of all who beheld it. The works were then under the superintendence of Primaticcio, to whom has sometimes been attributed the original design of this fairy palace, "surpassing," say writers of that period, "the description of the fabled abodes of Morgane or Alrine."

But the French are not willing to ascribe the plan of this edifice to an Italian architect. They give it a French origin, but can only suggest the artist's name, though one would suppose him to have been a man of so much eminence that no doubt could have existed about it; for Francis was not accustomed to employ artists, whatever their ability, who had not made a name. He patronised art for the sake of the glory it might shed on him and his reign; but his love of it never led him to foster rising or obscure talent.

One of the wonders of the Château de Chambord Charles especially admired was its double spiral staircase of 286 steps, rising in the centre of the edifice, from its basement to its highest point — the lantern, crowned by an enormous *fleur-de-lys*. It was a sort of puzzle. Eight persons could walk abreast up or down it, the ascending and descending parties never meeting, yet seeing each other.*

---

* The "Grande Mademoiselle" de Montpensier mentions this staircase in her memoirs, and the amusement of her father at

It was on a window-pane of an apartment of the Château de Chambord that Francis, in one of his fits of melancholy — when years and dissipation began to tell on him, and ladies smiled less beamingly upon him than in days of yore — is said to have written with the point of a diamond those oft-quoted lines, conveying a reproach which he of all others was least entitled to utter:

"*Souvent femme varie
Bien fol qui s'y fie.*"

But Brantôme, the early portion of whose memoirs are so little to be relied on, being nothing but scandal a generation or two old, of which personally he knew nothing, may be considered authentic evidence in this matter — one of small importance, certainly. He says that when he visited Chambord — which was when, in the reign of Henri III., the château began to be much neglected — he asked to see the window-pane on which Francis I. had written the above. The person in charge, apparently a friend of Brantôme, took him to a small room adjoining the chapel, and he gives as the inscription :

"*Toute femme varie,*"

nothing more. This seems more likely to be cor-

---

her efforts to come up with him when he was descending. For, although she could see him, she vainly tried to meet and get within reach of him.

rect than the lines usually given. Marguerite, it is said, was with the king, and what he wrote was a reply to some remark of hers. In the dreary mood he was in, he may have fancied this devoted sister changed towards him like others, and thus have expressed his feeling.*

The king, however, entertained Charles V. for some days at Chambord with great magnificence and profuse hospitality, which he repaid by admiration of all he saw in the immense park and grounds of that vast domain. As for the château itself, though only the donjon-keep and one pavilion could be said to be finished, Charles declared that he saw in them "an epitome of all that man's genius and industry could accomplish." This was flattering to Francis; but he would rather have heard him speak of Milan. He was pledged not to utter the word himself; and Charles apparently had for the nonce abjured politics and business, in order the more thoroughly to enjoy the pleasures and festivities so lavishly provided for him.

From Chambord they went to Fontainebleau, where again all that imagination could suggest was adopted to vary and invent new pleasures. The welcome of the imperial visitor at Orléans has

---

* This window-pane is said to have remained intact for upwards of a century, when it was removed by order of the Grand Monarque, who was fêting Madame de la Vallière at Chambord — her indignation being excited on reading so slanderous a reproach on her sex.

Palace of Fontainebleau.
Photo-etching from a photograph.

already been referred to; but the enthusiasm of the Parisians on his entry into the capital on the 1st of January, 1540, exceeded all that had preceded it. "The emperor alighted at Notre Dame, where a *Te Deum* was sung in honour of his arrival. He was afterwards installed in the Palais des Tournelles, and supped with the king in the great hall of St. Louis — five hundred gentlemen attending, ranged on opposite sides of this spacious apartment."

Charles had an enormous appetite, and ate voraciously. What a fine subject, then, for serious and speculative thought was presented to those five hundred gentlemen wall-flowers, whose high privilege it was to gaze on their royal master and the imperial guest, as grand officers of the household — preceded by heralds and followed by the chief officers of the culinary department to the entrance of the banqueting-hall — bore in the savoury and artistic productions of the royal cooks and confectioners, served on golden dishes (borrowed, probably, of some of the nobility, for Francis was always selling or melting down his plate).

They might, like M. Michelet, have found difficulty in believing that a man with so gluttonous an appetite could really be a great man — "such habits," continues that historian, "announcing the absence of great ideas and generous sentiments which should otherwise fill the soul." Doubtless. Yet men of spare appetites, even in these days of high culture and civilisation, are not, as a rule, more generous in their sentiments or more lofty in their ideas than the larger consumers of food.

Charles V. was not a great man. He was a man ambitious of conquest, caring not how much blood was shed or thousands of human beings sacrificed to accomplish his ends — which were often mean and base enough — though his grand and final object was to hold sovereign sway over Europe. Francis I. had similar but more restricted views, but set no greater value on human life than his rival. He was even a greater scourge to his generation than Charles, from his unexampled depravity. The king and his guest were indeed worthy of each other.

Charles was fond of the Rhenish wines, preferring them to the wines of Spain. It is not, however, recorded that he then indulged too freely in this respect. It was of vital importance to him to keep his head clear. But at one of the banquets given by Francis, the king's cupbearer is said to have enquired if his majesty would take Burgundy. Momentarily the question was startling, but Charles quickly replied that he would. Then suddenly Brusquet, one of the court buffoons, jumped up by his side from under the table. "Cousin," he whispered, rather loudly, "you mean you would take it if you could." Charles was not pleased.

After a week or ten days spent in jousts, and masques, banquets, and balls, and *fêtes* — which, being carnival time, were more noisily enthusiastic than usual — the emperor began to be desirous of continuing his journey to Ghent. The corporation of Paris then presented him with a silver statue of Hercules, said to have been of the height of a tall man. The lion skin partly enveloping the figure was represented in gold. The famous sculptor, Jean Cousin, was also commissioned to make a bust of the emperor to commemorate his visit.

He had been received and entertained in truly royal fashion; yet he was beginning to have doubts that all would be carried out loyally to the end. The same court fool, Brusquet — some writers say Triboulet, but whichever of these fools it may have been, he carried about with him what he called his calendar of fools, on which he had placed the emperor's name, deeming him a fool for trusting himself in France. "But," said the king, to whom Brusquet had shown his calendar, "suppose I allow him to pass through it without let or hindrance?" "Then, cousin," replied Brusquet, "I efface his name and put yours in its place." This would, of course, come to the ears of some of the emperor's suite, and would not fail to reach his. For court fools, who were not quite such fools as they seemed to be, were often employed to tell disagreeable truths under the mask of folly.

The young Duc Charles d' Orléans, in the

thoughtless gaiety of youth, one day jumped on the croup of the emperor's horse, and throwing his arms around his imperial majesty, laughingly exclaimed, "Now you are my prisoner." Charles thought this act suggested by some project of the sort that had been discussed among the courtiers.

He evidently grew rather anxious, and justly so when Francis himself — whom one must still believe incapable of contemplating so base an act — had the folly and bad taste to say to the emperor, directing his attention to Madame d' Étampes, "You see that fair lady, my brother? She is of opinion that I ought not to allow you to leave Paris until you have revoked the Treaty of Madrid." "If the advice is good," replied Charles, apparently unmoved, "it should be followed."

If this anecdote may be considered trustworthy (but few of this period are so) it exonerates Madame d' Étampes from the accusation of having kept up an active correspondence with the emperor from the time of the meeting at Aigues-Mortes, informing him of every occurrence at the Court of France that could be of interest or advantage to him. That he made a point during his prolonged journey through France of paying her the most courteous attention, and of endeavouring to conciliate her by political disclosures relating to his intentions towards the young Duc d' Orléans, in whose welfare, for reasons of her own, already intimated, she was interested, there can be no doubt. He would readily perceive that a woman of her ability and foresight would be more likely to be gained in that way than by presents and complimentary speeches.

The Court of France, with its rival factions, its intriguing favourites, mistresses, and courtiers, must have presented a striking contrast to the solemn Court of Madrid, where no heretic *maîtresse-en-titre* disturbed, by her superior influence, the serenity of the Empress-Queen Isabella. "For," remarks his panegyrist, Amadée Pichot, "Charles was the most faithful of husbands, and that, too" (which he seems to think enhanced his hero's merit), "as a contemporary of Henry VIII. and his wives, and Francis I. and his mistresses."*

The emperor, however, played a very able part at this intriguing dissolute Court of France; for if he succeeded in gaining an ally in the mistress, he also obtained a supporter of his interests in the arrogant De Montmorency, whom he seduced by a show of deference to his opinions, and an apparent conviction, almost as strong as his own, of his surpassing merit and infallible wisdom. It was probably well for the emperor that the constable was pleased with his flattery — a plot to arrest him at Chantilly having, it appears, been actually concocted between the dauphin, the King of Na-

---

* Charles was at this time a widower. Isabella died in the preceding year. They are said to have lived in great harmony, Charles being much attached to his queen.

varre, and the young Duc de Vendôme. To give effect to it De Montmorency's concurrence was needed, which he very rightly refused, whatever motive may have prompted him.

The dauphin had retained so vivid a recollection of the rigour and restraint he had in his childhood been subjected to, during his and his elder brother's four years' residence in Spain as their father's hostages, that he was deterred only by the king's injunction from openly exhibiting the rancour he bore the emperor. Charles was well aware of it, and is said to have intended to make such concessions in favour of the younger brother, of whom Henri was supposed to be jealous, as would tend to increase the coldness existing between them, and attach the Duc d'Orléans to the interests of Spain.

It does not appear that he attempted the conquest of either Catherine or Diane. Having devoted himself to the duchess, he scarcely could do so with any hope of success. He, however, did not forget Marguerite — having in view the putting an end to the quarrel respecting Navarre by uniting it to Spain by a marriage. His arrangement with Francis that treaties and marriages were not to be discussed while he was in France precluded anything beyond an indirect reference to the very high destiny awaiting little Jeanne d'Albret. This could have but one interpretation — that Jeanne was to be the bride of young

Philip, Prince of the Spains, and Navarre her marriage portion. This seems to have flattered Marguerite more than her husband — if we are to suppose that he was concerned in a plot to arrest the emperor.

But at last the imperial traveller resumes his journey amidst great demonstrations of friendship. The king accompanies him on his way as far as St. Quentin. The princes and the constable take leave of him only at the frontier, and return thence to Paris. But the ambassadors enter Valenciennes with him. It is the first city under his dominion, and there he is required to ratify his promises to the king. He pleads the urgency of delaying no longer the punishing of his rebellious subjects; but as soon as he is at leisure he will fully satisfy the king. With this promise Francis is perforce compelled to be for awhile content.

A numerous escort awaited the emperor at Brussels, and on the 26th of February, his birthday, he entered the unfortunate city of Ghent in great state, and followed by a large detachment of troops. Ghent was his natal city; but he had no thought of showing clemency towards it. The inhabitants had been sorely discouraged by the result of their appeal to Francis, which in the eyes of the emperor was, perhaps, their greatest crime. Resistance was useless; they submitted at once, throwing themselves on his mercy.

At once he proceeded to pass judgment on

them. Fourteen of the principal inhabitants were beheaded; others were hanged on the market-place. Their property was confiscated, and the city deprived of all its rights and privileges, and condemned to a double fine or penalty — "the *amende honourable* and the *amende profitable.*" In fulfilment of the former the municipal authorities were ordered to implore the pardon of the emperor on their knees, barefooted, bareheaded, and with ropes round their necks. The *amende profitable* consisted in the payment of a very large sum of money to the emperor, besides the tax which had been the cause of the rebellion; and 6,000 gold caroli annually for the building of a fortress and the support of a garrison to keep the town in subjection.

"Thus perished the glory of the wealthy city of Ghent. Its commerce soon passed to Antwerp, its republican spirit to Holland" (H. Martin). The Duke of Alba would have had the illustrious old city razed to the ground. But Charles forbore further to devastate and wreak vengeance on his birthplace.

Supposed to be now at leisure, the French ambassadors again requested the emperor to furnish those guarantees to which he had pledged himself in fulfilment of his promises to the king. He simply replied that "he had made no promises." But as he was not yet prepared for war, he explained to the ambassadors a project to be submitted to the king respecting an arrangement that would eventually give Burgundy, Navarre, and other places to Spain by the marriage of the Duc d' Orléans with his daughter the Infanta, and Jeanne d'Albret with his son Philip.

Francis was enraged. He declined his proposals; refused to visit him, as had been arranged, at Brussels, and, to prevent any further attempt at negotiation on the subject, he sent for Jeanne d'Albret, and, though opposed by her parents, married her to the Duc de Clèves (Guillaume de la Marck), whom the emperor had deprived of a portion of his domains, and, consequently, was his sworn enemy. To make this marriage-knot secure against any future attempt to untie it, a ridiculous ceremony was gone through, similar to that which took place when Anne of Brittany was secretly married by proxy to the Emperor Maximilian. The same fate awaited it — it was set aside when convenient. The little bride was but in her eleventh year, and after her marriage returned to her governess.

The emperor replied to this contemptuous rejection of the great alliance he had desired for Jeanne, by the formal investiture of his son Philip as Duke of Milan — a terrible blow to Francis. However, as war was then as inconvenient to him as to the emperor, the ten-years' truce remained in force — and the king vented his wrath on his favourites and courtiers.

The superb De Montmorency was banished to his estates, and deprived of the various posts he held in the royal household, though not of any part of his ill-gotten wealth, as he should have been. De Brion thus saw the fall of his enemy. But as he is described as a man of amiable character and humane feeling, it was probably no gratification to him. The constable solaced himself in his enforced retirement by encouraging the progress of the arts, in enlarging and decorating Chantilly, and building Écouen; calling into requisition the services of many of the most famous artists, native and foreign — among the former Bernard Palissy, of whom he was one of the first patrons.

Francis, in his rage, did not stop at disgracing De Montmorency. He made quite a clearance of his court, banishing from it all who had seemed to favour the imperial alliance. It is almost surprising that he did not banish his wife. Madame d'Étampes suggested new men to fill up the vacant posts, and still reigned supreme over the mind of the now capricious, suffering, wrathful, gloomy king of France.

CHAPTER VII.

Wider Becomes the Breach. — Improved in Health and Spirits. — Benvenuto Cellini. — Tramping the Country. — Now I Take My Leave of You. — Cellini's Pilgrimage. — Brought Back in Triumph. — Cellini an Abbot. — The Duchess's Hair-dresser. — The God of War, but No Venus. — The Gates of Fontainebleau. — Cellini Leaves France. — Expedition Against Algiers. — A Terrific Tempest. — Again the Storm Rages. — A Favourable Conjuncture.

THE lavish hospitality with which Francis had received his rival; the sumptuous *fêtes* he had given in his honour; the friendly feelings that seemed to animate both emperor and king, and the mutual professions of confidence and esteem with which they parted, gave promise of a lengthened peace rather than renewal of hostilities. But wider and wider became the breach between them, from the moment that Charles, throwing off the mask he had assumed in France, declared there were no promises on his part to ratify.

Francis, however, having wreaked on his favourites, his ministers, his brother-in-law and sister, the wrath he felt towards the emperor, being now, and perhaps by that very process, somewhat improved in health and spirits, divided his time between his pleasures and his preparations for war. The larger part was of course given to the former, though the latter were on a scale of unusual magnitude. His habits were now, on the whole, more those of an old man, fractious and infirm, and loving his ease; yet there were moments — or, if it be permitted to use the term, "*bons quarts d'heure*" — when this old, worn-out monarch of forty-six engaged in the chase (a passion with him still) with all the vigour of bygone days.

He and his court were also, as of old, ever on the move — more to his own satisfaction than theirs — for it was not only Venetian ambassadors who found in these royal rambles less pleasure than fatigue and expense. Even one whose energy, daring exploits, hairbreadth escapes, and strangely turbulent adventures should have made him proof against far greater discomforts than camping out in the open air on a wet or windy night — as was sometimes the case on these jaunts when weather suddenly changed — complained bitterly of the discomforts of thus journeying from place to place under, to him, the sullen skies of France.

This was that wild, harum-scarum, but most renowned and skilful sculptor and engraver, Benvenuto Cellini, who at this time returned to France — from which he had fled, disgusted with its climate, shortly before the emperor's visit. In Italy, as usual, owing to his impetuous temper, he soon got in trouble, and once again into prison, whence he made several desperate but ineffectual attempts to escape. The intervention of Francis and Cellini's friend, Cardinal Ferrara, procured his release, and a summons from the cardinal brought him post-haste and full of brilliant expectations to Fontainebleau.

There he saw the king, whose knee, he tells us, he kissed, while he thanked him for the part he had taken in restoring him to liberty, assuring him that "such meritorious actions were set down in the books of the Almighty before any other virtuous deeds whatever." Francis seemed gratified by this assurance. But when Cellini placed before him the famous silver cup and basin he had designed and chased for the cardinal, the king declared that, although he had seen all the *chefs-d'œuvre* of the artists of Italy, he had seen none that could compare, for beauty and grace of design and perfection of chiselling, with this new specimen of Cellini's skill. "I will think," said Francis, "of some great and curious piece of work which you shall execute for me. Meanwhile, repose after your fatigues, and take your pleasure."

"The king," says Cellini, "was, as usual, on the eve of departure, so we" (he and his two men) "followed the court, and truly we were in great straits while we did so. The king, in time of peace, travels with upwards of 1,200 horses, and a retinue of several hundred persons. Sometimes the halt was made in places where scarcely a house was to be met with, when we were compelled to put up with wretchedly uncomfortable tents, and to live like gipsies." Cellini thought it derogatory to a man of his talent to be tramping the country in the king's suite — unnoticed, unemployed.

Always dilatory, Francis thought more of his amusements than of the great work he had promised the artist, while Cellini, in his feverish impatience, thought of nothing else. What was its nature? When and where was it to be begun? How much longer must he wait for the king's commands concerning it? — were questions he put to the cardinal, and prayed him to speak to the king, reminding him of his promise. This Ferrara took the first opportunity of doing. "It was a pity," he said, "to let a man of such genius lose his time, he being also so very anxious to get to work." "Arrange about his salary," replied the king.

This piece of good news, as the cardinal thought it, he communicated to the artist. "I propose," he said, "that a salary of 300 crowns be given you, which I think will be abundantly sufficient, and you may leave the management of it to me, as I am always ready to assist you."

Scarcely could the superb Cellini restrain his indignation until the cardinal ceased speaking. Then, with all the dignity of speech and manner he could summon to his aid, he answered: "Your reverence sent me an express order to Ferrara to ride post to France — as though riding post was a part of my business. But if you had then said that 300 crowns was the salary that awaited me as a suitable one for my services, I should not have moved, or have thought it worth my while to do so for double that sum. But since God has made you the instrument of my deliverance from imprisonment, with all my heart I thank you for the great blessing for which I am indebted to you. I shall always pray for your reverence, in whatever part of the world I may be — and now I take my leave of you."

"Go wherever you please!" exclaimed the cardinal, in a passion; "one cannot serve a man against his will."

Right or wrong, and it was as frequently one as the other, when Cellini had decided on doing a thing, he did it. He now called for his two workmen, Paolo and Ascanio; informed them, to their surprise, of his immediate departure, dismissed them from his service, gave them his blessing and money for their journey home. For himself, he proposed to make a pilgrimage to the Holy Sepulchre, his object being to model while there a figure of Christ, "approaching as nearly as possible to the Divine beauty which had been displayed to him in a vision of the Saviour."

His horse was soon saddled, his saddle-bags soon ready. Off he rode, intending to get some thirteen or fourteen leagues on his pilgrimage that day. He had ridden about two leagues, when he entered a wood, and had fallen into a dreamy sort of contemplation of the beauty of the scenery around him, from which he was suddenly aroused by the sound of horses' hoofs. He turns to see who are his pursuers. It is a company of seven or eight horsemen, and, expecting that he is about to be assailed by robbers, he draws his rapier, and facing them, waits their attack.

As they approach, he perceives that his man Ascanio is one of the party; he then recognises others, and finally the cardinal himself. They are come to bring him back. For the king was frantic with rage when he heard that Cellini had left.

"Gone to Jerusalem," as his workmen said — "deeply wounded in his self-love, his artist-pride, by the offer of a salary of 300 crowns." "Three hundred crowns!" exclaimed the king — "I give him 700; the same salary as Leonardo da Vinci had; and let messengers be instantly sent in pursuit of him. Take him 500 crowns for the expenses of his journey from Ferrara, and tell him that he will receive extra payment for all the work he does for me."

This was such good news that the cardinal, who had been the cause of Cellini's flight, thought fit, as a further inducement to him to return, to be the bearer of it himself. He had known him long; therefore doubted whether Cellini — so well aware of his own great merit as an artist, and naturally of so vain and so impetuous and turbulent a spirit — would condescend to change his newly formed plans. But he was obedient to the command of the king, to whom he was escorted back in triumph. Thus did the celebrated Benvenuto Cellini enter the service of Francis I., continuing in it some four or five years from that time.

Twelve silver candlesticks, representing six gods and six goddesses, of the height of three cubits each — which Cellini says was about the height of the king * — was the "great and curious work in which Francis first employed him; and so well pleased was he with the designs, the celerity, and *con amore* with which the artist worked — for Cellini was always diligent and almost always in love. with his own productions — that before the work was completed he ordered a large sum of money to be sent to him.

The cardinal, who seems to have been strangely averse to this famous workman in the precious metals being too well paid for his labours, contrived by some means to get the order revoked. Perhaps the state coffers were empty, or the king may have repented of his hasty generosity, and the cardinal have taken on himself the blame of its non-fulfilment. At all events, his majesty

---

* This must have been an error — if the cubit was not more than eighteen inches. Four cubits would be more likely, as Francis was nearly six feet in height.

compensated the disappointed artist by making him an abbot. "If the revenue of one abbey is not enough, let him have two," he said, "or three." Thus worthily did the king exercise his power of filling vacant benefices.

Cellini was less successful in gaining the favour of Madame d'Étampes. He offended her first by turning her hair-dresser out of the court of the old Palais de Nesle, and throwing his blocks, his wigs, his pomade, and all the paraphernalia of his trade into the street after him. The king had given this château as a studio and residence to the artist, who found that many persons had made their home in it and its principal courtyard, without any right to do so. They seemed disposed rather to dislodge the artist than to allow him to dislodge them.

He complained to the king, who replied, abruptly, "Who are you, and what is your name?" Cellini was mute with astonishment. The question was repeated. "My name," he answered, "is Benvenuto Cellini." "If, then," said the king, "you are that same Benvenuto who has been described to me, act like yourself. You have my full permission." A word to the wise is sufficient. Cellini soon cleared his palace of intruders, a few angry brawls ensuing, a few broken bones, and just a little blood-letting from the artist's free use of that favourite weapon, his rapier.

Francis was perhaps in want of a new sensation, a new pleasure, when he told the excitable artist to act like himself, so much was he amused by the details of Cellini's reckless proceedings. He visited him in his studio, accompanied by the queen, the duchess, and his courtiers, to see the designs for the bas-reliefs that were to ornament the fountain of Fontainebleau. Cellini had introduced the figure of the king as the God of War, which was generally admired both for its martial *pose* and the resemblance to Francis in feature. Nowhere, however, could the prying eyes of Madame d'Étampes discover a Venus under her own form and likeness, and the omission did not please her.

To recover her favour Cellini determined to present her with an elegant silver-gilt vase, exquisitely engraved, and chased in fanciful and graceful designs. On arriving at her hôtel (afterwards l'Hôtel de Luynes) the duchess sent him word by one of her women to wait until she could receive him.

Up and down the anteroom, in an irritable mood, he paced, until, his patience quite exhausted (no very long time, it may be presumed), he went off in a terribly indignant state of mind, and presented the offering intended for the duchess to the Cardinal de Lorraine.

This incident afforded much amusement to the court. The king laughed heartily, and rallied Madame d'Étampes on the loss of her vase. But she was highly incensed at "the insolence of that mad fellow," and probably would have prevailed on the king to resent the act by some heavy mark of his displeasure, but that the dauphin and Madame Marguerite, the king's daughter, interceded for him.

Cellini was then desirous of leaving France; but the king would not hear of it, and instead of permission to leave sent him letters of naturalisation, the meaning of which he did not comprehend. Besides, the king commissioned him to make the bronze gates of Fontainebleau. He would have also employed him to fortify Paris had not Madame d'Étampes urged him to send for Bellaminta, an engineer of Siena, as a fitter person to undertake such a work. This seems reasonable advice, and the duchess was then his chief adviser — the king having cleared his court of all his old favourites. But Cellini attributed the suggestion to her enmity towards him.

She, however, again visited his studio with the king and the court to see the bronze gates, which received their due tribute of admiration, Francis declaring that they "could not have been more beautiful had they been intended for the gates of Paradise."

This work concluded, again the artist expressed a wish to revisit Italy — on leave of absence, to see his relatives. But Francis was still unwilling to part with him, and was irritated by the request, to which he replied that "Cellini was a blockhead for making it." Cellini afterwards availed himself of some misunderstanding with the cardinal that the king gave him permission to leave, and at once took his departure. Francis lost in him not only an artist of great genius, but a *protégé* whose eccentricities and turbulent spirit were a source of great amusement to him. Consequently he was allowed to commit with impunity many strange acts that would have brought severe punishment on another who had not, like Cellini, the gift of investing all he did with a certain air of wild romance.

He had many quarrels and lawsuits on hand when he left. He had fought several duels, and it was his custom after all these brawls, and escapades, and successful use of his rapier, devoutly to return thanks to the Almighty for his triumph and escape unharmed. Between him and Primaticcio, whom Madame d' Étampes favoured, there was open war; and indeed amongst the Italian artists generally there appears to have been great jealousy of feeling and much intrigue and treachery.*

While Francis was building and decorating palaces — employing one set of artists to make

* On returning to Florence, Cellini was employed by Cosmo de' Medici, for whom he executed his great work of Perseus and Medusa, also a Christ on the Cross, besides many bas-reliefs for the adornment of his patron's palace; also vases, medals, etc. Cellini afterwards prepared himself for the priesthood, as though intending to return to France to take possession of his abbeys as an ecclesiastic. Subsequently, however, he changed his mind, and took a wife. The fire of youth and manhood

modern statues, another to buy ancient ones in Rome — Charles V., in an attempt to add to his military glory, dimmed by the campaign of Provence, suffered a terrible disaster by an expedition against Algiers. Rejecting the advice of Andrea Doria and other experienced captains to defer the expedition until the spring, the emperor piously sought the Pope's blessing. Thus fully armed, as he conceived, against all that the turbulence of equinoctial gales could do to put obstacles in his way, he embarked in the Gulf of Spezzia at the end of September for Majorca, where a numerous fleet and army were assembled again to conquer the Turks.

Charles imagined that Algiers would be a conquest as easy as it was important. It was poorly fortified, and the approach of his formidable fleet and army was expected to so fill with terror the hearts of the Mussulmans that, remembering Tunis, they would surrender at the very first summons. They, however, replied, when that summons was made, that "they would defend themselves and their city to the death."

At once Algiers was invested. But on that very evening, while disembarking their artillery — which was lost in the sea — the more formidable

somewhat subdued in the evening of life, but never wholly extinct, Cellini lived henceforth in his own country. He had five sons and daughters. In 1570 he died, much honoured and respected. His countrymen buried him with great pomp in the chapel of the Nunziata.

artillery of the elements was let loose on the Spanish fleet. One of those terrific tempests which sweep the African coast at that season arose in full fury, and continued through the night. At break of day, having partly subsided, all the inhabitants of Algiers, Turks and Moors, a tribe of Bedouins assisting, rushed out to attack the wretched soldiers who had disembarked on the previous day, and had passed the night without provisions or even the partial shelter of a tent.

Desperately they were assailed — the storm again raging with redoubled violence — and desperately they resisted, amidst the crash and roll of thunder, blinding flashes of lightning, rain descending like a cataract, "the sea and the waves roaring." The vessels meanwhile were helplessly tossing to and fro in the bay, dashing against the rocks, or sinking, overwhelmed by the irresistible force and fury of the waves.

Upwards of a hundred small vessels and several large ones were either sunk or wholly wrecked, the sea around being covered with their fragments, and the dead bodies of the soldiers and sailors who were on board of them.

During a lull in the storm Andrea Doria succeeded in conducting the miserable remains of Charles's grand armament to a safe anchorage, where also were re-embarked the few survivors of the unfortunate detachment that had landed before the bursting of the storm. The emperor resisted the advice of the Duke of Alba and the famous Fernandez Cortez, who commanded one of the galleys, to renew the attack on Algiers. They looked for a calm probably after the storm; but were destined again to encounter a tempest and further losses ere the ports of Italy and Spain were reached, and Charles, who landed at Carthagena, could once more hide his disappointment, grief, and shame in Spain.

This thorough defeat of the emperor and the exhaustion of his resources, together with the victory gained over his brother Ferdinand by Solyman in Hungary, seemed to the French king a favourable conjuncture for the renewal of hostilities. A plausible pretext was afforded him in the recent murder of two of his secret diplomatic agents — waylaid by order of the Spanish general, Del Guasto, for the purpose of obtaining their despatches, addressed to Solyman and the seigniory of Venice. The emperor pronounced the deed justified; but the king determined to avenge it. "He could not allow so gross an insult to be offered him with impunity." War was therefore declared, apparently in very insulting language (*grosses et atroces paroles*), and was resumed with fury.

CHAPTER VIII.

A Formidable Host. — The Pope Reproves in Vain. — A False Rumour. — The Consequence of Delay. — The Rebels of La Rochelle. — Francis Shows Mercy. — A Satisfactory Conclusion. — Very Agreeable to God. — The Psalms of Marot. — The Inauguration of the Ruff. — A Marriage Annulled. — The Comte d'Enghien. — Blaise de Montluc. — "And Win We Will." — A Generous Offering. — The Victory of Cerisola. — The Hero and His Army Recalled. — The Siege of Montreuil. — Accused as a Traitress. — Marching on Paris. — Preparing to Defend the City. — The Treaty of Crépy. — French Pride Humiliated.

HE great army, 120,000 strong, which Francis had raised by burdening his people with taxes, was considered so formidable a host that with it the king might go forth and conquer, independent of allies, in whatever direction he might choose. He was, however, in close alliance with the Grand Turk, and diligently seeking that of the Protestant kings of Denmark and Sweden, as also of the princes of Germany. With the two former he succeeded in effecting treaties. The latter, because of his continued persecution of the reformers, and his friendly relations with the infidel, were more disposed to hold aloof.

Henry VIII., irritated by the nonpayment of his pensions, and still more so by the attempt of Francis to establish a rival influence to his in Scotland, evinced an intention of joining Charles against him. A few months later he did so, and Charles — rigid Catholic, intolerant and unsparing persecutor of all heresy — scrupled not, now that it suited his purposes, to ally himself with the schismatic Henry, even in defiance of the angry reproof of the pope.*

The object of Francis I. was to retake Luxembourg and Roussillon. To accomplish it he divided his 'army into two corps, and gave the chief command of them to his two inexperienced sons, each under the nominal guidance of a general of maturer age, skilled in the art of war. The result was, in both cases, unfortunate. The young Duc d'Orléans left his army after disbanding a portion

---

* It was at about this time, when on the eve of a war with his uncle, Henry VIII., that James V. of Scotland died. During his illness, which had been but a brief one, being informed that his wife had given birth to a daughter, he exclaimed, "It was by a woman that the crown of Scotland came into our family, and by a woman it will be lost!" Henry gladly seized this opportunity of uniting the crowns of England and Scotland, by endeavouring to obtain from the regent, Marie de Guise, and the Scottish Parliament the promise of the hand of the infant queen, Mary Stuart, for his son Edward, Prince of Wales, then five years of age. But the queen-regent and the Catholic party opposed this design, in the interests of France, the king sending them troops, money, and military stores; thus enabling them to renew the war with England.

of it, and went off post-haste to Roussillon ; leaving the Duc d' Guise, with greatly diminished forces, to contend with the troops of the Governess of the Netherlands (Charles's sister), who retook Luxembourg and other places which had surrendered to the French.

The Roussillon division was commanded by the dauphin and Admiral d'Annebaut. A great battle, it was reported, was about to be fought at Perpignan ; and the desire of being present at it had led the Duc d' Orléans to forsake his own *corps d' armée*, which had been engaged in successful sieges — very tame affairs, as it seemed to the youthful commander-in-chief, compared with a general fight. The rumour of an approaching great battle was, however, a false rumour. None took place, and the duke, on his arrival, met with no gracious reception from the king, who himself had but just appeared on the scene of this expected action.

The Roussillon expedition was near ending as disastrously as the emperor's attack on Algiers. For the heavy autumn rains and swollen mountain torrents began to flood the valley where the army was encamped. The command of the king to raise the siege of Perpignan — invested, but without effect, by 40,000 men — was scarcely issued in time. Marching was already difficult ; a large portion of the artillery was embedded in the ground, and of necessity abandoned ; and the floods overtaking a part of the rear-guard, many of the men, while endeavouring to swim, were drowned.

More activity at the outset might, it appears, have secured favourable results for France. But the young princes had already adopted the habits of their father, and could not move without the encumbrance of a numerous retinue of attendants, a long train of mules, pack-horses and wagons, for the transport of furniture to the seat of war, and the luxuries of a life of ease and revelry more suited to the palace than the camp. Much delay was the consequence, which the emperor, who better understood the value of time, turned to account by preparing for effective resistance.

From the scene of this unfortunate campaign the king, accompanied by a detachment of troops, hastened to La Rochelle. The inhabitants of that city and of the isles of Ré and Oléron, where the trade in salt and salted provisions was carried on to a great extent, had rebelled against a further increase of the *Gabelle*, or salt-tax, which the king, in his constant need of money, had raised in amount from time to time, until it now threatened the ruin of their commerce. The collectors of this tax had been rather roughly treated by the excited people; payment was refused, and the military were called in to quell the tumult and arrest the refractory burgesses.

On the king's arrival, a similar scene took place

to that which occurred at Ghent, when Charles V. appeared there to punish rebellious citizens who dared to dispute his right to tax them to their last florin, if such should be his will.

"Fettered, and in cages," the deputies and chief citizens, who had rather encouraged than sought to suppress the revolt, were brought before their king. Francis was seated in a chair of state placed on a daïs in the courtyard of the hôtel prepared for his reception. Kneeling before him, barefooted and bareheaded — while the tears and sobs of the people collected around testified to the deep sympathy they felt in the fate of their unfortunate fellow citizens — the deputies and others confessed themselves in fault, and implored the monarch's clemency.

None, it would seem, expected mercy; for Francis I. was known to be no less cruel and despotic than Charles V.; no less disposed to believe that opposition to his will was crime of the deepest dye. The barbarity of Charles towards the citizens of Ghent had been deservedly condemned throughout Europe. Francis, therefore, decided on the politic act of showing mercy for a similar offence. One would like to think that he was inspired by pity. But, alas! pity or the "quality of mercy" dwelt but rarely, very rarely, in the hearts of the kings and great ones of the earth of that period.

But what a relief to the poor trembling people

when, in reply to the appeal for clemency, the monarch replies, "I will neither take your lives nor your property, as the emperor took those of the people of Ghent for a less offence than yours — staining his hands with their blood. I prefer the hearts and good-will of my subjects, and since you acknowledge your offence, are repentant, and return to your allegiance, I desire you to forget the past — for I shall never at any time remember it. I pardon you entirely, and it is my good pleasure that all fines and corporal punishments be remitted, prisoners released, and the keys and arms of your city restored to you, the troops, horse and foot, ordered to leave, and that you be entirely reinstated in your liberties and privileges."

Scarcely can the people believe their ears. Are they in a dream, or have they awakened from a vision of fancied grief to a reality of intense joy. Soon, however, as with one voice, the prayer of the assembled multitude rises towards heaven, invoking blessings on the head of their merciful sovereign, "May health and length of days be granted him, and prosperity attend his undertakings!" The bells ring out in full peal, the cannon are fired, bonfires are lighted, and the joyous proceedings are brought to a close by a supper and ball at the Hôtel de Ville, given to the king by the chief citizens and ladies.

Francis remained three days with "his good people," assuring them, "on the word of a gentleman," when he bade them farewell, "that they had gained his heart, and he thought he also had theirs. I leave you," he said, "for another part of my kingdom, in order to defend it. You will defend this, I know, for I have the most perfect confidence in you." Thus, in mutual satisfaction, ended the king's visit, begun so unpromisingly for the people of La Rochelle.

It was one of the very rare incidents of the reign of Francis I. to which he might be supposed to recur at times with pleasure. And as, at this period — when attacked, as was of frequent occurrence, by illness — "he began to be anxious about reaching heaven," it is wonderful that he should not have sought to attain that goal by fresh acts of mercy rather than by those deeds of atrocious cruelty and persecution by which he strove to propitiate the sanguinary being of his imagination he misnamed God. If the hands of Charles V. were stained with the blood of his people, no less deeply dyed in that of his subjects were those of Francis I. But, as if in atonement for mercy extended towards the overburdened taxpayers, he returned from La Rochelle only to issue more rigourous decrees against the unfortunate heretics, "whom to denounce," as the faithful were told, "was a pious act very agreeable to God."

It was supposed that Francis was now and then disturbed by qualms of conscience respecting his alliance with the Turks (the *Fleurs-de-Lys* and the

Crescent were then floating side by side before Nice), but that his zeal in the extirpation of heresy would, he trusted, be accepted by God and all good Catholics as a set-off against it. So zealous was he for the "true faith" that even the old court favourite, Clément Marot, recently restored to full favour, and his translation of the Psalms of David also flatteringly received, fled once more to Geneva, fearing that he, too, might be consigned to the stake by some caprice of the king.

The "Psalms of Marot," as they were called, were at first approved by Francis. All the ladies and gentlemen of the court sang them. They had not been set to music, but, as the metre served, the singers adapted them to the tune of any popular hunting-song, march, minuet, or other air, lively or solemn. The fanatical Cardinal de Tournon denounced this heretical psalm-singing. The Sorbonne stepped in, condemned the work, and bade the author "take heed to his ways." Marot laid the warning to heart, and wisely decamped.*

The Duc de Clèves and Gueldre, an inveterate enemy of the emperor, and almost the only ally

---

* Marot did not remain long in Geneva. The habits of life and almost dissolute manners he had contracted at the court to which he had so long been attached, prevented him, notwithstanding his adherence to the doctrines of the reformers, from adopting that sombre and austere mode of life which

Francis now retained in Germany, had gained some slight successes, which the king promised to support by sending him a detachment of troops. Before, however, doing so, and renewing, as he proposed, his own attack on Luxembourg, his health being slightly improved, he repaired with his court to Rheims. In the neighbourhood of that venerable old city and its pleasant surroundings, some weeks were spent in the customary courtly amusements.

Very grand *fêtes champêtres*, where the ladies displayed many fanciful and elegant *toilettes*, and Queen Eleanor inaugurated the ruff; numerous gay hunting-parties; much feasting, much dancing, with some occasional jousting and tilting, made up a very gay summer. The ladies returned to Blois, and Francis and his sons, with a host of gay cavaliers, set off for the seat of war.

Henry VIII. and Charles V. had united their forces against France, and the former had sent his ally eight or ten thousand English troops, with whom Charles had completely crushed the Duc de Clèves and Gueldre. Always a merciless conqueror, without a spark of generous sentiment,

---

Calvin imposed on the reformers of Geneva. Marot therefore retired to Turin, under the protection of the French generals, and died there some few months after the battle of Cerisola (1544), which he celebrated in a short poem — the last strain of the dying swan (Martin).

the emperor humiliated his vanquished enemy to the full extent of his power. His submission was made on his knees, of course; and for permission to retain a corner of his domains, under Spanish supervision, he was required to renounce his alliance with France, and to return to the Catholic faith, which he and his subjects had abjured ten years before. Other indignities were also heaped upon him.

Francis I., whose bad faith was the cause of the duke's defeat, was exceedingly annoyed by his submission to the emperor, which he thought precipitate, though conquered by a superior force he had not the means of resisting. In consequence thereof the marriage, which three years back he had been at much pains to prevent the parents of Jeanne d' Albret from invalidating at any future time, he now informed the duke (who had sent for his bride, she having attained the age of fourteen, was null and void. At all events the King and Queen of Navarre were pleased with this decision, and their young daughter is said to have been no less so.

Nice having capitulated, the French and Turkish galleys withdrew to Toulon; the king, unwilling to have a garrison of Turks in Nice, giving them permission to winter in that port. The Comte d' Enghien, François de Bourbon, who had charge of the French galleys, being released from that duty, hastened to Piedmont, now the seat of war, carried on with great barbarity. This young soldier,* who at twenty-two years of age already possessed many of the qualities of a great general, was entrusted by Francis — who could discern talent, if he did not always encourage and employ it — with the command of a corps of ten thousand men, to keep in check the Spanish commander, Del Guasto, but not to risk a battle without orders.

With much activity the count performed this duty throughout the winter. But, as usual, he was left without money to pay his troops and carry on the campaign. A very elaborate plan, which Del Guasto proposed should result in the taking of Lyons by the imperialists, was frustrated at the outset by the young French general's prompt occupation of Carmagnola and siege of Carignano. A battle seemed imminent, which he was far from wishing to avoid. But on its result depended the fate of Piedmont, which he dared not risk without the king's consent. A Gascon officer, Blaise de Montluc, † was, therefore, despatched to inform Francis of the critical position the young general was placed in, and to request both money and orders.

With his accustomed dilatoriness, the king detained the impatient Gascon nearly three weeks

---

* Brother of Antoine de Bourbon, who afterwards, by his marriage with Jeanne d' Albret, became King of Navarre, and father of Henri IV.

† The author of the vivacious military memoirs, "*Les Commentaires de Montluc.*"

before summoning him to attend a council of war, assembled to discuss the reply he was to carry back to Piedmont. The elder military men were opposed to risking a battle. The recent disastrous results of entrusting responsible commands to young officers would naturally influence their opinions, and they unanimously urged the king to refuse D' Enghien permission to fight.

The gallant Captain Montluc meanwhile was gesticulating and stamping with rage, in his agony lest the king should yield to their advice. At last his opinion was requested. The pent-up ardour and enthusiasm of the Gascon soldier then burst forth in a torrent of eloquence, which, assisted by his gestures — as of one using his arquebuse and pike in battle — and his assurances in the name of the whole army of the marvels they would achieve, dispelled the effect of the prudent counsels of those who had spoken before him, and carrying the king along with him seemed to compel his consent.

The old generals, perceiving that Montluc's boldness of speech and chivalric bearing had found favour with the king, the Comte de Saint Pol, addressing him in the name of the council, said: "Will you really, sire, allow the words of this madman to alter your prudent resolution?"

"On the word of a gentleman, good cousin," replied the king, " Montluc has given me so many good reasons for changing my mind, that I scarcely know what to do."

"Suppose they should lose?" said the count.

"Why always repeating 'Suppose they should lose?'" exclaimed Montluc. "Say for once, 'Suppose they should win!' — and win we will!" he cried, with enthusiasm.

"I perceive," said Admiral d'Annebaut, "that you are inclined, sire, to give D'Enghien permission to fight. Do this: ask counsel of God."

The king then joined his hands, and raised his eyes to heaven; and, after a few moments of pious meditation, cried aloud, as though inspired by Montluc's enthusiasm, "Let them fight, and be victorious!"

Without delay, Montluc carried the king's permission to fight to the anxiously expectant young general; also his promise that Martin Du Bellay should follow immediately with money to pay the troops. No sooner was it known that the Comte d'Enghien had permission from the king to give battle to the Spaniards, than "a hundred or more" of the young nobility and gentlemen either accompanied Montluc, or hastened to follow him, to join the French camp in Piedmont. Nor did they go empty-handed. Each took a sum of money for the general; knowing, doubtless, how unmindful Francis was of the needs of his army, and how prone were the hired troops to demand payment at the moment of going into battle, and to decamp if they were not promptly satisfied — often leaving their commanders at the mercy of the enemy.

Under those circumstances D' Enghien thought himself justified in accepting the generous offering.

The battle of Cerisola, fought on Easter Monday, the 14th of April, was begun by Montluc and his arquebusiers. There was desperate fighting and terrible slaughter on both sides; but victory ultimately declared for the French. The enemy's colours and artillery were captured; also the military chest, the Spanish commander's silver plate, a large sum of money, and five or six thousand breastplates. Three chests of manacles are also said to have been found in the Spanish camp, destined by Del Guasto for shackling his prisoners and sending them off as slaves to the imperial galleys.

He was, however, so thoroughly beaten himself by the youthful general — whom as a commander he despised — that, becoming bewildered by his signal defeat, he fled from the battle-field with five or six hundred of his cavalry. He had boastfully promised the ladies of Milan that, for their amusement, he would bring back the Comte d' Enghien and the young nobles who had joined him fettered and laden with chains. On leaving Asti he had particularly enjoined the inhabitants of that town to close their gates against him if he did not return victorious. They obeyed his injunction to the letter, and refused to receive the vanquished general.

No such brilliant victory as that of Cerisola had been gained by the French since Marignan

(Melegnano).* Yet, while it served to establish the prowess and military reputation of the Comte d'Enghien, as it was not followed up, France reaped little or no advantage from it.† The young general desired to carry his conquests further, and to retake Milan — asking of the king but 6,000 infantry and punctual remittances for their support to accomplish this exploit. It was a favourable moment for it, and the ladies of Milan and the inhabitants of the duchy generally were prepared to give such a reception to the Comte d'Enghien and his gallant cavaliers as would have cut to the heart the boastful Marquis del Guasto.

To retake Milan was an enticing project to Francis I.; but Charles V., allied with Henry VIII., was marching on France with the old design of dividing the kingdom with him. Francis and his generals were therefore of opinion that the defence of the country was more imperative than seeking new conquests. A part of the victorious army was recalled. Nevertheless, the count had succeeded in taking two or three small towns, when the Spanish general — convinced at last that the young soldier was an enemy not to be contemned

---

* No victory equal to it did they again obtain over the Spaniards until, a century later (1643), another Comte d'Enghien of twenty-two, a young hero of the same family, completed at Rocroy the annihilation of those famous Spanish bands which had received from his ancestor their first terrible check at Cerisola.

† Montluc; Servan; Martin Du Bellay; Henri Martin.

— proposed a three months' truce, which was approved by both emperor and king. The Comte d'Enghien then returned to France in quest of more fighting.*

But the command of the army that was to confront the emperor and the King of England and to save France from her invaders, was given to the king's two sons. The dauphin, apparently alarmed at the importance of the task assigned him at this threatening crisis, suggested to the king the expediency of recalling the constable De Montmorency — a proposal which so greatly enraged him that it brought on a fit of sickness. Henry VIII. had landed in person and was besieging Montreuil and Boulogne, instead of marching direct on Paris, as arranged between him and the

---

* The career of the Comte d'Enghien was prematurely brought to a close, in less than two years after the battle of Cerisola, by a deplorable catastrophe similar to that which placed the king's life in danger in the early part of his reign. The court was at Roche-Guyon (Feb. 7, 1546). The cold was severe, the snow falling heavily. The younger men of the court, weary of the confinement of the château, proposed a mimic siege with snowballs. Being agreed to, the attack and defence was carried on with that sort of frenzy peculiar to the rough amusements of the period. During the heat of the battle, some excited or very indiscreet person seized a chest filled with linen (*un coffre plein de linge* — Martin Du Bellay) and threw it from the window. It fell on the Comte d'Enghien and fractured his skull. After languishing a few days, the unfortunate young officer died, to the great grief of the king. The dauphin was supposed to have suggested this crime, from jealousy, and the Duc d'Aumale to have carried it into effect.

emperor. The latter, after some delay in the assembling of his army, and the taking of several towns that opposed him on his line of march, arrived before St. Dizier on the 10th of June with an army 50,000 strong.

The garrison of this town held out forty days. Its surrender was then obtained by stratagem — a ciphered letter to the governor giving the king's permission to capitulate, supposed to be sent by the Duc de Guise, whose seal was attached to it. Honourable terms, were, however, granted, the garrison marching out with arms and baggage, and taking with them four pieces of cannon. Charles, being anxious to get on to Paris, now called on Henry to fulfil his engagements and march on the capital.

The English king, however, declined to give up his sieges of Montreuil and Boulogne, even should the emperor arrange a peace without him — a conference being then held at La Chaussée, at the instance of Madame d' Étampes, of which a peace or long truce was the object. But the plenipotentaries could arrive at no satisfactory agreement. The conference therefore came to an end, and the emperor continued his march. His army was powerful in numbers, but provisions beginning to fail, and the troops, in consequence, likely to disband themselves, Charles, to obviate such a mischance, was preparing to beat a retreat toward Soissons.

But Madame d' Étampes (accused on very doubtful evidence *) is said to have twice played the traitress to the emperor's interests, first, by sending him the ciphers of the Duc de Guise to St. Dizier, and on the present occasion by informing him that the dauphin had immense stores in Épernay and Château Thierry — towns without garrisons, unable to oppose his entry. The only bridge by which his army could cross, the Marne, the dauphin had ordered to be destroyed, but "the execution of this order," she is supposed to have said, "she had contrived to delay, and the bridge was still open to him."

Profiting by this information, Charles continued his onward march. The frightened inhabitants opened their gates to the invader, and the imperial army, finding in Épernay and Château Thierry all they needed, in abundance surpassing their expectations, refreshed themselves at their ease, recruited their strength, and regained confidence and vigour.

Rapidly spread the news — "Charles V. and his Spaniards are marching on Paris!" Consternation seized the people, and the first impulse of all was flight. Old and young, rich and poor, assembled with their families, and with whatever they could carry away of their property, prepared to seek a refuge elsewhere. All sorts of convey-

---

* That of Cellini, Brantôme, and the historian Beaucaire; though, as remarked by H. Martin, neither Martin du Bellay nor the papers of Granvelle make any illusion to treachery.

Charles V.
Photo-etching from painting by Garavagha.

ances were called into requisition. The Seine was covered with boats, some so overladen with goods and passengers that many sank, and numerous lives were lost.

The king was ill at Fontainebleau, but hastened at once to his capital, and rode through all the streets, seeking, by words of encouragement, to allay the fears of the people. Some reassuring effect they certainly had, for, by one of those sudden revulsions of feeling, not peculiar to the French alone, the Parisians, recovering from the state of panic and wild terror into which the first announcement of the threatened invasion had thrown them, became resolute and defiant. The various guilds arose *en masse*, and 45,000 men, well armed, passed before the king, prepared to defend their city.

The army commanded by the dauphin was assembling on the heights of Montmartre, and troops from all parts were marching to the defence of Paris. The emperor was soon convinced that, abandoned by the English king, he could not venture to attack Francis in his capital. He therefore withdrew to Soissons, and reopened negotiations without success. After pillaging that town, he marched to Crépy, whither Admiral d'Annebaut followed him; the king—alarmed by the intelligence that Boulogne had surrendered to Henry VIII.—accepting the onerous terms of peace proposed by the emperor.

The Duchesse d'Étampes was supposed to have urged the king to this course, as the Duc d'Orléans, by the convention of marriage that supplemented the Treaty of Crépy, would occupy a throne almost as elevated as that destined for the dauphin. As the duke was his favourite son, this arrangement, which dismembered France in his favour, gratified the king no less than the duchess. The treaty was signed on the 18th of September. Francis not only agreed to renounce his alliance with Solyman, but to aid the emperor against him. The two monarchs also bound themselves to labour in concert for the extermination of heresy, and the reestablishment of harmony in the Church.*

The dauphin being required to sign the Treaty of Crépy, from paternal reverence dared not refuse. But some days after he secretly, at Fontainebleau,

* How zealous Francis was in fulfilling this part of the treaty was too soon apparent in that fearful crime which stamps his memory and his reign with indelible disgrace — the massacre of those peaceful Christian people, the Vaudois, "on whom was inflicted every torture that hell itself could dream of." In order to exonerate from blame the monsters (Baron de La Garde, Baron d' Oppède, and their myrmidons) who had been guilty of these atrocities in the king's name, and who feared that after his death they might be called to account for their demoniacal deeds, Francis, at the suggestion of the fanatical Cardinal de Tournon, by letters patent 18th June, 1545, declared his "approval of all that had been done against the heretic Vaudois," "accepting before God and man the responsibility of that dread crime." Physical suffering, that made him gloomy and irritable, has been the poor excuse offered for the unhappy monarch.

protested against it in the presence of several of the nobility. The Parliament of Toulouse, in January, 1545, followed his example; and generally the terms of peace excited considerable irritation. Yet the first news of peace being signed, and of the retreat of the emperor, was received in Paris and throughout France with great joy. But this expression of pleasure could not prove lasting. French pride was too much humiliated, and it was too clearly perceived that France had been at the mercy of her enemies.

CHAPTER IX.

A Pledge of Sincerity. — A Journey Heavenward. — Death of Martin Luther. — The Great French Fleet. — The Ship on Fire. — Cannonading the English. — The Baron Sinks the *Mary Rose*. — Powerful on the Ocean. — Death of the Duc d' Orléans. — Resentment towards His Heir. — An Eavesdropping Fool. — In a Furious Passion. — A Prayer for Pardon. — Étienne Dolet. — Vain Expectation. — "*Un Jeu de Mots.*" — Weary of Warfare. — A Mass for Henry VIII. — The End Draws Nigh. — Beware of the Guises.

FRANCIS now clung with all his heart to his alliance with the emperor. That he was wholly devoted to the Catholic reaction none now could doubt, from the magnitude of the pledge he had given of his sincerity in the Vaudois massacre. Furious applause, therefore, was heaped on him in Spain — "the country, *par excellence*, of great human hecatombs." On the other hand, all, whether Catholic or Protestant, who possessed the slightest feeling of humanity or Christian sentiment, stood aghast at the enormity of the crime committed in the face of Europe by authority of the "most Christian king." But he was satisfied; fully assured that every act of rigour towards the heretics was a step in advance on his journey heavenward.

Notwithstanding continual persecution, reform had made considerable progress of late, as well in France as in Germany and Switzerland. To the horror of the emperor, the Austrian and even some of the Spanish nobility began to talk of liberty of conscience as a right. There was a Hussite revival in Bohemia, and, to the grief of Charles's righteous spirit, heresy had invaded the Netherlands, and to such an extent that his sister, Maria of Austria, dared no longer put in force his atrocious decrees against it (Martin).

At any cost, then, the rolling torrent of heresy must be stemmed; and the long talked of general council, which was expected by the Pope to amicably settle all differences, was appointed to meet at Trent on the 15th of March, 1545. It was afterwards deferred month after month, by the dissension between the Pope and the emperor, for nearly a year. An event then occurred which both at Trent and at Rome occasioned the liveliest joy, and seemed to many of the assembled prelates to inaugurate the operations of the council with a promise of the happiest results. This was the death of "the father of heresy."

Martin Luther died on the 10th of February, 1546, at his native town of Eisleben. He was sixty-three years of age. Profound sorrow naturally prevailed in the Protestant states of Germany, which Charles V., with his hired troops, was then overrunning.*

Francis I., meanwhile, had not been idle. By forced loans and other devices he had raised a large sum of money, with which, besides greatly increasing his army, he had equipped what then was considered a very fine fleet. With it he proposed to make a descent on the southern coast of Scotland, after an engagement with the English fleet, and effecting a landing on some part of the English coast. By this means he expected or hoped to alarm Henry into an immediate restitution of Boulogne. At the same time, being desirous of emulating the zeal of the emperor, he thought that, while seeking to further his own interests by attacking the renegade Henry VIII., he would be serving those of the Roman Church against the heretics no less effectually than Charles V. was doing in Germany.

Some of the vessels of the French fleet were of improved construction. They could be propelled either with sails or oars, and were also provided with port-holes — the invention of a Breton shipwright. There were, besides, fifty or sixty "large

---

* "It is credibly asserted," says Oderic Raynaldi, the annalist of the Church, "that on the day that scoundrel (*scélérat*), the most odious of the heresiarchs, died, many persons who had been possessed with devils were liberated, because the devils then left them to accompany the soul of Luther to the gulfs of the infernal regions. But they soon after returned to those unfortunates who for awhile had been dispossessed."

round vessels," and a number of the largest merchant ships armed for war. The command of this fleet was confided to Admiral d'Annebaut, who, it appears, was the first French admiral who for very many years, if ever, had been called upon to fulfil the functions attached to his title, or to command a ship (Sismondi). But Normandy and Brittany had excellent seamen. The Breton captain, Jacques Cartier, had recently discovered Canada, having in the preceding year sailed round Newfoundland, and, contrary to his expectations, found it to be an island. Lieutenants then would be forthcoming, possessed of those nautical acquirements which the military admiral had not. Otherwise, this first attempt to engage in maritime war with the English could hardly have been so successful — small as were the results — as French writers represent it.

A sad misadventure, however, occurred at the outset, by which the ladies and gentlemen of the court, who accompanied the king to Havre-de-Grace to see the fleet get under way, had a narrow escape of their lives.

The king gave a splendid *fête* to the Duchesse d'Étampes on board the *Carraquon*, the admiral's ship — a vessel of 800 tons, carrying a hundred bronze guns of small calibre, and reckoned a wonderfully swift sailer. The king's cooks — who always formed a part of his retinue — prepared the banquet. Cooking in a ship's galley was of course less convenient than in the kitchen of a royal château, or even in the open air on one of the royal gipsy jaunts. Doubtless, in the preparation of such a repast, no less ample than *recherché*, they were pressed for space — "cabin'd, cribb'd, confined." At all events they contrived to set the ship on fire.

Fortunately the galleys that formed the naval force of France in the Mediterranean had been ordered round to Honfleur. They were under the command of Baron de La Garde — a man whom the king delighted to honour. The court and a part of the crew of the *Carraquon*, also the military chest, were saved by these galleys. But "when the fire had burnt down to the lower part of the vessel, the cannon one after another went off, discharging their bullets in all directions." Of course the galleys could then take off no more of the crew, and the Baron de La Garde prudently gave the burning ship a wide berth.

He who had driven back men, women, and children into the flames with a pitchfork, when attempting to escape from them, had no mind to lose his own valuable life by a random bullet. So the *Carraquon* burnt on to the water's edge, or until the fire reached her powder-magazine, when she exploded and sank, "having on board several hundred soldiers and sailors," who, strangely enough, seem to have made no effort to save themselves.

This serious contretemps did not prevent the fleet from putting to sea. The various divisions of which it was composed were to assemble before the Isle of Wight. The English fleet in the roadstead of Portsmouth is represented as composed of "sixty fine large vessels, perfectly equipped and appointed for war; besides many smaller ones— long, narrow, and of great swiftness." The French fleet, at a respectful distance, opened a cannonade on the English, "who," say the military chroniclers of these events, "being unable to sustain the shock, withdrew to that part of the Channel where on one side they were protected by forts built on the heights, and on the other by shoals and sand-banks."

Nothing could draw them out into the open sea. "The Baron de La Garde boldly braved and defied them in their very anchorage." One would be inclined to think that the English contemned their foes, if not told that the aforesaid "baron and his galleys sank the great ship *Mary Rose* with all her crew, and further dismasted and cut down the English admiral's ship, *Henry the Great*," and would certainly have annihilated the fleet of those cowards "had not a land-breeze sprung up and driven them down in full sail on their dauntless aggressors."

Yet they would not fight, though a reinforcement of forty vessels came to their aid. Admiral d'Annebaut in despair landed a detachment of troops on the Isle of Wight, with orders to burn and destroy all before them. He, however, refrained from taking possession of and fortifying it, as advised by his officers. Leaving the English coast, the French fleet set sail for Boulogne for the purpose of disembarking some four or five thousand soldiers at Outr'eau for the camp of Marshal Biez, who had orders closely to surround Boulogne, and cut off its communication with the sea.

The great French fleet returned to port in about a month from the time it left Havre-de-Grace, very proud of its demonstration at the back of the Isle of Wight, but attempting no descent on Scotland. "France," say French writers, "at least has shown herself powerful on the ocean." This was the only result of her first great naval campaign, but the "chevalier king" regarded it as the crowning glory of his reign.

Within a month of the return of his fleet (8th of September) a great grief fell on Francis I., in the death of his younger and favourite son, the Duc d'Orléans. It was the unfortunate result of a foolish act of his own, while with the armies then laying siege to Boulogne and Montreuil.

A contagious epidemic was raging amongst the soldiers, and the prince, to show how little he feared an attack of the disease, said to be plague or typhus fever, entered a house with some of his companions where several persons had just died of it. The bedding they had used he turned over and over, cut open the beds with his sword, and, taking feathers from them, scattered them over himself and the young men with him. So vigourously did he exert himself at this strange occupation, laughingly exclaiming, as he tossed each handful of feathers into the room, "Never did a son of France die of the plague!" that he returned to his hôtel tired and heated, and lay down on his couch to rest. From it he never arose. Fever supervened, and three days after he died. He was in his twenty-third year.*

The death of this prince annulled the Treaty of Crépy, which was based entirely on his marriage with a daughter or niece of the emperor, and the territory to be given up by the king and emperor respectively to form a new kingdom for him. It also put an end to Madame d'Étampes's hopes of a secure retreat when her rival, Diane, should begin her reign. Francis was anxious that some new treaty of amity should replace that of Crépy, as the question of the cession of Milan might again be the cause of a war. Admiral d'Annebaut was, therefore, despatched to Madrid to confer on the subject with the emperor or with his plenipotentiary. He found Charles so wholly occupied with his projects against the Lutherans that, without any discussion of the question, he replied to it by a verbal message: "If the king did not recommence

---

* Other accounts ascribe his death to the very dissolute life he led, which had already undermined his constitution.

war, he was not disposed to disturb the good understanding existing between them by the last treaty."

Some undue elation was probably shown by the dauphin's partisans at the unlooked-for rupture of a treaty that was to deprive the future sovereign of a whole province of his kingdom, and this Francis attributed to rejoicing on the part of Henri at his brother's death. He had never regarded his second son with the same feeling of affection as the eldest and the youngest; and since Henri had become his heir he exhibited a sort of resentment towards him.

Jealousy was supposed to exist between the brothers. Yet there does not appear to have been any enmity, but merely emulation, and that with reference to military distinction, which neither seems to have been endowed with the ability to acquire. The death of the Comte d'Enghien, to whom Francis was much attached, occurred at about this time, and was attributed very unjustly, as some writers have thought, to a suggestion of the dauphin. But some colour was given to the suspicion by the fact that the king's dislike of his heir was, to all appearance, intensified by that unfortunate catastrophe.

Vincent Carloix, the editor of "Vieilleville's Memoirs," relates an anecdote of the dauphin having, at a banquet to which he had invited his friends and chief favourites, allowed himself to be drawn into speaking of what he proposed doing when he should be king — the changes he should make in the different departments of the government, and his household, and how he proposed to distribute the principal offices of state amongst his favourites then present.

One of the court fools, Briandos (there appear to have been three of those wretched creatures), had coiled himself up in an obscure corner of the apartment, where, without being seen, he could hear all the conversation, to which he eagerly listened. By and by he contrived to leave the dauphin's apartment unnoticed, and stealthily to enter the king's. Francis was occupied with two or three of his ministers. Briandos, taking advantage of a brief interval in the conversation, exclaimed: "God preserve you, François de Valois!"

"*Compère*," said the king, "where did you learn that mode of address?"

"*Par le sang Dieu*," he answered, "I have just now learned that you are no longer king. You, too, M. de Thais," addressing the master of the horse, "are supplanted by M. de Brissac. Saint-André, also, is first chamberlain," he said to another; and so on throughout the great offices of the household.

"*Par la Mordieu*, François," he continued, "we shall soon have the constable here again, commanding *en maître*, so beware how thou playest the fool! Fly, I advise thee! fly, or I swear by heaven thou art a dead man!"

When the meaning of Briandos's whimsical excitement was explained to the king, he burst into a furious passion; called for the captain of the Scotch guards, and, with him and thirty or forty of his archers, went straight to the dauphin's apartments. But as the festive party had dispersed, having been warned of what had occurred, the king expended the full force of his wrath on the *valets de chambre*, the pages, the *laquais*, and other attendants, dealing about heavy blows with a halberd on all he could catch, as they fled from corner to corner of the banqueting-room, endeavouring to make for the door or to reach a window, to save themselves from this desperate attack upon them by jumping out of it.

Tables and chairs, furniture and tapestry, all he could find in the adjoining rooms and antechamber, Francis, in his violent anger, broke and destroyed — effacing even the names of the *fourriers*, subaltern officers of the dauphin's military staff, whose names, it appears, it was customary to write over the doors.

The dauphin, in consequence, absented himself from court for several weeks. From the efforts that were made during that time to effect a reconciliation, and induce the king to recall him, one might infer that he was generally beloved, except by the queen, who knew his feeling towards her brother. The princesses and ladies, even Madame d' Étampes, with the princesses and the nobility, lost no opportunity of urging the king to forgive his son.

At last pardon was granted, but only on condition that he brought with him neither Saint-André nor any other of his companions who had assisted at that evening's festivity, so greatly marred by the malice of Briandos. What became of that malicious fool, history seems to have forgotten to record.

The king's health continued to decline. He had not improved his chances of life by the outbreak above mentioned. His violent rage had visibly told on him. He, however, solaced himself by rigourous persecution, and 1546 was prolific of martyrs burnt at the stake in France.

The most distinguished of them was the *littérateur* and printer, Étienne Dolet, the author of "*Commentaires sur la Langue Latine,*" and of many poems, and the translator of the "Dialogues of Plato." In 1542 or 1543 he had been accused of heresy and atheism, by the Inquisitor-General of Lyons, who further charged him with the horrible crime of having eaten meat on days when it was prohibited by the Church.

Dolet had then a friend at court, the Bishop of Mâcon, the king's reader, who interceded for him as a young man of great ability, with the promise of a brilliant literary career before him. The "Father of letters" could hardly decline to be merciful in such a case. Dolet, like Berquin, escaped when first denounced, his books only being burnt on the Place Maubert. The burning zeal of Cardinal de Tournon would willingly have sent the bishop to the flames from which he had snatched a victim. He was compelled to content himself with reproaching him for his daring act, as a Catholic bishop, of defending heretics and atheists. The bishop replied "that in pleading for the unfortunate he had performed a bishop's duty, while the cardinal had taken upon him the functions of an executioner."

In 1544 Dolet was again denounced; this time on suspicion of having introduced prohibited books from Geneva into France. Aided by friends, he escaped to Piedmont, where he addressed some poetical epistles to the king and Madame d' Étampes. For the purpose of printing his "Dialogues" and other works, he secretly returned to Lyons, where he had left his family. He was shortly after arrested and his writing seized. The Sorbonne found in the "Dialogues" a phrase which seemed opposed to the doctrine of the immortality of the soul, and at once condemned the translation.

The Parliament, therefore, sentenced the translator to be tortured on the rack, then hanged, and afterwards burnt, together with his heretical books. "Should he venture to utter any blasphemy or do aught to create scandal, his tongue was to be cut out, and he burned alive."

Dolet appears to have expected that the king would once more save him from the fate to which the wretched fanatics of the Sorbonne and the Parliament had condemned him. Vain expectation! Learning and the arts no longer interested Francis I. as formerly, and Dolet's sentence must be carried out to the end.

He is said to have borne his sufferings with heroical firmness; so much so that the spectators —though one would scarcely credit those who were willingly present at such a scene with the possession of much feeling — sympathised deeply with him, and were greatly affected. Perceiving this, as he mounted, or — his limbs being dislocated and broken on the rack — was borne to the scaffold, he said, extending his hand towards the people :

"*Non dolet ipse Dolet, sed pia turba dolet.*" *

Dolet was thirty-seven years of age. Many epitaphs were written on this distinguished victim of the Place Maubert. "His friend Rabelais avenged him in a different manner" (if he did

---

* A clever *jeu de mots*, more concisely expressed in Latin than in either French or English. " Dolet n'est point *dolent*, mais ce peuple compatissant est *dolent* pour lui." " Dolet is not *doleful*, but these compassionate people are *doleful* for him."

not rather insult him) "by publishing at the foot, as it were, of his funeral pile the second book of Pantagruel, '*avec privilége du roi*' !" "Rabelais," says M. H. Martin (who gives the greater part of these particulars), "must have been as unprecedentedly clever as audacious." He must indeed; but with two cardinals for friends, one of whom had just obtained for him the curacy of Meudon, what might not be accomplished? Cardinal Du Bellay, and afterwards the powerful Cardinal Jean de Lorraine — persecutor and sceptic — were the protectors of this coarse licentious writer.

Francis I. was now chiefly anxious for peace with England. In both the French and English armies typhus was still raging; yet during the past year unceasing skirmishing had been kept up at the gates of Boulogne and around Calais and Guines. Though comrades were dying around them, and pestilence was daily thinning their ranks, there was not one among the survivors who desired to quit his post. Nor did the nation complain of the expense of this harassing war — for it was war against England, therefore a popular war — it being not only the heartfelt wish of every Frenchman, but a point of honour with him, to compel the English to evacuate the territory they held in France; Boulogne at all events, and Calais — though the realisation of the hope had been long deferred — would follow by and by.

Henry VIII. and Francis I. were, however, both

growing weary of this continuous and expensive yet petty strife — the latter because he desired to give more attention to the proceedings of the Pope and the emperor, who, seeking to suppress heresy from different motives, were striving to accomplish it by different means. Overtures of peace were, therefore, made to Henry, whose health was failing him, and who, being unwilling to have his youthful successor hampered with a war, consented to a negotiation being entered into. It resulted in a treaty, by which Boulogne was to be restored to France in eight years, on a payment of five million *francs* being completed within that period.

Before the necessary arrangements for giving effect to the treaty were concluded, Henry VIII. died, 30th of January, 1547.* Francis was informed of the event on returning to St. Germain, after a lengthened journey, or series of journeys, he had undertaken to ascertain the progress made in the construction of fortifications on several parts of the east and northeast coast of France. He was much saddened by Henry's death, and, notwithstanding the English king's separation from the

* The issuing of a general pardon was contemplated on the death of Henry VIII. But the Earl of Hertford and Sir Anthony Browne (Master of the Horse) were of opinion that it would be better to defer it until the coronation of Edward VI. — "the late king, being in heaven, having no need of the merit of it."—" State papers." Yet Henry is said to have died full of terrible apprehensions of what awaited him in futurity.

Church, ordered a solemn funeral mass to be said for him at Notre Dame; much to the scandal of all good Catholics.

The Court of France, once the gayest in Europe, was now the gloomiest. The king seemed to regard Henry's death as an announcement that his own was at hand. As if to retard the grim tyrant's approach, though languishing in hopeless torture, he still wandered from château to château even more persistently than before — yet experiencing in these frequent changes an increase rather than an alleviation of suffering. He knew that his death was impatiently awaited; that it was not on him but on his successor, whom he hated, that all eyes were now turned, and his survival, as it were, of himself he keenly felt and resented.

It was not the court only that was gloomy. Throughout the kingdom the sinister decline of this reign was felt — the torturing and burning in the king's name of suspected heretics, now of every-day occurrence, causing terror and general depression.

The treaty with England was renewed and signed on the 11th of March between Francis and the Duke of Somerset, Lord Protector of England during the minority of Edward VI. The king was even then thinking of levying fresh troops in France and Switzerland for a new campaign. But his malady greatly increased; a burning fever attacked him, and, on arriving at Rambouillet from Fontainebleau, he was compelled to take to his bed. He now felt that his end was nigh, and the dauphin was immediately summoned to his bedside. The king advised him to diminish the taxes; to retain Admiral d'Annebaut — a man of incorruptible honour — as his minister; not to recall De Montmorency, and, above all, to beware of the ambitious and audacious self-styled princes of the House of Guise. He is said to have expressed some remorse for the massacre of the Vaudois, and to have urged his son to make inquiries respecting it, and if possible some reparation.

"*Il s'en va, le galand! il s'en va!*" whispered François de Guise, as from the anteroom of the dying king's bedchamber he and Diane watched for the last moment of his agonised struggle with death, and heard his warning "*Gardez-vous des Guises!*" Francis I. died on the 31st of March, 1547, in the fifty-third year of his age and thirty-third of his reign.

CHAPTER X.

Welcome News. — The King's Private Council. — Worshipping the Favourite. — François de Guise. — Henri II. — The Serious Business of Life. — In Swaddling Clothes. — Such is Our Good Pleasure. — Rapacious Favourites. — The Favourite's Favourite. — Cato, a Boudoir Knight. — The Double Funeral. — An Embarrassing Complaint. — A Peep into Purgatory. — The Tomb of Francis I.

SO little respect did the new monarch pay to his father's dying injunctions that he scarcely waited until his last breath was drawn ere he left Rambouillet to meet his favourite, De Montmorency. Knowing that Francis's death would be the signal for his return to power, the constable, when the welcome news that the king was no more was brought to him, set out from Chantilly without a moment's delay. Together he and Henri repaired to St. Germain, and once more the management of state affairs was placed in his hands. The late king's ministers were immediately dismissed — esteeming themselves fortunate that to disgrace, or dismissal, persecution was not added; such being the usual course, whether deserved or not, when the sun-

Francis I.
Steel engraving from an old portrait.

shine of royal favour was withdrawn from a minister or other member of the government.

An ordinance of the second of April announced the reorganization of the king's private council and of the Council of State. In the list of the former appeared the names of three of the ambitious "princes" (a title they now assumed, but which Francis would not concede to them) of the House of Lorraine — the Cardinal Jean de Lorraine and his two nephews, François de Guise, Comte d'Aumale, and Charles de Guise, Archbishop of Rheims; Albon de Saint-André; De Montmorency, the constable, of course; Henri d'Albret, King of Navarre; Antoine de Bourbon, first prince of the blood; and Robert de la Marck, son of the famous Fleuranges and the son-in-law of Diane de Poitiers.

The private council met in the morning, the Council of State after dinner. The members of the former were members also of the latter, which was further increased in number by four cardinals — one of whom, De Châtillon, was a nephew of the constable; three dukes, one of them a Guise; two bishops and a president. The Guises and the De Montmorency party, with Saint-André, who had been Henri's favourite companion from boyhood, alone possessed any real influence. They abhorred each other, but prudently forbore to make any open display of their mutual antipathy — content to unite for awhile in worshipping the all-powerful favourite, and under her auspices to follow each his own ambitious views while secretly thwarting those of his rivals.

The Guises had further secured the support of Diane by asking in marriage the hand of her second daughter, for Claude de Guise, third son of the duke. This alliance, far more than any supposed friendship of Henri II. for François de Guise, enabled these most aspiring young men of the junior branch of the Guises to put themselves on an equality with the arrogant De Montmorency, and eventually to surpass him in credit, as they greatly surpassed him in ability and political intelligence. For the attainment of their aims this numerous family (Duc Claude de Guise had seven sons) are said to have acted in concert, the younger sharing the aspirations and fortunes of the elder, and all manœuvring as one man.

The eldest, François de Guise, Comte d'Aumale, possessed great force of character. His military reputation was well established, and he was popular with his troops. When successful he was very magnanimous, but implacable and ferocious in danger. He was then twenty-eight. Charles, the next brother, was two or three years younger, but was already Archbishop of Rheims.* The

* This ecclesiastical dignity was ceded to him by his uncle, Cardinal Jean de Lorraine, in order to appease public indignation, very strongly expressed, at the large number of rich benefices held by that prelate. The bishoprics of Metz and

brothers generally have been described as very shrewd, genial, gracious, *spirituel*, seductive. Always dignified, and "so elegant and stately that other princes in their presence appeared to be people of inferior station;" but to the Archbishop Charles has been assigned the doubtful honour of preeminence as a court flatterer.

"In him were united all the talents and all the vices compatible with hypocrisy. He was learned and witty, a subtle politician, an eloquent orator. At court he was supple and complaisant, the humble servant of the king's mistress. In his archbishopric he was the pious bishop and father of the Church, sternly reproving every slight indiscretion of his *curés*, and thus playing the double part everywhere customary with the Guises. In character François and Charles de Guise resembled each other only in their vast ambition. The former was the hero, the latter the diplomate — the lion and the fox of the family, whose formidable association so elevated their race, that in the third generation they could climb no higher but by an assault on the throne." (Henri Martin.)

Henri II. had attained his twenty-eighth year a month previous to his accession. He was a handsome man, handsomer probably than Francis, in symmetry of person and regularity of features.

Verdun were also resigned at the same time. But they, too, were not allowed to go out of the family. They fell to the share of Louis de Guise.

But his face is said to have been expressionless, and his eyes, though fine, had that vague, wandering glance denoting indecision and feebleness of purpose. Yet he excelled in all the athletic sports of that day. As a runner, few could compete with him in rapidity, or in the height of his bounds as a leaper. He was a perfect horseman, riding with ease the most restive animals. In an assault of arms he was a formidable antagonist for the most practised fencers; and in tilting, a game of which he was exceedingly fond, he rarely failed to carry off the victor's wreath.

Similar feats are attributed to Francis I. in his earlier years, and indeed they were common at that period to all young men of family. "One might say," writes Giustiniani, "that they were born with swords in their hands;" war continuing to be their only occupation through life, in fact its whole serious business, as warlike games and the chase were its chief pleasures.

As a ruler, Henri II. had all the failings of Francis I. He was too idle-minded to attend to the government of his kingdom, or to give thought to affairs of state beyond following the advice or directions of the grasping favourites whom he allowed to control him. These favourites were by no means so frequently subjected to the changes of mood and caprices of temper as were the advisers and favourites of the late king. Henri, being more the slave of habit, was seemingly more constant in his favouritism. He was apparently, too, of a more amiable temper ("*prince débonnaire*"), but his amiability was the result of weakness rather than goodness, and did not prevent him from indulging at times in violent gusts of passion; while of the cruelty of his disposition he gave ample proof during his reign by the horrible decrees which, in his fanaticism and senseless bigotry, he issued against the reformers; urged on, doubtless, by the ferocious zealots who surrounded him.

Henri was less dissolute than Francis, yet far from constant to either wife or mistress — if Diane really was his mistress, of which some doubt exists. She herself was not ambitious of bearing the title of *maîtresse-en-titre*.* Her influence over him was certainly unbounded, but may be attributed to the power which her stronger mind and greater ability, aided by much fascination of manner and long retention of personal beauty, exercised on one so weak as Henri II. — so willing to be held in leading-strings, or to be put into the "swaddling clothes" (*maillot*) of which Francis I. warned him when bidding him beware of the ambitious scions of the House of Lorraine.

---

* An unauthenticated correspondence, attributed to Diane de Poitiers with Francis I., is the only ground for the accusation that to save her father's life she became the king's mistress. M. Mignet, after much research concerning this correspondence, rejected it as utterly untrustworthy.

No less ravenously eager than the Guises was the Connétable de Montmorency in grasping places and pensions for himself and his five sons. But while his object was the accumulation and hoarding of wealth, that of his rivals, after heaping it up, was to scatter it with a lavish hand. They were courtiers of the multitude as well as of the king; princely in their liberality as well as graciously affable towards all their inferiors and dependents. Thus they gained partisans who might be useful in the furtherance of their schemes — as yet somewhat vague, though illimitable in their aim.

The dignity of duke and peer (Duc d' Aumale), conferred on François de Guise at this time, was objected to by the Parliament of Paris as contrary to the laws regulating the institution of the peerage in France. "There had been twelve judges in Israel. Twelve apostles had been appointed by Christ; and Charlemagne had decreed there should be twelve, and no more, peers of France — six temporal, six spiritual." That number was then complete. However, the difficulty was surmounted by a formula setting aside all objections — "Such is our good pleasure."

That Archbishop Charles, notwithstanding his twelve or fourteen benefices, might also receive some special mark of the king's favour, a cardinal's hat was obtained for him at Henri's solicitation; while at the request of Diane — who would have felt much hurt had her son-in-law been passed over without some assurance that he possessed a share of the king's good graces — all the vacant estates in the kingdom were given to Claude de Guise, Marquis de Mayenne.* Hardly could a gift have been made that occasioned so much inconvenience, or that excited more rancour and resentment among so large a number of persons as were thus suddenly dispossessed.

Honours and wealth for himself and family fell, also, in copious showers on Anne de Montmorency, and on Henri's young soldier friend, Saint-André, whom he graced with the marshal's *bâton* and appointed grand chamberlain of the royal household, with the disposal of various offices wherewith to gratify a host of poor relations. One could almost pity the poor, weak king, so besieged on all sides by his rapacious favourites, whose expectations of wealth, place, and power were beyond his ability, if not his will, fully to satisfy.

The sweeping changes in the royal household would have extended to the ladies of the court, could De Montmorency have dared to act, or advise the king to act, as his wishes prompted him. Some changes, of course, there were. Queen Eleanor left France to reside with her sister, the Governess of the Netherlands, Dowager-queen of Hungary. Madame d' Étampes, after giving up

* " All estates in the actual occupancy of persons who bore no corresponding title being considered vacant."

her jewels — not to the nominal queen, Catherine, but to the queen who ascended the throne with Henri, Diane de Poitiers, which made the sacrifice more bitter to the deposed favourite — retired, as "invited," to one of her estates, where, having embraced Protestantism, she afforded protection to its persecuted professors. It is the historian Mézeray who mentions this latter fact, but he adds: "Some historians contend that she did not fall so low."

De Montmorency would have been even more glad to see the friend with whom hitherto he had been leagued — Madame Diane, as she was now called — also displaced. Not to put Catherine on her vacant throne, or because his moral sense was shocked by present arrangements; but because she usurped his post of first favourite, which, when Henri became king, he had expected to occupy without a rival — whether a Guise or a maternal friend. Dissembling his resentment, he sought the next best post — that of the favourite's favourite — none more assiduously paying court to the brilliant, if not youthful, "Madame Diane," now Duchesse de Valentinois, than the arrogant Anne de Montmorency.

The classic mania of the day not only led to the assumption of Greek and Latin terminations to ordinary surnames, but frequently to the affectation of taking some hero of antiquity as a model of life or conduct. De Montmorency appears to have favoured this custom, and to have adopted Cato, the Censor, for his example, under the delusion that the character of this Roman sage was in some points in harmony with his own. What these points were it would be difficult to say. The rigid principles attributed to the Cato of ancient times could have nothing in common with the rapacity and corruption of Anne de Montmorency, whose bloodthirsty cruelty deserved also a harsher name than an "austere manner," ascribed to his model. But for the nonce Cato is transformed into a *boudoir* knight.

As soon as court arrangements were complete for entering on the new reign with *éclat*—outgoing ministers and fallen favourites slinking off without beat of drum, the incoming ones, with colours flying, taking their places — the obsequies of the late king, for which great preparations had been making, were solemnised. At the same time the young Duc d' Orléans, who died in September, 1545, was finally interred. At the sight of the two coffins — that of his brother being borne before the king's — Henri appeared much affected. But this evidence of emotion the courtiers about him thought it right immediately to check, and that by reminding him that his brother had been his enemy.

The Treaty of Crépy, that was to dismember France for that brother's benefit — for only thus indirectly was he, or rather Francis, who subscribed to such a treaty, his enemy — immediately recurred to the king, and (according to Vieilleville) from lamentation he passed to insult, applying the term *bélître* (rascal or rogue) to his dead brother.* This double funeral was, however, a splendid pageant. It drew crowds of sightseers into the streets, if not many mourners. Few indeed must have been the number of those who regretted such a king as Francis I. There may have been some sanguine persons who hoped for a change for the better in the new reign. If so, they were destined soon to discover that hope had told them a flattering tale.

In the funeral oration of the late king all virtues, all talents, were ascribed to him. Art, science, learning, had lost their great patron in this powerful sovereign and humble Christian, whose stainless soul had needed not the purifying fires of purgatory, but "had passed direct from its earthly tenement to the plenitude of joy in paradise." So bold an assertion did not meet with unqualified approval. The preacher, argued the doctors of the Sorbonne, in thus covertly denying the existence of purgatory, must be tainted with the Lutheran heresy, though a bishop of the holy Catholic Church.

The reformers rejected this tenet of the Roman faith; but if it were shown by one of that faith

---

* "*Voilà donc!*" he exclaimed, "*le bélître qui fait l'avant-garde de ma félicité.*"

that some souls were exempted from sojourning in purgatory, though only those of saintly kings, what lamentable results might not follow! It was thought expedient to draw the attention of the king to what had occurred, lest, possibly, he might solace himself with the hope of a similar exemption. Henri was considered a more devoted son of the Church, more devout than Francis had been, notwithstanding the cruel persecution he sanctioned in the latter years of his reign, and he probably was a stricter observer of its appointed forms and ceremonies.

He was rather at a loss what reply to make to the complaint of the Sorbonne; and evidently was displeased, — perhaps with the doctors for not deciding the question for themselves, and either canonising Francis, or burning the offending preacher, if they desired it, instead of embarrassing him with their doubts.

A Spanish officer, named Mendoza, who had been some time in the service of France, happened to be present. It was he, indeed, who had introduced the delegates from the Sorbonne into the royal presence. Seeing the king's perplexity, he ventured to say, "Sire, your royal father, of blessed memory, was not accustomed, as your majesty knows, to sojourn long in any place; and if he did take a look into purgatory, it is certain that the devil himself would never have prevailed on him to make any stay there."

Surely this man's head depended on a smile or a frown. Courtiers looked grave, and the king seemed undecided which it should be; but after musing for a moment, and then glancing at Mendoza, who was anxiously awaiting the sovereign's approving nod, felt compelled to laugh — all present, of course, dutifully following suit. Here the story ends. How the Sorbonne took the jest no one seems to have been at the pains to inquire or to record. But it may be considered certain that no victims were offered up in sacrifice on this occasion, either to the royal Saint Francis or in defence of the doctrine of purgatory.

But Henri had not only decided on giving Francis I. the grandest funeral — that of Anne of Brittany perhaps excepted — that the French had ever witnessed. He proposed to erect a splendid tomb to his memory, surpassing, in the grandeur of its proportions, and the richness of its sculptural decorations, all such monuments as had hitherto been erected in France. It took many years to complete the magnificent tomb, on which every French artist of note was employed.

It was designed by the celebrated architect, Philibert Delorme. The bas-reliefs were the *chefs-d'œuvre* of Pierre Bontemps and Ambrose Pesret. The large bronze figures were the work of the famous sculptor, Germain Pilon — then fast rising into celebrity, and rivalling Jean Goujon, who at that time was at the height of his fame and his powers. The latter was the favourite artist of Diane de Poitiers, whose image he has immortalised. She had the merit of recognising his great talent, when neglected — and never duly appreciated — by Francis I., and employed him to execute the sculptural decoration of her splendid Château of Anet, which Philibert Delorme was rebuilding for her.

Under Henri II.'s reign Jean Goujon, although a Protestant, enjoyed great favour; and the fame his distinguished talent merited even subdued the fanatical zeal of the constable, whose Château of Écouen was enriched with many specimens of the graceful fancy and skill of the heretic artist.

CHAPTER XI.

Diane Takes the Helm. — The Queen and the Favourite. — Diane in Despair. — Catherine's Debts. — Reserved for Greater Deeds. — The *Procès* of Jean de Brosse. — A Guise to the Rescue! — Not Mercy, but Justice. — The Loss of a Triumph. — A Judicial Duel. — A Slanderous Report. — The Beau and the Athlete. — The *Coup de Jarnac*. — Anger and Resignation. — The Vanquished Foe. — A Crime to Be Expiated. — Excellent Servants of the Crown. — The Lady of Cental.—The Snares of the Heretics. — The Justice of Heaven.

"MADAME DIANE" now guided the helm of state and reigned supreme at court, apparently with as much satisfaction to Catherine de' Medici as to Henry himself. Some modern writers have spoken of Catherine as "the young and haughty Italian beauty so strangely neglected by the king, and compelled to follow the triumphal car of a superannuated *belle* of forty-eight." But on the authority of those gossiping Venetian ambassadors — whose functions seem to have comprised that of court newsman to the seigniory of Venice — it may be asserted that Catherine at this time, so far from being haughty, was in manner very retiring, or rather, perhaps, cold and reserved. For the spirit of the Medici was recognised in the habit she had imposed on herself of constant dissimulation.

She was on friendly terms with "Madame Diane," whom she always thus addressed as though she were a royal personage. Diane had, indeed, some pretensions to being of royal descent — her family claiming the ancient sovereign princes of Aquitaine as their ancestors. Ever since her arrival at the Court of France, Catherine had been made to feel very bitterly her plebeian birth, and the wonderful condescension of Francis I. in uniting her, for his own political purposes, to the son he disliked, and whom he never expected to inherit his throne. Even as queen, the *grands seigneurs* and their ladies saw in her only the Florentine banker's daughter. But, by and by — Catherine had faith in her astrologer — by and by these slights would have to be accounted for.

If she had had beauty in her favour, possibly she might have triumphed over Diane. But she had not become personally more attractive since her marriage at the age of thirteen. She was now twenty-six. The "short, thickset girl" had developed into a very stout woman, below the middle height. Her appetite was enormous, and she indulged it freely; but to keep down the ever-increasing *embonpoint* resulting from it she took long walks and rides, which appear to have caused her much effort and fatigue, without accomplishing their object. Her complexion was pallid, sallow, and unhealthy, and she was now the mother of three unhealthy children — the eldest, the dauphin Francis, about four years of age.

The physicians spoke discouragingly of her state of health. They shook their heads and doubted if she would attain middle age. Diane was in despair. When Catherine had an illness threatening to be dangerous, Diane was unremitting in her attentions to her. She is supposed to have dreaded the probability of Henri taking a second wife in the event of Catherine's death. Not that she expected any diminution of her influence over him to result from it ; but she did not like her temper ruffled — it was destructive to beauty. And in what royal house was a second Catherine to be found? Where a princess so submissive, so grateful for small attentions which, at his favourite's suggestion, her husband paid her? Catherine's death might prove the end of Diane's reign ; either she would, for her own beauty's sake, abdicate, or she might possibly be deposed.

Though Catherine dared not meddle, as she would have liked to do, in public affairs of importance, she could solace herself in encouraging art; the love of which she had inherited, with other less amiable qualities that distinguished the Medici. She was very liberally disposed ; but, as her means were not ample as Diane's, she incurred heavy debts by a thoughtless lavishness in rewarding those who pleased her. No grant from the king or the state appears to have been made for their settlement. They were left for the chance of what the womb of time might bring forth to remove the restraint of her position.*

Catherine was fond of pleasure, and liked the rambling life of the court, to which Francis I. had so accustomed his family and his courtiers that, although gradually they fell into less unsettled habits, frequent change of place and residence long continued to be the rule. Whatever Catherine became later in life, after having so long lived unconsidered and in the shade, a silent spectator for twenty-five years of scenes of corruption, vice, and licentiousness unsurpassed at any court of Europe — even the papal one — she did not at this period exhibit any signs of that Machiavelian genius she subsequently displayed.

It is singular that she did not contrive to resent in some way the usurpation of her queenly rights by Diane. But perhaps only her life would have satisfied her vengeance; for it is difficult to believe that such a woman was content to be abased by her rival. The perfume of Italian gloves, the refreshing coolness of a sorbet, or the bright blade of a

---

* That such was the case may be inferred from a remark of Giovanni Michiele, immediately after she became queen-regent in 1559. He says: "Accustomed to give with a prodigal hand, she has been for some time considerably in debt and her affairs in disorder. Now her dowry is 300,000 *francs*, double the sum hitherto granted to dowager-queens. She has therefore sufficient now to pay her debts and to spend liberally."

stiletto might alone occur to her as a means of gratifying her resentment; but to employ them in her then humbled position would have been at the hazard of her own life. She refrained then, believing herself reserved for greater — as she certainly was for even more terrible — deeds.

The banishment of Madame d' Étampes from the court, and the transfer of the crown jewels to Madame Diane, did not, it appears, entirely appease this lady's angry feeling towards her former rival in favour and court influence. Her contemptible husband, Jean de Brosse, Duc d' Étampes, was induced to commence a *procès* against her for the amount of his salary as Governor of Brittany, of which he had borne the title, and she, he asserted, had received its emoluments. For twenty-one years he had held this post, and now for the first time preferred this claim.

The king was prevailed on to give evidence in his favour, so that his success and Madame's ruin seemed certain. But the king's evidence was found to be more prejudicial to the character of his father than to his father's favourite. That his son should voluntarily come forward publicly to censure him was thought monstrous, and excited general reprobation. Henri himself was smitten with remorse, and the *procès* of Jean de Brosse at once was put an end to.

But another charge — a more serious charge — was preferred against Madame d' Étampes, — if proved, involving the loss of her head, and that of the Baron de Longueval, the agent who was said to have been employed by her in her treasonable correspondence with Charles V. Nothing was really proved against her; not that her condemnation would have been less certain on that account; but these proceedings, like the former, were suddenly, for reasons of state, brought to a close. Certain revelations were threatened, compromising the constable, and likely, if enquired into, to transfer the charge of treason to him. When Charles V. was in France, the guest of the king, in 1539, De Montmorency, in his fanatical zeal for the Church, and approval of the emperor's persecuting spirit, is said to have shown him the private correspondence of the Protestant princes with Francis I., seeking his aid against him. This the king was made aware of, and, together with De Montmorency's urgent advocacy of the imperial alliance, contrary to the opinion of every other minister, caused his downfall at the moment when he thought himself most powerful.

François de Guise turned his knowledge of this circumstance to account, and Madame d' Étampes was saved; not from any interest he took in her, but because it gratified him to thwart the aims of De Montmorency. But the baron — is he to be the scapegoat in this affair? Is his head to fall? It seems likely — and better so than life spared, with permission to drag it out in a dark dungeon.

But again comes a Guise to the rescue! It is the pious young cardinal-archbishop. De Longueval has a fine estate in the neighbourhood of Laon, and the archbishop has taken a fancy to it. He mentions that fact. He does not offer to buy it. What is the use of money to a man who is about to lose his head? And it would be of no benefit to his family, as his estates would be confiscated. De Longueval, therefore, offers the prelate his château and domain of Marchais; he accepts, and in return guarantees that the baron's head shall remain on his shoulders, and further that he shall be free.

Forthwith he visits the king, and, as is his sacred duty, points out to him the iniquity of putting to death an innocent man — the crime he was accused of not having been proved against him. He sues not for mercy, he says, but merely requires the king to do an act of justice. As Henri usually thought that what his advisers recommended was the very thing he had himself determined to do, he the more readily complied with the archbishop's request. The Baron de Longueval's innocence was declared to be fully proved, and the prison doors, that had been closed on him for some months, were, as the archbishop had promised, duly opened.*

---

* "The Cardinal Charles de Guise obtained the Château de Meudon in a similar manner from Cardinal Sanguin, Madame d' Étampes's uncle."— H. Martin. Thus was justice administered at the brilliant period of the Renaissance.

The baron walked forth a free man; minus his estate certainly, but it was better than being minus his head.

The courteous archbishop, in his sacred character of peacemaker, had yet to soothe the ruffled spirit of Madame Diane. What became of the Duc d'Étampes and the Baron de Longueval she cared not; but that the duchess should escape was the loss of a triumph she had looked forward to over a supercilious rival, who had publicly declared that she was born on the very day Diane was married.

The secretary of state, the Sieur de Bayard, had been deprived of his office and thrown into prison,* for referring jestingly to her age; but the greater culprit was to escape with impunity. The archbishop reminded her of the deep humiliation of the late king's favourite, and prayed the incensed Diane to be satisfied with that and the final banishment of Madame d'Étampes from the court. It may be presumed that she yielded to his appeal for the fallen favourite, as no further proceedings were taken against her.

Her name was, however, again brought forward in connection with an affair of honour, as it may perhaps be called, of rather old date, which had remained unsettled because of the late king's refusal to allow it to be decided by a judicial

---

* "Where he ended his days."— H. Martin.

duel. This mode of determining disputes in the Middle Ages, by command or authorisation of the king or judges, was of such rare occurrence in the Renaissance period, that practically it was regarded as abolished. Louis XII. had entirely prohibited it; and Francis I., by once in the early part of his reign authorising and being present at a contest of that kind, had given great offence to the magistracy and the clergy.

The quarrel which, on the present occasion, the parties concerned were desirous of deciding by such a duel, was one of considerable rancour. Twelve years had not sufficed to allay the anger of their feelings, the challenge having been thrown down and taken up in 1535, when the late king's eldest son, the dauphin Francis, was living. It appears that the dauphin one day rather abruptly enquired of a young man of family, but of slender means — Guy Chabot de Jarnac, nephew or cousin of the Admiral Chabot de Brion — how he contrived, his father having married a second time and his allowance from him therefore reduced, to live in so extravagant a style and to dress so sumptuously on his small income.

It was suspected that Madame d'Étampes supplied this relative of her favourite friend, the admiral, with the requisite funds for making so brilliant a figure at court. The question annoyed the young man, it seems; and with some confusion he replied that his stepmother was good enough to add to his father's allowance for his maintenance. The dauphin, a thoughtless, dissipated youth, immediately set afloat the story that De Jarnac had boasted of being the lover of his stepmother, who supplied him with money.

By and by this tale came to De Jarnac's ears, and his father's also. The dauphin was, of course, far too great a personage to be called to account for this slanderous report. De Jarnac, therefore, publicly declared that "whoever had attributed such an assertion to him had told a dastardly lie." One of the dauphin's favourite companions stepped forward and took up the gauntlet that De Jarnac had thus thrown down. The meeting was arranged; but the king, whose consent to the duel was required, peremptorily forbade it. The dauphin went to the wars, and his death soon after ensued. La Châtaigneraie survived, and when Henri II. ascended the throne, both he and De Jarnac were as eager for the combat as ever.

Not only was their duel authorised by the king, but almost imposed upon them by decree in royal council, countersigned by a secretary of state. It was to take place on the 10th of July at St. Germain, where all the *noblesse* of France were convoked to celebrate the victory of La Châtaigneraie and the death of De Jarnac, which Henri both desired and expected. The ancient ceremonial was revived with all its formal pomposity. Witnesses, seconds, and sidesmen were appointed;

but the combatants were very unequally matched, except perhaps in courage. For Chabot de Jarnac was a man of slight frame, more of the beau and gallant than an athlete like La Châtaigneraie, who is said to have regarded his antagonist with the feeling of contempt that a lion might be supposed to feel for a dog.

So much did the king share this feeling that a grand supper was provided, of which he defrayed the expense, though the courtiers and other guests were invited in the victor's name to spend the evening after the combat in revelry. François de Guise and two of his brothers were La Châtaigneraie's seconds; the Bourbon princes offered themselves as De Jarnac's. Henri refused, and they expressed their disapprobation of the unfairness of the arrangements by withdrawing from all participation in them. The Connétable de Montmorency was *Juge du camp*, and, although he would not, like the Bourbons, declare for De Jarnac, to annoy the Guises, of whom he was beginning to be exceedingly jealous, he decided against them in favour of De Jarnac's demand to be provided with the heavy defensive armour customary in such encounters.

The king is a spectator of the combat, and is finally to pronounce the victor "confirmed in his rights." He sits on a raised daïs, Madame Diane beside him. Catherine may be on the other side, but her name is not mentioned. The provincial nobility attend in full force to witness this renaissance of the ancient customs of chivalry. The Parisians, too, have flocked to St. Germain, and left the capital to take care of itself. This vast multitude crowding the terrace awaits the combatants in breathless expectation.

They arrive; they enter the lists; they salute each other. La Châtaigneraie's first passes fall harmlessly on De Jarnac's armour. De Jarnac, evidently a less skilful swordsman than his adversary, yet contrives adroitly enough to parry his thrusts, and by an unexpected blow, which wounds him in the back of the leg, brings him, utterly disabled, to the ground.

Such a result of their combat was contrary to all expectation. But the victor spares his vanquished foe. He does not take his life. Three times he kneels before the king. "Sire," he says, "esteem me now a man of honour. I give you La Châtaigneraie's life." But Henri, mortified beyond measure, remains motionless and mute. Eloquently, but in vain, he continues to address the silent, angry monarch; then, turning from him, he boldly appeals to Diane, from whom he seems to have had some assurance that the king was not prejudiced against him. "Madame," he says, "you told me so."

But Henri's conduct towards the unexpected victor shows so plainly how very far from impartial he was in this matter that a feeling of indignation pervades the mass of spectators. They are said to have trembled with rage, and to have given such unmistakable indications of it that the poor weak king, trembled too — but with fear; and to this he yielded with as good a grace as the awkwardness of the position permitted.

"You give me the vanquished man's life?" he said.

"Yes, sire."

"You have done your duty," he replies; "and, as is your right, your honour is restored."

De Jarnac then, according to the prescribed ceremonial, ascended the royal daïs, and the king, resigning himself to playing his part in this scene with more courtesy than before, embraced him, and, in the pedantic style then in vogue, told him he had "fought with the courage of Cæsar and spoken with the eloquence of Aristotle."

But if he succeeded in dissembling his anger at De Jarnac's unexpected victory,* he evinced no desire to conceal his displeasure at La Châtaigneraie's failure to achieve the triumph he was so certain of. Coldly and haughtily he passed the wounded man, as he left the field with his retinue — expressing not the slightest interest in him, or deigning to turn his eyes towards the spot where, attended by the surgeons, he was lying. La Châtaigneraie was cut to the heart. De Jarnac had

---

* The "*coup de Jarnac*" has ever since remained a proverbial expression in French, for any unexpected blow or event.

spared his life, placing the granting of it in the king's hands. But his vanquished foe refused to accept it. He tore the bandages from his wound, and died from loss of blood.

The assembled crowd, meanwhile, disregarding the presence of the court, thoroughly sacked the tents in the grounds of the Château of St. Germain, where great preparations had been making for feasting and revelry to follow the completion of the judicial duel, or murder. The king sent his Scotch guards with their halberds to disperse the rioters, and this last attempt at reviving the customs of chivalric times ended in a fearful affray, in which many persons were wounded and some few slain.*

This duel and the preceding *procès* were not the only affairs standing over from the last reign to be settled by the inept monarch to whose hands France and her destinies were now confided. One of infinitely greater moment than the quarrel of De Jarnac and La Châtaigneraie, or the treason of Madame d' Étampes, called urgently for the attention of the king and the government — the enquiry into the massacre of the Vaudois of Provence, and the due punishment of those concerned in it. Outraged humanity cried aloud for the expiation of that horrible crime that had disturbed even the worthless Francis I. on his deathbed — certain as

* See Michelet, "*Histoire de France;*" and H. Martin, "*Renaissance et Reforme.*"

he had made himself that heaven was his heritage, where probably he looked to continue playing the despot; but over subjects orthodox as himself, and more submissive to excessive taxation than the French.

Henri II. had not hitherto been required to give much heed to the Reformation. He simply contemned it. He was solemn and devout to an extent that Francis was not, and regarded the reformers as the dregs of the people. What to him were those ignorant, obstinate, heretical peasants, the Vaudois, compared with those excellent servants of the crown denounced as their persecutors? — such men as that orthodox prelate, Cardinal de Tournon; the Comte de Grignan, Governor of Provence; the Baron Meinier d'Oppède, first President of the Parliament of Aix; and that valiant and useful officer, the Baron de La Garde, who had been captain of the Mediterranean galleys, had sunk the English admiral's ship *Henry the Great*, and now displayed his military genius as commandant of a detachment of troops.

The king was disposed to let this lamentable affair rest, and to fling to the winds his father's deathbed injunction, inspired by qualms of conscience, to enquire into the conduct of these men. To revive the matter was but to revive the scandal attaching to his father's memory for the part he took in it. And this, perhaps, was true. But the widowed Lady of Cental, to whom belonged the country that had been ravaged and depopulated by the Vaudois persecution, brought her complaint before the king, and demanded judgment against the monsters who had so cruelly robbed, tortured, massacred, her inoffensive vassals.

Of necessity, then, the king must take cognisance of the matter. La Garde and D' Oppède were arrested, besides three commissioners of the Parliament of Aix, who had been most active in the work of extermination. This afforded the Guises another opportunity of adding an estate or two to those already so honourably acquired. They had, when first preferred, vehemently urged the claim of the Lady of Cental to be avenged on the murderers of her people. But whether her estates were too entirely ravaged to be worth their acceptance, or she was indisposed to incur further loss to secure their aid, or other motive actuated them, suddenly they abandoned the lady's cause to give their support to De Grignan.

The château and domain of the Governor of Provence formed a very fine property. He was not, however, prepared, though he trembled for his life, to cede his estate to François de Guise, or other of the brothers; but he could bequeath it to them. This he did — reasons why he should not be included in the Vaudois enquiry having been made clearly apparent to Henri — and at De Grignan's death it became the property of the Guise family.

The Pope also interfered on behalf of the infamous D'Oppède, whom "his holiness" dared to term an "illustrious defender of the faith, persecuted for his religious zeal"—zeal and religion as understood, of course, at the Vatican. Prayers, too, were ordered to be offered up to God (instead of to Satan) for the preservation of this fiend, and his "happy escape from the snares of the heretics." The king referred the decision of the matter to the Grand Chamber of the Parliament of Paris, who took upwards of two years to make up their minds as to whether or not the atrocities perpetrated by those demons in human form, and at which every feeling of humanity revolted, should receive their due measure — if that were possible — of retributive justice.

After many animated discussions, it was finally determined that, with one exception, there should be a general acquittal. Such was the fanaticism of the age that, even among those who were not extreme in their opinions, an unwillingness prevailed to accord to heretics such signal satisfaction as this case seemed to demand. The condemnation of the attorney, Guérin, who was hanged on the Place de Grève, was less for his participation in the horrors of the massacre than because it was discovered that he had falsified some documents connected with it, issued by the Parliament of Aix.

This, discovery or invention, also furnished the

Parliament of Paris — much to their satisfaction — with a pretext for evading to cast the stigma of reproach on the Parliament of Aix for the contents of those documents, which authorised the Vaudois persecution. De La Garde and the much-maligned and virtuous Baron d'Oppède were reinstated in their several employments, and thanksgivings to the Deity that had preserved them from harm were sung in many churches.

"But the justice of heaven," says De Thou, "soon after supplemented that of the earthly judges, the baron being carried off by a violently painful internal complaint." Another account adds that "a Protestant surgeon, who was called in to perform some operation, assisted in hastening his departure by the use of a poisoned probe." If it really was so, it is a pity that one can neither approve the deed nor lament the victim.

CHAPTER XII.

The Real Power in the State. — Summoning His Vassal. — Misty Visions of the Future. — Coronation of Henri II. — Insurrection in Angoumois. — The Common Cause of Guyenne. — A Wicked Gabeleur. — Festivity and Barbarity. — A Vain Appeal for Mercy. — "The Great Soldier." — A Striking Contrast. — Congenial Surroundings.

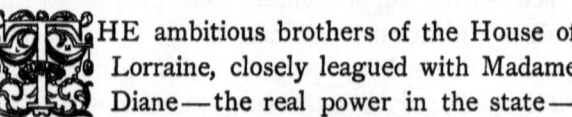HE ambitious brothers of the House of Lorraine, closely leagued with Madame Diane — the real power in the state — and using the king as a tool for the more effectual carrying out of their deeply laid and far-stretching schemes, now, in furtherance of them, sought to embroil the weak monarch both with the emperor and with England.

Henri abhorred Charles V. Time could not dim the vivid impression his memory retained of the harshness he and his brother had been subjected to during their Spanish captivity.* The king was, therefore, easily persuaded, under pretence of the necessity of asserting and maintain-

---

* A recent atrocious act of cruelty on Charles's part had strengthened this feeling—little inclined as was Henri himself to show mercy. By his order a number of lansquenets, who had served in the French army, being taken prisoners, had their feet chopped off. Even his son Philip—the future Philip II.— pleaded for these poor men, but pleaded in vain!

ing his rights of suzerain of Flanders, to repeat an act of folly similar to that which Francis I. had once been led into.

Henri was to be crowned on the 27th of July, and Valois, the principal herald-at-arms of France, was despatched, by order of the king, to the emperor to inform him of the event, and "to summon him, as his vassal, to appear at Rheims on the above date, in his quality of Count of Flanders, and in discharge of his duty as a peer of France." The emperor, much provoked, replied, in his irritation, "he would be at Rheims, as required, with 50,000 men to aid him in the discharge of his duty." But Charles at that moment was too fully occupied by his quarrel with the Pope, his efforts to exterminate heresy, and the recent success of his arms over the Protestant princes of Germany, to fulfil his promise of attending Henri's coronation with a retinue so numerous. Nothing, therefore, resulted from these bravados but a mutual increase of angry feeling.

War with the emperor in Italy was looked forward to, to achieve for the Guises both power and glory. They are said to have aspired to the conquest of the kingdom of Naples, with the view of retaining possession of it themselves — asserting their right to it as heirs of the House of Anjou, through some distant female connection. The crown of France, too, floated before their longing eyes in misty visions of the future.

The child-queen, Mary of Scotland, was their niece, and a project was then on foot in that country to betroth her to the heir of the crown of Denmark, with the object of preventing the union of Scotland with England. But the Guises, desiring to secure for France a queen of their own family, proposed her betrothal to the youthful dauphin. At the same time, to divert the attention of the English ministers to other matters, they induced the king to refuse to ratify the treaty respecting Boulogne, concluded between Henry VIII. and Francis I.

Meanwhile, the coronation wholly engaged the thoughts of the court and people. Thirty-two years had elapsed since that of Francis took place —at night, and without any outward pomp to render it memorable; so eager was he to join the army assembling at Lyons when Louis XII. died, and to march on Italy to recover "his heritage." On this occasion the old ceremonial was revived. A brilliant scene, indeed, must have presented itself to the admiring gaze of Diane and Catherine, as together, under a "canopied tribune," they beheld the handsome monarch, in his royal robes, kneel before the archbishop — the assembled peers, at the same moment, rising and removing their plumed hats — to receive the sacred oil; and, following that ceremony, the crown from the prelate's hands.

After his coronation, Henri, attended by a numerous retinue, visited the fortified towns of France. Many ladies and gentlemen of the court accompanied him, and a large body of troops ; more like an army than the escort of a sovereign with his court, making the tour of his dominions for recreation in time of peace. The king reviewed the garrisons after inspecting the fortresses ; much to the delight of the ladies of the court, who, though sometimes accompanying Francis I. on his flying visits to his armies, had rarely witnessed any grand military spectacle, especially during his latter years.

After visiting the frontier towns of Piedmont, this numerous party of pleasure passed on to Turin ; the king's escort everywhere exciting surprise, apparently because of its unusual decency of equipment and attempt at a uniform. Some suspicion, however, was created in Italy by its numbers, as, joined by a garrison or two from neighbouring towns, the escort would at once be transformed into an army. Plots and counterplots were then rife, as generally they were, at Genoa and Milan ; but nothing of sufficient importance seems to have warranted the interference of the French, as the vigilant Duc François d'Aumale was of the party, and no encounters of a hostile character occurred.

But while at Turin information arrived of a serious insurrection then at its height in Angoumois and Saintonge. It began at the small town of Lorignac, where the people had resisted an increase of the Gabelle, or salt-tax, and had beaten and put to flight the collectors of that impost. The peasantry of the surrounding country rose in arms, and threatened not only the "Gabeleurs," but the gentry of the district who had given them shelter, and whose châteaux had, in some instances, already been attacked, plundered, or burnt. Emboldened by success and daily increasing numbers, they marched on Château-Neuf, forced its prison doors, and liberated several peasants of the canton. These poor men were confined there for the crime of having failed to provide themselves with the regulation quantity of salt which every family, by an edict of the Gabelle, was ordered to buy at the king's storehouses at an exorbitant price.

The Governor of Guyenne, Henri d' Albret, sent a company of infantry to disperse the insurgents. But the foe they had to encounter was an overwhelming multitude of armed and excited peasantry, before whose advance and frantic cry of "Death to the Gabeleurs!" the troops sent against them were soon compelled to retreat. The insurrection continued to spread; calmed a little in one town, it extended to the next. La Rochelle, which had taken so prominent a part in a former revolt against the Gabelle, and had escaped punishment so unexpectedly, alone refrained from joining the present one.

At length it reached Bordeaux. Exempt from the tax of the Gabelle, the inhabitants of this city had no direct interest in the quarrel. But several thousands of the insurgent inhabitants of smaller towns and villages of the province of Guyenne, of which Bordeaux was the ancient capital, having entered the city, the humbler class of the Bordelais were led at least to sympathise with their countrymen in what they termed the common cause of Guyenne.

Unfortunately, the lieutenant-governor, having convoked a meeting at the town hall of the chief members of the various tribes or guilds of Bordeaux, addressed them in terms so menacing, telling them that gibbets were ready for any who joined in this insurrection, that indignation was aroused; and one of their number, a rich merchant named Guillotin, exclaimed that "the people of Guyenne had done right to seek to recover by arms the liberty of their ancestors." At once the tocsin was sounded. The arsenal was invaded, and arms delivered to the people. The lieutenant-governor fled to Château Trompette — the fortress — but having the imprudence to leave it once more to speak to the people, a band of insurgent peasants that had just entered the city fell upon him savagely and killed him, as a "wicked Gabeleur," afterwards throwing his body into the river, bidding him "go salt the fishes there."

On the first intelligence of this serious insurrection reaching the king, he despatched both the Duc d' Aumale and De Montmorency, each with a small force, chiefly lansquenets, to quell this sedition and restore order. He and his court awaited the issue at Lyons, into which gay and flourishing city he made his public entry.

The event was celebrated with unprecedented magnificence, the native and foreign population vying with each other in their efforts to invent new methods of doing honour to the new reign and their young sovereign. For the first time he passed under triumphal arches, tastefully and elaborately ornamented; saw columns and obelisks raised in his honour, though of victories there were none yet to inscribe on them. The Italians gave theatrical spectacles, naval combats on the river, and athletic sports after the manner of ancient Rome, with other entertainments of a novel character, taking the place of the ceremonial formerly observed at royal entries.

But while all was gaiety and festivity at Lyons, horrors unspeakable were enacting at Bordeaux, by order of the sanguinary constable, who was revelling in blood and human suffering. The insurrection had been effectually quelled before his arrival, by the efforts of La Chassagne, president of the Parliament of Bordeaux. While endeavouring to soothe the irritation of the people, he was seized by some of the insurgents, who compelled him to swear, while a dagger was held to his throat, that he would be their captain and march at their head to the fortress.

Having taken the oath, he turned his newly acquired authority to account in bringing about a more peaceful state of things; and this, together with the dejection and weariness that suddenly succeeded the violence and uproar that for a time had prevailed, restored the calm and order that prior to this rebellion had reigned in Bordeaux. The insurgents from neighbouring towns were expelled, and the gates of the city closed.

This information was sent to the king, and it was hoped that he would avail himself of the event of his recent coronation, and his public entry into the principal cities that was to follow it, for showing mercy and pardoning what had occurred, as Francis had done for a similar revolt at La Rochelle.

But the march of the troops was not countermanded, and terror seized every heart when it became known that the inhuman De Montmorency — whose very name caused a thrill of horror in every breast — was on his way to Bordeaux with a detachment of lansquenets. In order to propitiate him, the authorities of the city sent to Langon a magnificent boat, ornamented with his armorial bearings, and begged him to use it for his conveyance to Bordeaux. They also entreated him, as all was now perfectly peaceful, to leave the lansquenets outside the walls. He replied: "It was not for them to dictate terms to him; that he would enter Bordeaux neither by boat nor

gate, but with the keys he had brought with him"
— pointing to his twenty pieces of cannon.

A breach was made in the walls, and through it he and his troops passed into the city — the latter pillaging and ravaging as though they had entered the country of a conquered enemy. "Bordeaux was declared deprived forever of its privileges, franchises, liberties, and immunities; its town hall, municipal council, church bells, justice, and jurisdiction." "With their own hands the authorities were ordered to prepare the fire that was to consume the charters and privileges of the city, also to raze the town hall; to pay a fine of 200,000 *livres*, besides the expense of keeping up the fortifications and the two fortresses."

All this, however, was as nothing compared with what was to follow — the sickening horrors invented by the demon De Montmorency for torturing and putting to death the people concerned, or not concerned, in the late revolt. It seems amazing that they did not rise *en masse* and inflict on the monster a punishment of his own devising — one of the "red-hot crowns," for instance, "followed by breaking on the wheel, or tearing to pieces by four horses."

The Duc d'Aumale — François de Guise — did not immediately effect the junction of his small *corps d'armée* with that of De Montmorency; but turned aside from his direct route to pacify the people of Saintonge and Angoumois. They had

Anne de Montmorency.
Photo-etching from painting by Chasselat.

laid down their arms, and made no opposition to his march; while he, refraining from punishing what was now past, advised them in conciliatory terms to abstain from such violent measures for obtaining redress of their grievances in future. This conduct, contrasting so strikingly with the constable's, is said to have been in pursuance of his system of courting popularity, and a reputation for generosity and magnanimity. But however selfish his aim may have been, a system that led to kind and generous acts must certainly be far better than one whose sole results were deeds that eternally disgraced humanity.*

The constable remained several weeks at Bordeaux, and executions occurred daily, amounting before he left to near five hundred. The scene around him — gibbets, racks and wheels, red-hot irons and burning piles, together with the shrieks of his victims, music to his ears — was too congenial to his tiger-like nature, easily to tear himself from it. At last his lansquenets, gorged with blood and plunder, took their departure. But it

* Two years after, Henri restored to Bordeaux and other towns of the revolt the privileges, immunities, town hall, church bells, etc., of which they had been deprived. He was impelled by the fear of what might happen, in the event of a war with England, if Bordeaux — long an English city — should remain under the stigma of disfranchisement. He also sold to these provinces, oppressed by the Gabelle laws, an exemption from the forced purchase of salt for 200,000 gold crowns, and abandoned his own monopoly for a fixed tax on the article. — H. Martin.

was long, very long, ere the valiant deeds of the "great soldier," Anne de Montmorency, were forgotten at Bordeaux or throughout the province of Guyenne.

CHAPTER XIII.

A Delusive Dream Dispelled. — Marriage of Jeanne d'Albret. — The Ceremony at Moulins. — The Semi-royal Betrothal. — Marguerite's Last Years. — The Bride and Her Pages. — The Bride's Mother. — The Widow's Garb. — The King's Costume. — Antoine de Bourbon. — The Wedding Banquet and Ball. — La Balafré. — Ambroise Paré. — Journeying North. — An Excellent Bringing-up. — The King's Entry into Paris. — A Proof of His Orthodoxy. — The Wickedness of the Age.

HERE was no longer any hope that the daughter of the King of Navarre would ever sit on the Spanish throne — a hope which both he and his queen had once fondly cherished. The resentment of Francis I. towards the emperor had dispelled that delusive dream of exaltation and splendour momentarily imagined for Jeanne d'Albret; and again his anger had set her free from bonds with which he afterwards closely fettered her, contrary to her own and her parents' wishes. Since then Jeanne had lived in happy freedom from betrothals and engagements, and had learned to regard her escape from a marriage with the haughty, gloomy bigot, Prince Philip of Spain, as a mark of providential care.

The heiress of the little kingdom of Navarre

was now nineteen, and was about to give her hand to Antoine de Bourbon, Duc de Vendôme, and first prince of the blood — in the event of the failure of male heirs to Henri II. — heir to the throne of France. The ceremony was to take place at the Château de Moulins, where the Constable Charles de Bourbon had once lived in great state. It was one of the few domains of that immense property, confiscated by his revolt, that Francis had restored to his heirs.

Thither Henri II. and his court repaired, on leaving Lyons, to celebrate the nuptials of his cousin Jeanne, and at the same time the betrothal of the Princess Anna of Este, daughter of the Duke and Duchess of Ferrara, to the Duc d'Aumale, who by this distinguished alliance with the granddaughter of Louis XII. placed himself and his family in much closer relationship with the royal House of France. The duke arrived from the scene of the revolt with a fresh halo of popularity, and with him the constable, followed by a unanimous yell of execration.

The ceremony which royalty and the court had assembled to witness, and to honour and grace by their presence, was not, perhaps, solemnised with the splendour with which the former magnificent owner of the princely abode of Moulins had celebrated the christening of his infant son and heir — splendour that had so greatly aroused the jealousy and wounded the self-love of Francis I.

Many circumstances of the moment combined to render it rather a private family affair than an event of national importance.

Henri had not yet made his public entry into Paris and the principal cities of the kingdom. The revolt of Bordeaux and its sad results had put all idea of festivity out of the question there, and thrown a gloom over other towns looking forward to receive the new monarch. For Bordeaux, as described by Navagero (Venetian ambassador), about that time was one of the handsomest and most populous of the provincial towns, and the inhabitants, he says, "of a very gay and lively temperament." Henri was also in need of money. The salt-tax had not been paid; and although 400,000 gold crowns had been found, to the astonishment of most persons, in the late king's private coffers, that sum (which, it afterwards appeared, was drawn from the bank he had established at Lyons for the receipt of deposits at eight per cent.) had been absorbed, partly for the needs of Madame Diane, — what remained, by the expenses of the coronation.

Nevertheless, the company attending the royal marriage and semi-royal betrothal at Moulins formed a brilliant and effective gathering. It was almost the last occasion of Queen Marguerite's appearance in the court circle of France; she no longer possessed either influence or credit there. The death of Francis; the departure of Queen

Eleanor; the accession of "Madame Diane" to share the throne of Henri II.; the return of her sworn enemy, De Montmorency; the power of the Guises, and the ceaseless intrigues and counter-intrigues of all parties to secure a preponderance in the government, and the largest share of places, pensions, estates, and titles,* — were so many motives for her exclusion on the one part, and for retirement on her own. There was, however, nothing new in this state of things. It was the old system; but the working of it had fallen into new hands, and, as it seemed, even more rapacious ones.

So Marguerite, who was now fifty-six, kept to her own little Court of Navarre, and the society of her daughter; except occasionally when she retired for prayer and meditation to a religious house, of which she was nominally chanoinesse, or, as Brantôme seems to have heard, abbess. He therefore says "she died a good Catholic." But Marguerite had adopted the principles of the Reformation; yet she said that, "if her heart was right with God, the form of worship was of little moment."

Jeanne d'Albret, as the adopted daughter of

---

* "It is reported by Vieilleville that both the Guise and Montmorency families employed secret and paid agents in various parts of the kingdom, to give them immediate notice of the death of every person holding an office or benefice." — Martin.

Francis I., was brought up strictly in the Roman faith. Francis feared the influence of her mother's sentiments. But the energy of Jeanne's character led her, after embracing Calvinism, far beyond her mother in her profession of it, and in the observance of its prescribed forms. She was, however, too intelligent and too amiable to be harsh or coldly bigoted; but she gradually became graver in manner, and dressed with greater simplicity, especially after her mother's death,* than was customary in the Court of France.

But Jeanne d' Albret is a charming vision of a youthful bride, as she stands at the altar of the chapel of Moulins, arrayed in white and silver satin brocade, her hair flowing loosely over her shoulders, but confined at the forehead by a circlet of pearls with diamond clasp, as was usual at that time for brides of high degree. Her long, heavy train, embroidered in silver and seed-pearls, is borne by four young pages in costumes of blue velvet and silver, white satin shoes with blue rosettes, and blue velvet toques with small white plumes. The great width of the deeply pendent sleeves (another distinguishing mark of the *toilettes* of ladies of rank, women of inferior station being permitted far less latitude in this respect), heavily embroidered to match the train, seem, from their weight, almost to need the services of two more

* Marguerite d' Angoulême, Queen of Navarre, died December 21st, 1549.

pages to support them. A stomacher of pearls
and diamonds; a *cordelière* of the same; silver-
embroided satin shoes, and veil of Italian silver
tissue, rather narrow, but falling very low on
the back of the dress, completed the bridal
costume.*

Marguerite was always remarkable for the elegance and suitableness of her *toilettes*, often cor-
recting by her superior good taste the fondness
of Queen Eleanor for elaborate ornamentation.
Lake, or dark crimson (*laque foncée*), appears to
have been her favourite colour, as she frequently
wore it on great occasions. On that of her daughter's marriage she wore a *cotillon* or underdress of
that shade, of rich Venetian satin embroidered and
fringed with gold. This *cotillon*, called by the
Venetians a *carpetta*, was always, it appears, a
handsome and expensive garment; ladies of the
upper *bourgeoisie* were permitted to wear it.

Over it the Queen of Navarre wore a long train
of velvet of the same colour, lined with white satin
and fringed with gold. Her *coiffe*, to which was
attached a long veil of gold tissue, was of netted
gold riband, bordered with jewels — diamonds and
rubies probably, her stomacher, *cordelière*, earrings,
necklace, etc., being composed of those gems. Her
train-bearers wore costumes similar to those of the
bride's pages; the only difference was in their
colours — crimson and white. Other ladies, of

---

* The Venetian ambassador, Lippomano.

course, were similarly attired — Catherine de' Medici with great splendour. She was exceedingly fond of dress, as were also the Italian ladies in her suite; inclined, too, to exaggerate the fashions of the day, however absurd, even to a further expansion of the *vertugadin* — precursor of the *panier* — which to Catherine, considering her increasing stoutness, could scarcely be becoming. Rouge was not then in favour; on the contrary, the paleness of the cheek, if it did not proceed from ill health, was considered an added charm to beauty. The hair was also arranged, or a *toupet* put on, to give an appearance of width to the forehead.

One lady, however, would be distinguished from the rest by the widow's garb. This was "Madame Diane." She had worn it from the time of her husband's death in 1531, and continued to wear it as long as her own life lasted. Further to mark her sense of her great bereavement, she employed the most distinguished artists of the time to erect a superb monument to the memory of the Comte de Brézé, with whom, apparently, she had lived in perfect amity for nineteen years.

The widow's colours were black and white, the dress buttoned up high to the throat, with a long-sleeved camisole having a large collar thrown back. All perfectly plain, without ornaments or lace. A small black veil of tissue was worn at the back of the head; a larger one, covering the shoulders and falling low at the back, was put on when going out. But Diane, though she wore the widow's colours, did not confine herself to the pattern prescribed by sumptuary laws. Black and white velvets and satins, made after the fashion that most became her style of beauty. Also black and silver tissues; a *coiffe* of netted ribands, or of velvet bordered with pearls. No other ornaments, and no other colours.

The king, who mostly wore black, and sometimes black and white, in compliment to Diane, on the occasion in question was attired in a *pourpoint*, or vest of black velvet, slashed with white satin, with short skirts or basques, and a cloak of the same material, embroidered in broad stripes of gold. Trunk-hose of white silk, very large, and rounded with horse hair or wool, a band of gold braiding attaching them to the long, white silk stockings. White silk shoes, with black rosettes. A black velvet toque, with a white plume of two or three feathers placed on the right side, and bordered with four rows of black and white pearls. His cravat was of fine lace, and a pouch or purse (*escarcelle*) on his right side was fastened by gold chains to an embroidered waist-belt. It was used for the same purpose as the pockets now made in the dress itself.*

The princes and other persons of distinction would be similarly dressed, the bridegroom wear-

---

* "*Costumes historiques:*" P. Lacroix.

ing blue and white velvet and satin; many jewels in his plumed hat, many rings on his fingers, a jewelled pouch at his side, and a massive gold chain passing twice round his neck.* Notwithstanding his effeminate fondness for jewels — a weakness of many men of that period — he was a brave and valiant prince when at the head of his troops. But in the council-chamber of Henri II. he made a less brilliant figure. Both he and his brothers — the young Prince de Condé excepted — were wanting in the firmness and decision of character which might have enabled them, to the benefit of the state, to have counteracted the grasping, ambitious views of their more energetic and unscrupulous colleagues. Still, as first prince of the blood, his presence, small as was his influence, presented an obstacle to the efforts of the Guises to place themselves in nearer connection with royalty, and to take rank with princes of the blood. As King of Navarre, expectant, in right of his wife, Antoine de Bourbon might at all events be less in the way than hitherto.

It was on his betrothal to the Princess Anna of Este† that François de Guise first publicly as-

* Antoine de Bourbon was exceedingly fond of jewellery, and even wore earrings years after his marriage, and when a snowy beard rather prematurely gave him a venerable air. This was in striking contrast with the simple tastes of his grave Calvinist wife, who nevertheless possessed great influence over him.

† Granddaughter of Lucretia Borgia, whose beauty she is

sumed the name of Anjou, together with the title of prince. The king did not oppose this usurpation on the auspicious occasion of his betrothal, but soon after, to the extreme indignation of the Guise family, the first President, Lizet, of the Parliament of Paris refused that title — which, as he said, "in France belonged only to royalty" — to the Cardinal de Lorraine.*

The wedding banquet and ball, with the general rejoicings of the household and peasantry of the domain of Moulins, comprised the whole of the marriage festivities. No marriage present was given by the bridegroom's father — or whoever may have represented him — to the bride's mother, as appears, from the remarks of the Venetian ambassador, to have been the custom in Italy but not in France. Two celebrated men were born of these marriages, both of whom were destined to be assassinated — Henri IV. of France, and Henri,

said to have inherited. The Duc d' Aumale regarded her only as a granddaughter of Louis XII. and cousin of Henri II.

* Having one day some public business to transact with the king's council, where the cardinal presided, Lizet was required to make his statements standing and uncovered. But, as the head of a sovereign court, he declined thus to lower the dignity of his office before any one but the king in person. Henri feared the Guises, and, on being appealed to, Lizet was told to do as the cardinal desired. But he persisted in his refusal. The cardinal thereupon declared him a rebel against the royal authority, and suspended him from the exercise of his presidential functions. Lizet replied by resigning his office, to which a more pliant successor, recommended by Madame Diane, was appointed.

Duc de Guise, sometimes erroneously named the "Balafré."

The term *balafré*, signifying a long, deep wound or scar on the face, was applied as a surname— "*Le Balafré*" — to François de Guise, who, in 1545, in one of the skirmishes between the English and French at Boulogne, received a wound from a javelin, which pierced his right cheek just below the eye, and entered his head to almost the depth of six inches. In the violence of the shock the javelin broke, the short, sharp steel-pointed end, with some splinters of the wooden shaft, remaining in the wound. Although so severely hurt he was not unhorsed, and even retained strength and consciousness long enough to get back to the camp.

The surgeons gathered around him, and declared their opinion that the wounded man would die under their hands at the moment the fragment of steel was drawn from his head. One alone among them — a young man of twenty-eight, who had already acquired distinction in his profession by his able treatment of some dangerous wounds in the course of the war — had confidence in his own ability to extract the lance, and in the fortitude and courage of the patient to undergo the operation. He placed his foot on his head, and with a pair of fine pincers drew the fragment of steel from the wound, with a hand so firm and sure that no serious result occurred, and the sight of the eye was not injured. A deep scar remained on the face of François de Guise, and gained him the surname of "*Le Balafré*." That he recovered with no further permanent harm than some damage to his good looks was esteemed by many a miracle.*

The able surgeon who wrought it was the famous Ambroise Paré, who effected great reforms in the surgical art of that day. The French call him the "Father of modern French surgery." "Until his time, wounds received from firearms were considered poisonous, and it was the general practice to cauterise them with boiling oil, which was more frequently the cause of death than the wounds themselves. He introduced, also, a more effective and less painful method than hitherto had been customary in cases of amputation. The success of his method and his great celebrity made no change in his unpretending mode of life. He was a reformer, and was accustomed to say, piously and modestly, of those whose lives he had saved, "I took care of him; it was God who cured him" (Martin).

On leaving Moulins, the queen and the ladies of the court were escorted to Blois; the king, accom-

* Yet a similar accident is said to have occurred to Francis I. many years before, while engaged in an assault of arms. Similar surgical skill was attended with similar successful results. A few inches of cold steel in the head apparently was a trifling matter to those heroes. But fortunately the offending weapon never pierced the brain. See vol. i., p. 222.

panied by De Montmorency, the Duc d' Aumale, the Archbishop of Rheims, and other members of his council, journeyed north. Henri was anxious to be in nearer communication with Scotland, which, after the defeat of the Earl of Arran in September, 1547, and the refusal of the Scottish Government to fulfil the treaty promising the hand of Mary Stuart to the Prince of Wales, now Edward VI., had entered into close alliance with France.

Influenced by the dowager-queen, Mary of Guise, the regent had offered the hand of the child-queen to the dauphin Francis, and a French squadron was then cruising near the west coast of Scotland, waiting an opportunity of carrying her off to France. There, "under the vigilant eyes of Catherine de' Medici," assisted by the Guises, Mary was to be trained up a model Queen of France and Scotland, and, perchance, of England. Mary was secretly conveyed to Dumbarton, and put on board the vessel of the commander, Villegagnon, who, without mishap, reached Brest with her youthful majesty. To her early introduction to the most intriguing and depraved court in Europe, and to the immoral examples ever before her eyes during the next twelve years, many of the faults and consequent misfortunes of the later life of the ill-fated Scottish queen may, doubtless, be ascribed. She was but six years old when taken to France; her affianced husband was four and a half.

Hostilities continued on the frontier of Scotland and in the northern counties of England, the Scotch being aided by the French, but without any decisive result. Religious strife added exasperation of feeling to both parties, while towns were taken, lost, and retaken; the country ravaged, the crops destroyed; the peasantry reduced to dire distress, and blood flowed in torrents.

Another object of the king's northern journey was to prepare for profiting by those dissensions between the English and Scotch, by ejecting the former from Boulogne. The preliminary step appears to have been the despatching a rather peremptory command to the Lord Protector and Council of Regency to cease their attacks on the territory of "his daughter, the Queen of Scotland." He then returned to Paris, and made his public entry into that capital with more than the customary splendour. The Parisians having had information of the novelties introduced into the festive arrangements at Lyons, did their best to surpass them in brilliancy and variety, and to give their new monarch a grand reception as well as a cordial one.

To the usual procession through the city, the municipal authorities of Paris, vying with those of Lyons, had made many considerable additions. They had gone to the expense of providing a quantity of new silk banners, and increased the number of archers and men-at-arms. Many new costumes also appeared, with gold embroideries and braidings to an extent much beyond what certain regulations respecting them permitted. But for so auspicious an occasion it was thought they might well be overlooked as a temporary exaggeration for adding effect and splendour to the *fête*, and doing honour to the sovereign.

The ladies of the upper *bourgeoisie*, who filled the windows of the houses, appeared in very rich and elegant dresses, especially where there was a balcony the better to display them. Many were also resplendent with jewellery. All this show of wealth, indicating easy and affluent circumstances, the monarch noted well. He was of too solemn a temperament to be carried away by the enthusiasm of the people into sympathy of feeling with them.

He, however, could give his good people of Paris, on this special occasion of his first appearance among them in his quality of their sovereign ruler, a striking proof of his orthodoxy. It might serve both as example and warning to them in these days of heretical doctrines. Auvergne had become tainted with them, and several arrests had been made there. What better termination, then, could be devised to grace a grand and gorgeous festival and display the pious monarch's zeal than the public burning on the Place de Grève of half a dozen of these heretics? This horrible inauguration of his reign took place. But it shocked the feelings of many persons, and was regarded as of sinister foreboding.

On Henri's return to Paris, many new laws, many severe edicts, were enacted, and old ones, fallen almost into desuetede, revived. The disapprobation of the Parliament was strongly expressed at the extended jurisdiction of the provost of Paris, to whom powers were granted trenching on those of the superior court. "The wickedness of the age" was, however, fully admitted, and the law on that account registered. Arms were forbidden to all but the military. Robberies and murders had become so frequent, and the stiletto and that favourite weapon, the pistol (recently introduced from Italy), in such constant use, that the streets of ·Paris and other large towns were unsafe after dark. Severity was, therefore, necessary to repress these crimes, which were, however, more leniently punished than the crime of heresy.

Among the numerous edicts issued at this time was one that had been often renewed without avail — the interdiction to build any new houses in the faubourgs of Paris. The Parisians were always making efforts to enlarge their borders, which the king found it difficult to restrain. It was feared that the great city of forty or fifty thousand inhabitants would become overgrown and unmanageable if this tendency to spread in all directions should not be vigilantly repressed.

CHAPTER XIV.

The "Key of the Nation's Strong Box." — The New Coinage. — Too Many Counsellors. — Reform in Costume. — Ladies Exempted. — Henri II. a Reformer. — An Ungrateful People. — Defying the King's Decrees. — Catherine's Coronation. — The Court of Henri II. — The Heretical Tailor. — The Burning of the Heretic. — Death of Paul III. — Besieging Boulogne. — Public Entry into Boulogne. — Prince Débonnaire. — A Mass, a Ball, a Banquet.

WAR was now imminent — Henri's commands to the English government to cease their attacks on his daughter's territory not having been obeyed — and money was sorely needed. Madame Diane, as Michelet says, had "secured the key of the nation's strong box," by recommending one of her confidential agents to the post of treasurer. Little, indeed, could therefore be looked for from that source. Yet Henri had ceded to her, with the revived title of Duchesse de Valentinois, all the fines or fees which, on the accession of a new king, were levied on the holders of venal offices for the renewal or confirmation of their rights; also for the immunities and privileges enjoyed by certain corporations. She also obtained from him the disposal of the ecclesiastical benefices. Consequently, the king in his poverty, after selling a portion of the crown lands, "demanded a free gift of money from the loyalty of his good towns."

He increased also the current value of the coin of the realm, and gave orders for impressing it with his effigy instead of the cross of Saint Louis, then in use and more easy to counterfeit. He may have thought that his portrait was worth the difference between the real and nominal value of the coin. The people, however, did not think so; for very soon the complaint was general of a sudden rise in the price of provisions, of clothing, and all articles of domestic use. But from that time the gold and silver coins, with few exceptions, have always borne the bust of the reigning monarch.* The custom of placing the date of the coinage on each piece of money was reintroduced in this reign, with the addition of the numerical rank held by the king among sovereigns of the same name.

Apparently the expedients adopted for raising money were unsatisfactory in their results. The "good towns" had not responded so liberally as was expected to the demand for a "free gift." The army then levying required higher pay; or rather

---

* Louis XII. was the first King of France who ordered his bust to be engraved on the coin with the date. Francis seems to have discontinued the practice; Louis's coins being distinguished by the name of *testons* or *tétons,* because of his head being impressed on them.

refused to accept the coin at the current value put on it, unless the deficiency were made up to them by a nominal increase in the amount to be received. More crown lands were sold, and more judicial offices created, for sale to the highest bidder. So alarmingly numerous had the judges become, not only in Paris but in all the provincial parliaments, that to prevent the appointments purchased being nothing more than sinecures, it was decreed that the number of their holders should be divided, and serve alternately, relieving each other every six months.

But Henri had not forgotten the splendour he had witnessed on his public entry, and the display of wealth made by the principal merchants, their wives and daughters, who, as he conceived, lavished on their own persons and in luxurious living that which should supply the needs of the state — now demanding all that his subjects could be made to give up.

New and stringent sumptuary laws were therefore issued, and an endeavour was made to enforce the regulations which Francis I. during the two or three last years of his life had vainly striven to impose on the nobility, by inflicting heavy fines on their infringement. He who had introduced an excess of luxury ruinous to the state into the habits of the court, and set an example of reckless extravagance and prodigality, when racked by pain and suffering no longer could tolerate the same wasteful profusion. He was tired of the world, if not of life. The gay apparel of his courtiers seemed an offence to him, — a mockery of his own inability any longer to share in pleasures and pursuits which had brought all this expensive and elaborate finery into requisition. He had, however, the power to prohibit it, which may have afforded him some sort of satisfaction.

Accordingly, "the nobility and gentry were forbidden henceforth to wear any material woven, embroidered, or braided with gold or silver." The "sayon" (the overcoat of the military men), "the vest, cloak, trunk-hose, or other garment, must no longer be made of velvet or of silk, with gold or silver cordings." Many other articles of dress, rich and rare, were also prohibited, on pain of a fine of a thousand gold crowns — upwards of 7,000 *francs*. Francis was, however, so considerate as to allow three months, from the issuing of this strange decree, for the wearing out of the stock of dresses on hand, and the replenishing of the wardrobes of the court with garments of the prescribed material and pattern.

Very little effect was produced by this prohibition of luxury in dress. Few if any fines were paid, if levied. Francis had the gallantry not to interfere with the ladies' dress, but the ladies disapproved the change in that of the cavaliers. The king also from time to time rallied, and then set no example of moderation in dress himself. Probably, also, the gentlemen in vests and mantles of sombre-hued cloth and trunk-hose of plain linen; no plumes in their cloth caps, no fine Venetian point-lace, but muslin ruffles and cravats (if any thus habited ever appeared before him), were no less displeasing in his eyes than in those of the ladies. For it is certain that no such costume, even for a brief period, ever became general in the Court of Francis I., and that many of the nobility, who held no office in the royal household that made their presence there imperative, having for awhile absented themselves, reappeared, unreproved, in full splendour.

The dress of the women of the time, generally, is described as more simple than the men's, and their fashions less changeable. But Henri II., with the hope of obtaining fines, resolved to reform the ladies' *toilettes*, and to issue a decree regulating those of the men; more express in terms than his father's, and of greater extent. All classes were to be included in these ordinances, which entered so very minutely into the mysteries of female *toilette* that Madame Diane was suspected of having had some share in preparing or revising them. Her own elegant "weeds" were, of course, in no way altered by them.

The ladies of the upper *bourgeoisie* were treated with great rigour — deprived of the use of silk, and of the mask, always worn in the streets. The chaperon, which was to supply its place, must be

of plain cloth — not, as hitherto, of velvet, silk,
or any material they preferred. The sleeves of
their dresses must be narrower than those of their
betters, and always of black cloth. The wearing
of jewellery, of rich brocades, or gold and silver
in any form, entailed a heavy penalty. Even the
ladies of the court were limited to certain specified
materials for dress. The manufacturers of the
rich productions of the looms of Lyons and Tours
seemed, therefore, threatened with ruin.

"Francis had allowed three months for wearing
out the old finery, Henri only one week; but during that week many of the upper *bourgeoisie* of
Paris and their wives provided themselves with a
fresh stock of the prohibited rich costumes, and
when warned of the consequences of setting at
naught the king's decree, pleaded the hardship of
being compelled thus suddenly to put aside expensive clothing, and to prepare other of a different kind." * Both ordinance and fine were thus
frequently eluded. But when the former was
complied with in the outdoor garb, the rich *bourgeois*' lady appeared in full *éclat* in her own house,
and thus consoled herself for the slight publicly
put upon her.

But the ingratitude of Henri's "good people of
Paris," as well as of other large towns, for his efforts to make them prudent and keep their money
in their purses, was visible, and very audible, too,

* P. Lacroix, "*Vie Privée des Français, XVIème Siècle.*"

in their murmurs, when he began to ask for the transfer of their savings to him in the shape of new taxes. Yet there was another pageant in reserve for them. Catherine de' Medici was to be crowned before the king went to war.

, The French ladies of the court had been greatly annoyed on learning that the ungallant monarch had exempted the Italian ladies in the suite of the queen from the restrictions imposed on them. These Italian coquettes had not had the good manners to put any restraint on their love of fine clothing, but "continued to wear the richest gold and silver stuffs and satin brocades from the looms of India, or from Venice, and other Italian states." The queen and her ladies seemed to find both amusement and pleasure in thus eclipsing the more simply attired ladies of France. But the eclipse was of short duration. The resentment of the injured ladies was aroused. They determined on setting the king at defiance, and casting the restrictions of his sumptuary laws to the winds.

Catherine's coronation was the occasion chosen for the revolt. Some departure from the strict letter of the sumptuary laws would probably have then been permitted, that the great ladies of France might have less the appearance of attendants on the gaily dressed Italians; but a display of *toilettes* composed of the richest and most gorgeous materials that the looms of any country had hitherto produced, woven with gold, seed-pearls, and gems, in patterns of the most artistic design and exquisite workmanship, together with the blaze of jewels and forest of waving plumes, was an unexpected and dazzling sight. And not only did the dresses surpass in splendour and taste of arrangement those of the Italian ladies, but in grace and elegance their wearers are said to have surpassed their rivals also.

On the day of the coronation, on that of the public entry, and during the usual *fêtes* that followed, there was no falling off in the splendour of court dresses, or any change in the expensive ones of the well-to-do Parisian families. A contemporary writer remarks: "It was not easy on that occasion to distinguish the *bourgeois* from the courtier by his dress, the ecclesiastic from the cavalier, or the women of inferior station from the wives of the nobility."

This continued, and Henri's sumptuary law became a dead letter; so great was the objection to being dictated to in such a matter. There was, besides, the national fondness for dress. To this he was compelled to resign himself — making a virtue of necessity — which he did with the better grace, as no fines were likely to be forthcoming. The judges were unwilling to inflict pains and penalties for a crime of which the king set the example, and they were themselves not free. Henri was not averse to velvets, satins, and jewels in his own apparel; while in the luxury of the table the disbursement of the royal household exceeded his father's in lavishness, and the court of the monarch who began his reign by an attempt to repress excessive expenditure gradually became the most extravagant in Europe, without being remarkable for either brilliance or gaiety.*

It could scarcely be otherwise, composed as the court was at that time. Henri to the intolerance of Francis united dulness of intellect; he was therefore considered more devout. His mistress, or maternal friend and adviser, if less devout, was equally zealous for the faith, and an active persecutor. The Guises were the same, and De Montmorency was a perfect fanatic as an extirpator of heretics. When not engaged in sending poor wretches to the stake, and dividing among them the confiscated property (half of it being always Madame Diane's share), they were intriguing

* The richness of the materials employed in dress had attained at this period the very highest excellence and perfection of beauty. Lyons, in its gold and silver brocades, vied with Venice — Lyons, of course, being indebted to Venice and refugees from other Italian states for the great superiority and sumptuousness of her manufactures. The reputation which Tours had once enjoyed for her silk goods declined as that of Lyons increased. The velvets of the latter city were esteemed equal to the productions of Genoa — as they might well be; Genoese workmen being employed in their manufacture, and the silk used in it procured from Italy. These rich materials being in great request, and the price paid for them very high, the expenditure in dress was enormous.

against each other to obtain possession of every post in the state.

In his desire to free his kingdom from the "curse of heresy," Henri had established, as advised, a special chamber in the Parliament against heretics. It was named significantly the "*chambre ardente.*" The provost having soon after its establishment arrested, on a charge of heresy, a poor working tailor employed in some department in the royal household, Madame Diane and the cardinal, Charles de Guise, thought to provide a pleasant morning's amusement for the king by having this poor man brought before him to be questioned. His fear and trembling when ushered into the awe-inspiring presence of majesty would be most diverting to witness, and Madame Diane and the cardinal enjoyed by anticipation the scene expected to ensue.

But to their astonishment the man exhibits no fear, and replies clearly, discreetly, and without any sort of confusion to the questions put to him by both cardinal and king. However, Madame Diane must needs interfere with some very probing question. The man turns towards her. "Madame," he says, "content yourself with the evil you have wrought in France, and attempt not to meddle in so sacred a matter as the truth of God." Diane is speechless with amazement at the man's audacity. The king is furious, and resolved, he says, of see this insolent heretic burnt alive. On the morrow the pious king is to go in procession to Notre Dame, to renew there his oath to extirpate heresy. What more appropriate termination to that solemn ceremony than the offering up of this insolent fellow and two or three others, doomed like him to the stake, in witness to God of his sincere and burning zeal for the faith!

At a window of the Hôtel de La-Roche-Pot — which commands a full view of the place of execution in the Rue St. Antoine, and belongs to a son of the constable — sits Henri II., leaning on his elbow and surrounded by his courtiers. The torch has just been applied to the wood, and four criminals ascend the burning pile. Three of them are writhing in agony as the flames shoot up around them. The fourth stands calm and erect, apparently insensible to torments which, like the rest, he must then be suffering. It is the heretic tailor. He has espied the king, and his eyes are fixed on him in intense, immovable gaze. There is a fascination in that searching look which compels Henri to meet it, until terror seizes him, and, suddenly rising, he rushes from the fearful scene.

For some time his victim's earnest gaze seemed, he said, to pursue him day and night, and he vowed that never again would he witness the burning of a heretic. "He did not, however," remarks M. Martin, "vow that he would burn no more of them;" on the contrary, the persecution continued, and executions in the Rue St. Antoine and on the

Place de Grève followed with greater frequency than before. It was not, however, poor tailors and people of his class that the agents employed by the court to hunt up heretics were especially in quest of, but persons of substance, whose possessions were large enough to form an acceptable sum to the courtiers and ladies, to whom the king graciously conceded the privilege of sharing in the confiscations. It was cupidity, then, rather than increased religious intolerance, that prompted all this zeal for the Church and true faith.

At about this time Paul III. died, worn out with age (he was eighty-three), as well as by his interminable disputes with the emperor, and his violent and unceasing grief for the loss of his worthless son, Pietro Luigi Farnese — a man of the Cæsar Borgia type — who was assassinated at Placentia by two Italians, with the concurrence of the imperial Governor of Milan, whose life he had proposed to take. Paul was succeeded by the infamous Julian III., who was more disposed to enter with complaisance into the emperor's views than his predecessor had been.

But Henri at this moment was concerned with what was passing in Scotland and England more than in Italy and Germany, where Charles was at the height of his fortune. Having succeeded in subduing the princes of the Protestant League, he was meditating how he could further humble them, when the English Government, whose dissensions at home prevented them from sending troops to France, sought the emperor's aid against the French king, who, late in the autumn, had marched in person at the head of his army to besiege Boulogne. Occupied with his own interests, Charles declined to interfere.

Unfavourable weather prevented military operations, beyond building a fort (by the advice of Gaspard de Coligny) to command the entrance to the river and port of Boulogne, and the garrisoning of some small towns in the vicinity. It was proposed to besiege Boulogne in the spring, and the success of the French was deemed certain. The English Government appear to have been of the same opinion, as they proposed negotiation. This resulted in an arrangement to restore Boulogne at once, instead of — as agreed between Henry VIII. and Francis I. — at the expiration of eight years. The compensation for fortifications, etc., was fixed at 400,000 crowns. Francis had consented to pay two millions; also to discharge the arrears of and continue the perpetual pension granted to Henry VII. and his successors. This was now wholly abolished, which was indeed a great triumph for France. Peace was proclaimed between France, England, and Scotland on the 24th of March, amidst national rejoicing; and in the following month of May Henri II. made his public and triumphal entry into the town of Boulogne. Greater demonstrations of the people's satisfaction at the recovery of Boulogne could scarcely have been exceeded had Calais itself been included in this restitution of French territory. Gay-coloured banners and every bit of tapestry or bright-hued damask was brought into use for the external decoration of the houses while daylight lasted, to be succeeded by illuminations when the shades of evening fell on them. Reviews of the troops in garrison, and processions of the townspeople, in which a conspicuous part was borne by the fisher-folk — as it is to this day whenever they publicly appear in the ancient picturesque costume — continued for several days.

Fireworks, too, were not wanting — they seem to have come into great request on festive occasions at about this period; * and so great was the general joy, that even the dreary, handsome countenance of Henri II., much to its advantage, was lighted up by smiles; caught from the overflowing enthusiasm of the people, who bestowed on him the epithet of *"Prince débonnaire."*

In the following year peace with England resulted in a convention of marriage between Edward VI. and Madame Elisabeth, daughter of Henri II., a child three years of age. The announcement of this projected alliance was not

---

*The sum expended on fireworks at court festivals during the inauspicious reign of Henri II. is stated to have been considered enormous — 90,000 crowns — between £10,000 and £11,000.

received by the English with great favour. The tone France had assumed towards England in their political relations since the Treaty of Boulogne did not denote much amity. Then there was the question of religion. But the English Government, who, as was customary in such contracts, looked only to the exigencies of the time being, thought it better, in the interests of Protestantism and of the German princes — who sought Henri's alliance against the emperor— to remain on friendly terms with France. At all events, it gave the ladies and gentlemen of the Court of France a mass, a ball, a banquet, and fireworks; the now usual termination to such courtly arrangements — the burning of a few heretics — was on the present occasion omitted.

CHAPTER XV.

More Honours for the Guises. — Duc François de Guise. — Too Assiduously Attentive. — Claim of the Guises on Naples. — The Council of Trent. — A Penitent Pope. — About to Meet His Conqueror. — Rejecting "The Interim." — Fears for His Soul's Salvation. — A Pact with the Lutherans. — Catherine Appointed Regent. — Catherine's Murmurings. — A Very Bold Champion. — Duke Maurice of Saxony. — Summoned to Innspruck. — A Declaration of War. — The Cap of Liberty. — The Fathers Take Flight. — The Capture of Metz. — A Perilous Position. — The Castle of Ehrenberg Taken. — Flight of the Emperor. — On the Banks of the Rhine. — The Treaty of Public Peace. — In Haste for Revenge. — A Terrible Disaster. — The "Courtoisie de Metz."

Y the death of Duc Claude de Guise, in April, 1550, and in the following month that of his brother, Cardinal Jean de Lorraine, an increase of wealth and honours — helping more firmly to establish their influence in the government of the kingdom — devolved on the ambitious scions of the House of Lorraine. François de Guise then took his father's title of Duc de Guise, his former one of D'Aumale descending to his brother, Claude — Madame Diane's son-in-law. The cardinal-archbishop, Charles de Guise — who was comptroller-general of the finances —

immediately took possession of the numerous rich benefices possessed by his late uncle, adding them to those he already held, and assuming his title of Cardinal de Lorraine.

Other honours and lucrative posts, ecclesiastical and civil, fell to the share of three younger brothers. A fourth, a natural son, who — as then was customary in so many noble and royal houses — was acknowledged by the proud distinction of the "bastard" of the family, was provided for by nomination to that wealthy benefice, the Abbey of Cluny. Duc François de Guise was commander-in-chief of the French armies. Aware of the general dissatisfaction created by the rapid rise of his family to power, and the possession of enormous wealth, he was desirous of war to justify at least his own elevation by his great ability and popularity as a commander and, in contrast with De Montmorency, a humane and magnanimous one.

He was not, however, devoid of other and more ambitious views, in his desire again to embroil France with Italy, where, without actually declared hostilities, the Duc de Brissac held Piedmont only by ceaselessly observing the movements of the Spaniards, and by occasional skirmishes. De Brissac had been sent to Piedmont as governor, and with the rank of marshal of France, not because of his military ability, that had not yet been proved, important as was the post he held, but because of Henri's jealousy. He had, in fact, been too assiduous in his attentions to Madame Diane — still the most attractive siren of the court, though granddaughters were growing up around her. She had smiled graciously on De Brissac, as he wanted neither place nor pension. He was not an old beau, but one of the younger of the chivalric and *preux chevaliers* of whom Francis had deemed himself the first of the age, having also a great reputation for gallantry.

After his removal from the court to Piedmont, De Brissac proved himself a not unworthy rival of François de Guise. He was as strict a disciplinarian, and, more from natural disposition than vainglory, very humane, and full of thoughtful care for the soldiers' welfare. Left without provisions or money to pay his troops — the usual course with the French and other governments of that day — the Duc de Brissac, like the distinguished commander, Guillaume Du Bellay, whom he succeeded, supplied the needs of his troops and discharged their arrears of pay from his own private resources.

Since the Duc de Guise had openly assumed on his marriage the name and dignity of a prince of the House of Anjou, he had made his imaginary claim on Naples, as "his patrimony," less of a secret than formerly. The emperor had recently endeavoured to introduce the Inquisition into Naples as well as into the Netherlands, and the

Neapolitans had resisted the attempt as energetically as the people of the latter country had done. Consequently, great confusion and discontent reigned there. If the Pope could be prevailed on to sanction their schemes — the chances of war also proving favourable — this might be turned to account in furtherance of the views of the Guises.

It was, however, with no intention of promoting the claims of the Guises on Naples, which Francis I. had regarded as part of "*his* heritage," but to assist Ottavio Farnese to retain possession of Parma, that French troops were about to be sent into Italy, and orders forwarded to Maréchal de Brissac to attack the imperial possessions. The orders were promptly obeyed, though no declaration of war took place, and the two fortresses of Chieri and San Damiano fell into the hands of De Brissac, thus opening the way for the march of the French troops.

Ottavio Farnese, the grandson of Paul III., had received Parma from Paul's successor, in acknowledgment of the services of the Farnese party in securing his election to the papal throne. But no sooner had Ottavio taken possession of his duchy than he was deprived of it. The emperor had peremptorily required this of Julian III., though Ottavio was Charles's son-in-law, having married his natural daughter. But Parma must be closed to the French, being the only communication by land between them and the interior of the peninsula, not in possession of the imperialists.

The Pope, wholly subservient to the emperor, was neither able nor willing to defend Ottavio, who, having no troops of his own, made an appeal to France. Henri very readily responded to it. Julian had greatly offended him by convoking at Trent, and under the domination of the emperor, the general council which Paul had dissolved at Bologna. The French prelates, in consequence, would not attend it, or acknowledge its authority. But the displeasure or even the arms of the French king troubled the Pope far less than his edict prohibiting, under heavy penalties, the "sending of *annates* or any tribute-money to Rome or other papal dependency." This indirect attack on the emperor annoyed him greatly. De Montmorency had argued much against it, as he supported the Spanish alliance; but Diane's voice was for the Guises. They, therefore, prevailed. Julian soon discovered that war was a very expensive pastime. After three or four months of it he fully comprehended how grievous an affair he had on his hands. For the Venetians as well as the Dukes of Ferrara, Mantua, and Urbino favoured the French, being unwilling that Parma and La Mirandola should be in the power of the emperor.

Julian was at the end of his resources. He had borrowed money on the security of the papal jewels; his credit was exhausted, and none he applied to would advance him even 10,000 crowns he was sorely in need of. The emperor, on whose account the war was actually waging, as usual, had failed to fulfil his engagements, and had not even paid his own troops. Thus, yielding now to anger or fear, now to repentance or shame; desiring peace, yet shrinking from seeking it, the Pope at last wrote with his own hand a piteous letter to the king, depicting fully and eloquently the various emotions which agitated his mind.

The letter arrived at a favourable moment. Since the French troops had entered Italy, open and direct war had been declared against the emperor. Hostilities in Parma had, therefore, no longer an object, besides costing large sums of money wanted elsewhere. Advantage was, in consequence, taken of Julian's utter inability to continue the war, and a truce for two years signed with him. The emperor confirmed it, being in a frightful position himself, and in pressing need of the troops in Parma and all he could collect from other quarters. The great emperor was about to meet his conqueror, or, more correctly, to fly before him; and Henri II., to his great satisfaction, was shortly to march in person against his hereditary and much-abhorred foe.

France had been for nearly six years free from actual war with the emperor when, in 1551, the alliance and aid of Henri II. was sought by the

German princes. Several of the most influential of their number, headed by the Elector Maurice of Saxony, had secretly formed a league to resist by force of arms the "measures employed by Charles of Austria to reduce Germany to insupportable and perpetual servitude." Charles V. was on the point of becoming as despotic in Germany as he was in Spain. The long interval of peace, though not very profound — war being always threatened and attempts to provoke it frequent — yet was sufficiently so to enable him to devote himself to his favourite scheme of humbling the princes and free states of the empire. He had sown dissension among them, succeeded in breaking up the League of Smalkalde, and detained in prison, threatened with perpetual captivity, the Landgrave of Hesse and the Elector John Frederick of Saxony. They had been sentenced to death, having taken up arms against him. Frequently appealed to to release them, Charles declared that to trouble him further on their account would be to bring on them the execution of the sentence they so richly merited.

His political aims he believed to be now accomplished, and the spirit of German independence nearly, if not wholly, extinguished. But with this he was not content. The time had arrived, he thought, for the full and final extirpation of heresy, and the carrying out of his grand scheme of "establishing uniformity of religion in the empire."

The formula of faith, called "The Interim," which he had drawn up for general observance until the council reassembled, had been for the sake of peace accepted, with slight resistance, except at Magdeburg, which, for its obstinate rejection of it, was placed under the ban of the empire. But the prelates were assembling at Trent, and the full acquiescence of all parties in their decisions — given, of course, in conformity with the views of Charles V. — was to be made imperative.

This accomplished, the imperial dignity would be decreed hereditary in the Austrian family. Ferdinand had resisted this scheme at first, but afterwards yielded to Charles's and his sisters' reiterated requests that, though crowned King of the Romans, he would give place to the gloomy, haughty bigot, his nephew Philip, who excited no feeling but repulsion and a determination to oppose him when shown to Germany as her future emperor.

Henri II. had already renewed the French alliance with Sultan Solyman, and urged him to send his lieutenants to ravage the coast of Sicily — a suggestion he was not at all loth to follow. Yet the proposal of an alliance with the heretic German princes — though the league was not simply a Protestant one — met with strenuous opposition from that excellent Catholic, Anne de Montmorency. The persecuting king, too, anxious as he was to oppose his arms to those of the emperor, feared to do so in alliance with heretics, lest he should compromise his soul's salvation.

But the princes had offered him an irresistible bribe. They proposed — even declared they thought it right — that the seigneur king should take possession of those imperial cities which were not Germanic in language — as Metz, Cambray, Toul, Verdun, and similar ones — and retain them in quality of vicar of the Holy Empire. As a further inducement, they promised — having accomplished their own objects — to aid him with their troops to recover from Charles his heritage of Milan. This was decisive.

On the 5th of October a pact was signed with France by the Lutheran Elector Maurice, in his own name and that of the confederate princes, Henri's ambassador being the Catholic Bishop of Bayonne. Extensive preparations for war were immediately set on foot, and new taxes levied; for the king had promised aid in money also — a considerable sum monthly as long as hostilities continued.

He, however, deemed it expedient, before joining his army, to give some striking proof of his continued orthodoxy; first, by way of counterbalancing his heretical alliance with the Lutherans, and his infidel one with the Mussulmans; next, to destroy the false hopes founded on them by some French reformers. The heretics, during his absence, were, therefore, to be hunted down with the utmost rigour. The Sorbonne was charged "to examine minutely all books from Geneva, and no unlettered person was permitted to discuss matters of faith. All cities and municipalities were strictly enjoined to elect none but good Catholics to the office of mayor or sheriff, exacting from them a certificate of Catholicism before entering on the duties of their office. Neglect of this would subject the electors themselves to the pains and penalties inflicted on heretics."

A grand inquisitor was appointed to take care of the faith in Lyons, and the daily burnings on the Place de Grève went on simultaneously with the preparations in the arsenals, and no less vigourously. Thus was the king enabled to enter on this war with a safe conscience, the full approval of Madame Diane, and that of her allies, the Guises. De Montmorency, unwilling always to oppose the emperor, was compelled, lest he should seem less patriotic than his rivals, to add his voice, also, in favour of a project that promised the realisation of the views of Charles VII. and Francis I. that the natural boundary of France was the Rhine.

To her surprise, no doubt, Catherine de' Medici was appointed regent during Henri's absence. He could not actually name the Duchesse de Valentinois the representative of royal power; but he could place all power in her hands, and she would certainly not yield any part of it to the Queen-regent Catherine. He, indeed, fenced her round with so many restrictions that she was regent in little more than name; and lest she should go astray on being for the first time out of leading-strings, he named the several advisers whose counsels she was strictly to follow.

Hitherto so docile, and apparently well contented with the insignificant part she was allowed to play in her own court, Catherine now complained that not only no trust was reposed in her, but that she was made to appear an object of distrust, incapable of the duties nominally confided to her. These murmurings were rarely if ever heard, except in the presence of people of her own nation — either her attendants, with whom she was exceedingly familiar, or with the Strozzi or other of the many Italians who then frequented the French court, several of whom held offices in the royal household or posts in the government. Catherine strove to keep on good terms with the higher powers, and whatever were her emotions or her real feelings towards the usurping Diane, well knew how to throw an impenetrable veil over them.

It, however, happened on one occasion that the Seigneur de Tavannes was present when Catherine was betrayed into an expression of resentment at some slight she had received. The unrestrained indignation with which, in his memoirs, Tavannes speaks of the baneful influence of women in the affairs of the kingdom, though referring in the early portion especially to Louise of Savoy and the mistress of Francis I., was afterwards extended to Diane. She certainly equalled Louise in her rapaciousness, and, much to its prejudice, shared the government of the state with Henri no less than her predecessor with Francis. Tavannes sympathised with Catherine, and, quite seriously, it is said, "offered to avenge any wrong she had to complain of by cutting off Madame Diane's nose." He would willingly, he told her, "risk the consequences of that act to put an end to the vice and the misfortune of the King of France."

Tavannes's gallant offer, it appears, greatly amused Catherine. Of course she could not accept it, though she might not have been unwilling that the beauty which time was powerless to wither should be thus irremediably damaged; unless she would have preferred that instead of cutting off the favourite's nose he should have merely put it out of joint. This feat he had not the influence necessary to accomplish, and nothing was left to Catherine but to repay her bold champion's offer by grateful smiles and thanks.

To return to Germany and the emperor — whose complicated affairs are so entangled with those of France that they cannot be wholly separated, each in some measure forming the complement of the other: The command-in-chief of the German army was given to Maurice of Saxony — an able general, full of resource, daring and dauntless in the field, crafty and cautious in the cabinet as Charles himself. Throughout the winter he secretly assembled troops, preparing to take the field early in the spring, yet adroitly concealing his projects, and lulling into security "the most artful monarch in Europe."

The emperor had left Augsburg for Innspruck that he might at the same time watch over the council and the affairs of Germany and Italy. He was suffering from asthma, gout, and other maladies, chiefly brought on by his excesses at table, and rendered incurable by his inability to put any restraint on his immoderate appetite.*

In his retreat some rumours had reached him that the movements of Maurice of Saxony were suspicious, and that he was raising troops in Transylvania. But he gave little heed to this, or to warnings pressed on him by some of his partisans. For Maurice, to serve his own ambitious views, had in fact, though professing the reformed faith, aided Charles to acquire that power and ascendency, that almost unlimited despotism in Germany he now proposed to overthrow. For his services he had obtained the larger part of the electoral

---

* He is said to have drunk not less than five or six large bottles (litres) of wine daily at dinner, and to have eaten in proportion. See details in Mignet's "Charles Quint; son Abdication."

dominions of his unfortunate relative, John Frederick of Saxony; whose release, as also that of the landgrave, now formed part of his programme for delivering Germany from her fetters ere the imperial despot could — as Maurice saw he was prepared to do — rivet them on her. To renew the Protestant League, to place himself at its head and defy the despot, was more congenial to Maurice's restless, aspiring mind than to play the part of his lieutenant.

The winter passed away without any serious suspicions on Charles's part. To throw him off his guard Maurice had undertaken to subdue the Magdeburghers. The leniency of his conduct towards "those rebels," with whom he was secretly in league, did at last excite a doubt, in Charles's mind. Maurice was summoned to Innspruck, ostensibly to confer with him respecting the liberation of his father-in-law, the Landgrave of Hesse. But Maurice was far too wary to put himself in his power, and readily found some plausible excuse to delay his journey from time to time. But when, early in March, at the head of 25,000 men, thoroughly equipped, he announced that he was about to set out on his journey, the information was accompanied by a declaration of war. "It was a war," he said, "for the defence of the true religion, its ministers and preachers; for the deliverance of prisoners detained against all faith and justice; to free Germany from her wretched condition, and to oppose the emperor's completion of that absolute monarchy towards which he had so long been aiming."

To this manifesto was appended another from the King of France. Therein Henri announced himself the "Defender of the liberties of Germany, and protector of her captive princes," further stating "that, broken-hearted (*le cœur navre*) at the condition of Germany, he could not refuse to aid her, but had determined to do so to the utmost of his power and ability, even to personally engaging in this war, undertaken for liberty and not for his personal benefit." This document — written in French — was headed by the representation of a cap between two poniards, and around it the inscription, "The emblem of liberty." It is said to have been copied from some ancient coins, and to have been appropriated as the symbol of freedom by Cæsar's assassins. Thus singularly was brought to light by a king of the French Renaissance that terrible cap of liberty, before which the ancient Crown of France was one day destined to fall.

The declaration of the German princes and that of their ally, the King of France, fell like a thunderbolt on the emperor — so great was his astonishment and consternation at events so unexpected. With rapid marches Maurice advanced on Upper Germany, while other divisions of the army, headed by the confederate princes, hastened on towards Tyrol, by way of Franconia and Suabia, everywhere being received with open arms as "Germany's liberators." Maurice reached Augsburg on the 1st of April, and took possession of that important city — the garrison offering no resistance, and the inhabitants receiving him joyfully. There, as in other towns on his march which had willingly opened their gates to him, the Interim was abolished; the churches restored to the Protestants; the magistrates appointed by the emperor displaced, and those he had ejected reinstated. Money, too, was freely offered him, and the deficiency in his artillery supplied. At Trent the news that the Protestant princes, joined by several of the Catholics and Free States, "had taken up arms for liberty" caused a terrible panic. The Fathers of the Council, Italian, Spanish, and German, at once made a precipitate retreat, and this famous council without authority from Pope or emperor dissolved itself, to reassemble only after even a longer interval than before. When Maurice began his march Henri II. had joined his army at Châlons, and was on his way to Lorraine. Toul, on his approach, presented the keys of the city to the constable, commanding the vanguard — the king afterwards making his entry, and receiving the oath of fidelity from the inhabitants, having previously sworn to maintain their rights and privileges inviolate. After this easy conquest the French army continued its march towards Metz.

This old free republican city did not so readily as Toul yield to the French. The municipal authorities very politely offered provisions to the army, but declined to deliver the keys of their city to the constable. They were, however, willing to admit the king and the princes who accompanied him within their walls. "Troops were not permitted to enter Metz, whatever their nation." This was one of their privileges.

De Montmorency cared little for privileges, and violence would probably have been used, but that the Bishop of Metz, who was a Frenchman, prevailed on the principal burgesses to allow the constable to enter with an escort of two ensigns, each with his company of infantry. De Montmorency availed himself of this permission to give his ensigns 1,500 of his best troops. The city gates were thrown open, and the burgesses then perceived their error, but too late to remedy it. They were firmly repulsed when attempting to exclude the unwelcome visitors; there was, however, no bloodshed. The people were soon reconciled to the change; and the chief sheriff and town council on the king's entry having assembled under the cathedral porch, Henri there, in the presence of an anxious multitude who crowded around to hear him, made oath strictly to maintain their franchises and immunities. Thus easily was captured the former capital of the ancient Austrasian kings, which remained under the dominion of

France until separated from her by the misfortunes of the second empire.

The city of Verdun followed the example of Toul; so that Henri's defence of the liberties of Germany was thus far nothing more than a military promenade, with grand public entries, banquets, and general festivity. The inhabitants of Metz—like the rest of his conquests, French in language and manners—petitioned the king not to restore their city to the empire, of which it had been a vassal republic from the beginning of the feudal era; they feared the emperor's revenge. Henri, however, had no thought of relinquishing Metz; he was too well pleased with his new possession, and "proposed to make it one of the ramparts of France."

But, while Henri for the defence of German independence was making conquests and annexing them to his dominions, Charles V. had fled before Maurice's vigourous pursuit, and had only escaped capture by a mere mischance that briefly retarded his pursuer's progress. When Augsburg was taken, Charles felt that he was not safe at Innspruck. He was neither in a position to crush the rebellious princes, nor to resist the invasion of the King of France. Want of means had induced him to disband a large part of his army; Mexico and Peru for some time had failed to make any remittances to his treasury; the bankers of Venice and Genoa were not willing to lend him money, and it was only by placing Piombino in the hands of Cosmo de' Medici that he obtained from him the small sum of 200,000 crowns.

His first impulse was to endeavour to pass over to the route of the Netherlands by the valleys of the Inn and the Rhine; but as he could only move, owing to his gout, from place to place in a litter, he was compelled, from physical suffering, after proceeding a very short distance on his journey, to return to Innspruck. There he remained with a small body of soldiers sufficient to guard him personally — having sent all he could possibly spare to hold the mountain-pass leading to the almost inaccessible Castle of Ehrenberg. But, guided by a shepherd, the heights of Ehrenberg were reached by the troops under George of Brandenburg, after infinite fatigue and danger. The walls were scaled, and the garrison, terrified by the appearance of this unlooked-for enemy, threw down their arms and surrendered.

A few hours only separated Innspruck from Ehrenberg, and Maurice proposed to push on so rapidly as to anticipate the arrival there of any accounts of the loss of the castle, hoping to surprise the emperor and his attendants in an open, defenceless town, and there to dictate conditions of peace. The dissatisfaction of a portion of the troops at not immediately receiving the usual gratuity for taking a place by assault, occasioned a short delay in the advance of Maurice's army. He arrived at Innspruck in the middle of the night, and learned that the emperor had fled only two hours before to Carinthia, followed by his ministers and attendants, on foot, on horses, in litters, as they could, but in the greatest hurry and confusion.

The night was stormy; rain was falling in torrents when the modern Charlemagne, unable to move, was borne in a litter by the light of torches across steep mountain-paths with a swiftness most surprising; terror adding wings to the footsteps of his bearers, lest they and their gouty burden should yet fall into the hands of the heretic army, said to be in pursuit. But pursuit was soon given up, for the troops were worn and weary with forced marches and climbing the heights of Ehrenberg; they needed rest, and there was the imperial palace of Innspruck to pillage, Maurice having given it up to them.

Negotiations for peace were opened on the 20th of May at Passau on the Danube. The King of France was informed of this; it being found necessary to put some check on his proceedings; to remind him that he was the "Defender of the liberties of Germany," not Germany's oppressor. He and his army had advanced into Alsace, and De Montmorency had assured him that it would be "as easy to enter Strasburg and other cities of the Rhine as to penetrate butter." However, when they knocked at the gates of Strasburg and courteously requested that the Venetian, Florentine, and other ambassadors might be permitted to enter and admire the beautiful city, they found the Strasburgers insensible to these amenities — butter by no means easily melted; for not only they refused to gratify the *soi-disant* ambassadors with a sight of their fine city, but mounted and pointed their cannon, as a hint to their visitors that they would do well to withdraw.

Henri, perceiving that he would be unable in the present campaign to extend his dominions to the banks of the Rhine, contented himself, "before turning his back on it, with the fact that the horses of his army had drunk of the waters of that stream." The Austrasian expedition was less brilliant in its results than he had expected; nevertheless, whether he was to be included in the peace then negotiating or not, he resolved to retain the three bishoprics — Toul, Metz, and Verdun.

Meanwhile the conference of Passau, between Maurice and the princes of the league on the one part; Ferdinand, King of the Romans, and the emperor's plenipotentiaries on the other, proceeded less rapidly than Maurice desired. By prolonging the negotiation Charles hoped to gain time to assemble an army, when the Catholic princes might again rally round him. But even those who had not joined the league were exceedingly lukewarm towards their emperor; his despotism, they considered, being as dangerous to them as to the Protestants. Even his brother Ferdinand — who was on such excellent terms with Maurice that it would almost seem that he had connived at an enterprise he could not openly join in — is said to have seen with satisfaction the check put on Charles by the dauntless leader of the league.

But Maurice's propositions being at first rejected, and no counter ones proposed, he at once set off for his army to renew hostilities, as though the negotiations were closed. Charles doubtless renounced the realisation of the dream of his life with a pang of despair. That it should vanish at the very moment when he looked for its fulfilment, was anguish to him. But, pressed by Ferdinand, convinced, too, that resistance is useless, Charles yields an unwilling assent to the demands of the princes, and the " Treaty of Public Peace " is signed on August 2d. Henceforth "the two religions are to be on a footing of equality in the empire;" "Germany divided between Luther and the Pope," who are to live side by side in peace, neither interrupting the other. The ban of the empire to be withdrawn from all persons and places; the captive princes detained for five years, in prison if not in fetters, released, while many other matters relating to imperial encroachments are to be satisfactorily settled within six months.

"The defender of German liberty" was not included in this treaty. As he proposed to keep the cities he was to occupy but as vicar of the empire, he would have to fight a battle for them with Charles himself. Though compelled to renounce absolute sway over Germany, he yet thought it incumbent on him to reestablish the territory of the empire in its full integrity. His valiant sister, the Dowager-queen of Hungary, who governed the Netherlands so ably for him, was already diligently collecting an army for the destitute monarch of many kingdoms, and troops were on their way from Spain.

In spite of his infirmities, Charles was in such haste to chastise the French and revenge himself on Henri — having succeeded in raising an army 60,000 strong, besides 7,000 pioneers — that he rejected the prudent counsels of his generals, who begged him to wait until the spring, when Metz might be attacked with much greater advantage. But his excessive obstinacy, which had led to so many of his disasters, again prevailed. The Duc de Guise, now governor of Metz, had put the citadel into a state of defence. The garrison was numerous, and, as was usual wherever he commanded, thither followed all the young, ardent spirits among the great families of France.

The siege of Metz was a terrible disaster for the emperor. The extreme severity of the winter, a scanty supply of provisions, of clothing, and other necessaries, was soon followed by sickness, typhus, and many deaths. Desertions were numerous;

for the sufferings of the troops had quenched all ardour, and subverted all discipline. Desperate efforts to take Metz were continued for nearly three months without avail, when Charles, thoroughly disheartened, and unable to rise from his couch except for removal to his litter, raised the siege — abandoning the greater part of his artillery, which was half buried in the mud. "Fortune," he exclaimed, "I perceive is indeed a woman; she prefers a young king to an old emperor." The spectacle that met the eyes of the victorious defenders of Metz, on issuing forth in pursuit of the enemy, is said to have been one of so harrowing a nature that even rough soldiers, accustomed to the horrors of war, looked on the misery around them with emotions of deepest pity. There lay the dying and the dead heaped up together; the wounded and those who had been stricken down by fever stretched side by side on the gory, muddy earth. Others had sunk into it, and, unable to extricate themselves, were frozen to their knees, and plaintively asked for death to put an end to their wretchedness. Scattered along the route of the retreat lay dead horses, tents, arms, portions of the baggage, and many sick soldiers who had fallen by the way in their efforts to keep up with the hasty march of the remnant of the army — a sad and terrible scene indeed, in a career called one of glory.

François de Guise greatly distinguished himself

as a general, and added to his military renown by his defence of Metz; but far greater glory attaches to his name for his humane and generous conduct to the suffering, abandoned troops of Charles's army. All whose lives could be saved, or sufferings relieved, received every care and attention that he and the surgeons of his army could bestow on them. Following his example, instead of the savage brutality with which the victors were then accustomed to treat their fallen foes, kindness and good offices were rendered by all to the poor victims of the emperor's revenge for the loss of Metz.

So utterly contrary was such treatment to the practice of the age, that the generosity and humanity of François de Guise towards an enemy's troops passed into a proverb as the "*Courtoisie de Metz.*"

CHAPTER XVI.

Catherine's Indisposition. — The Rebuilding of Anet. — Diane's Boudoir Clock. — Bernard Palissy. — Chenonceaux and Chaumont. — Extremely Vexatious. — Progress of the Louvre, etc. — The Crescent Moon and Arrow. — Another Diane. — Premature Rejoicings. — Destruction of Terouenne. — Death of Maurice of Saxony. — Death of Edward VI. — An Offer of Marriage. — Worthily Celebrated. — Mary's Persecuting Zeal. — In the Event of Mary's Death. — An Apology for Mary's Cruelty. — No Decisive Results. — The Siege of Siena. — Starved into Surrender. — A New Model Republic.

AFTER the fatigues and horrors of war, banquets and balls, fireworks, tournaments, and the usual round of festivities followed. Catherine was relieved of her duties as regent; the chief event of her regency having been her order to arrest two preaching monks who, in the pulpit, had cast grave censure on the king's alliance with the German heretics. She had been seriously indisposed during Henri's absence, but the watchful care and maternal attentions of Madame Diane, who was summoned to Paris with all speed, had greatly contributed towards her restoration to health, if not to the bloom and beauty that distinguished her anxious friend.

When the king left Paris to join his army,

Diane departed immediately for Anet, to ascertain the progress making in the magnificent château he was partly rebuilding there, in default of his present of Chenonceaux to accompany the title of Duchesse de Valentinois — a title to which she made some claim, as having once been borne by a branch of her family. Anet was inhabited, if not actually built (as some accounts state), by Diane before Henri became dauphin; the king and the court on their travels having been sometimes received there. But on Henri's accession to the throne, and Diane's elevation to the first place at court, it was thought necessary that Anet should be enlarged, and adorned in the more elaborate Italian style that reached its greatest development in Henri's reign.* Although the works begun by Francis I. at Fontainebleau were still carried on, Cellini's bas-reliefs, executed for that royal residence, were sent by Henri to Anet, and some of the finest specimens of the skill of the sculptors of the period adorned Diane's sumptuous dwelling.

A wonderful piece of mechanism, a triumph of the clock-maker's art — which had attained to great excellence during the early part of the sixteenth century — had been made by the king's order. It

---

* Philibert Delorme is said to have been the original architect of Anet. But this must be an error, as he was of the same age as the dauphin Francis; consequently, but eighteen when Francis died. Delorme also passed his early years in Italy.

was an elegant clock, intended for the adornment of Diane's tastefully arranged and spacious boudoir. Completed during his absence, it awaited his and his court's admiration at Des Tournelles before its transfer to Anet. The clock was placed in the tower of a château — probably a miniature model of Anet. Around it appeared a thick forest, whence every hour there issued a stag, followed by a pack of hounds, which stopped in front of the château. The stag then stamped the ground with his foot, thus setting in motion the mechanism beneath it, and causing the clock to strike the hour. This feat accomplished, the stag made off again, with the pack in full pursuit, returning to the forest-glades on the opposite side.

Besides this whimsical yet magnificent clock, which was placed on a high stand of sculptured white marble, all that was artistic, beautiful, costly, and luxurious contributed to make Diane's home, situated in a lovely spot, the abode of art and beauty. Bernard Palissy, then in great repute, was much patronised by the new duchess. A mantelpiece of enamelled earth, with figures of life size on either side, was constructed by him for her château. It was said to be one of his finest works. Carpets of any considerable size were at about that time first woven in one piece, and the establishment of the Gobelin Brothers became the royal manufactory of carpets and tapestry for the court. That the choicest specimens of these and many other arts and industries of the day were to be found at Anet is not surprising, as Diane's influence over the king seemed to increase as time went on.

But Diane was herself a liberal patroness of the arts — more liberal far than the king, probably, her means being less restricted; for, besides the wealth she inherited, the many gifts of lands from the king and the facilities allowed her for the disposal of benefices, not a heretic of the ever-increasing number was burnt at the stake but a portion of his possessions, whether small or large, was assigned to her. She was a firm supporter of the pure faith of the Church, deriving from it a full purse and an easy conscience — the enjoyment of this life's pleasures and a passport to those of the next.

It appears that Catherine in 1550 had bought for herself the Château de Chaumont, in order to enjoy more freely there the exercise of hunting, by which she hoped to keep down her increasing *embonpoint*. At the same time Henri created Madame Diane a duchess, and gave her the Château de Chenonceaux. Chenonceaux was celebrated for the beauty of its situation and charming surrounding country, as well as for the grandeur of its château, begun by the Baron de Saint-Ciergues, who died before its completion. Catherine herself had taken a great fancy to Chenonceaux, and, in spite of her power of suppressing all indication of her real feelings, she could not on this occasion wholly disguise her jealousy and indignation that the château was not given by the king to her. Catherine resolved on revenge.

Too much under supervision at this period to venture on employing the poisoned bowl and the dagger, she adopted a more moderate course, that of compelling ·Diane to pay for Chenonceaux, as she had paid for Chaumont. The Baron Boyer de Saint-Ciergues had been induced to cede his château and its dependencies to De Montmorency, to ensure his silence concerning some fraudulent transactions while holding office in the government. As it was De Montmorency's own practice to fill his coffers at the expense of the state, he thought to avert the disgrace about to fall on him, when, some time after, his dishonesty was discovered, by presenting Chenonceaux to Francis I. The king accepted it, but it did not prevent the constable's fall.

Antoine Boyer, the baron's son, instigated by Catherine, then made urgent and pressing claims for the restitution of his patrimony; and finally, though Diane was not deprived of Chenonceaux, it was adjudged that, if with Boyer's consent she retained the domain, she must pay for it. This she did, though to her extreme mortification, as she had already completed the façade in the new style, and was building a bridge across the Cher, in communication with the château. But Henri — as if to compensate the fair Diane for the vexation which Catherine's spiteful jealousy might have caused her,* and the consequent delay it occasioned in the alterations and additions she proposed to make at Chenonceaux — immediately despatched several of the artists and their workmen employed at Blois, Chambord, and Fontainebleau, to hasten the completion of Anet — Diane's favourite residence.

Henri II. inherited his father's passion for building. The works begun by Francis I., often suspended, and resumed after long intervals, were carried on with far greater activity during Henri's reign. At the Louvre, especially, great progress was made. The west wing was finished, and the south wing nearly so, as far as the wicket gate opposite the Pont des Arts. The king's pavilion was also completed. Henri, who was the last king that resided at the Palais des Tournelles, made many alterations in it, but without removing the cause of its extreme unhealthiness, though Catherine attributed her frequent indisposition to it.

* Diane, however, rarely, very rarely, was betrayed into being vexed. To keep the mind calm, proof against the vexation sometimes caused by petty trials, was one of her remedies for the preservation of beauty. This serenity of soul, together with her early morning cold bath, her two hours' ride after it, and her return to her couch for an hour or two with a pious book in her hand to send her off into a pleasant doze, was her chief recipe for defying Time's heavy hand to impress wrinkles on her smooth, fair brow. Yet jealous Catherine and her Italian confidantes would sometimes speak profanely of Henri's fair friend as "the wrinkled old woman" ("*la vieille ridée*").

The Château of Saint Germain-en-Laye was also enlarged. The Châteaux of Blois and Amboise were not neglected; and at the vast and princely abode of Chambord many artists of repute and numerous skilful assistants constantly resided during Henri's reign. It was at Chambord he ratified the treaty with the German princes. The interlaced initials (H) which so often recur on the façade of the Louvre, and which may be either H C or H D, were no doubt adopted by Henri because of the ambiguity. The attributes of the chase, the crescent moon, the leverets, the stags, the head of Diane the huntress many times repeated, not only in the friezes of the Louvre, but in those of all the royal residences of the period, refer, doubtless, to Diane the enchantress — the enchantress who at forty enslaved the royal youth, then barely twenty, and held him a willing slave until his death, twenty years after.

When Henri became dauphin, he assumed as his device a crescent moon, with the motto, *Donec totum impleat orbem* — "Until she attains her plenitude or fills the earth." The meaning of this, Diane's device and motto are supposed to have explained. The former, an arrow; the latter *Consequitur quodcunque petit* — "It reaches all it aims at." So that when Henri and Diane ascended the throne the moon had reached the full; the arrow had reached its aim.

But another Diane — Diane of France — now

appears on the scene; youthful and beautiful, and just sixteen. She is betrothed to Horatio Farnese, the grandson of Pope Paul III., and her marriage is about to take place at Saint Germain-en-Laye. Diane of France, according to Brantôme, was the natural daughter of Henri II., and her reputed mother the Signora Philippa Duca, a lady of Piedmont. Henri had legitimatised this daughter, and the same authority asserts that he proposed to do so in the name of her real mother, "who," he says, "was the Duchess de Valentinois, Madame Diane de Poitiers." But Diane was indignant at such a proposal, and replied, haughtily, "I was born to bear you legitimate children," (meaning, probably, that her royal descent made her no unequal match for a king). "I have been your mistress because I loved you, and I will not suffer you by a decree to declare me your concubine."

The marriage of Diane of France is said to have been solemnised with great pomp, and to have been followed by a round of gaieties such as the Court of Henri II. had scarcely yet witnessed. Without being in any way less vicious, a sort of dull depravity, an affected air of seriousness — in compliment to the devoutly-minded king — had succeeded the more lively libertinism of the Court of Francis I. The immoderate gaieties of the court, then about to be unpleasantly interrupted, are, however, considered by some writers to have referred to no marriage whatever, but to have been rejoicings for the victory obtained over Charles V., and the great and crushing defeat he had sustained, as well in Italy as in Germany, which it was believed had finally laid his power low, and trampled his glory in the dust. The very existence of Diane of France, except in the fertile imagination of Brantôme, is doubted. Horatio Farnese, whom she is said to have married, and who had entered the service of France, having been expelled from Italy by Charles, was killed in battle a few weeks after his supposed marriage.

But whether the story of Diane of France be a myth or not, it is certain that the rejoicings, if intended to celebrate the final defeat of Charles V., were rather premature. The state of his health was reported as being so bad "that body and soul seemed anxious to part company." On raising the siege of Metz he had fled to Brussels with the remnant of his army. There, whenever he enjoyed an interval of ease from the torture he suffered from the gout, a longing desire for revenge seized him. An army was got together, his sister Margaret aiding him, and great indeed was the surprise of both Francis and De Montmorency on learning that the emperor, with an army of Spaniards and Flemings, was beseiging Terouenne. Situated on the borders of an enemy's territory, Terouenne was accustomed constantly to maintain an attitude of aggressive warfare. It was believed to be impregnable; yet it was taken, and its inhabitants, who had long been the terror of the surrounding country, were now put to the sword without mercy — some few Frenchmen being saved by Spaniards who had shared in the "*Courtoisie de Metz.*"

The total destruction of Terouenne was ordered, and so thoroughly was the order carried out that at the end of four or five days scarce a vestige of this ancient city remained. "It never rose from its ruins, and is believed to be the only instance of a French city having entirely perished" (H. Martin).

Marching onward, the imperial army — Charles borne in a litter at its head — attacked Hesdin, and, before the French troops, commanded by Henri in person, had time to march to its defence, the great emperor had sated his vengeance on this city and its inhabitants. All who were not taken prisoners were massacred, their dwellings burnt, the fortress blown up, and the country around devastated. The arrival of the French army checked his imperial majesty's further triumphal progress, though without, it is remarked, achieving much glory. Diane's son-in-law, Maréchal de la Marck, was taken prisoner, and Horatio Farnese killed. De Montmorency is stated to have been really ill with chagrin that the emperor should have been provoked to such reprisals — the result of not following his advice condemning the heretical alliance.

But another death, which must have been

pleasant news to the emperor's ears, though it caused consternation among the princes of the empire, occurred at this time. It was that of the "conqueror of Charles V., the empire, and the papacy"—the Elector Maurice of Saxony. He received a pistol bullet in the breast while heading a charge of cavalry in a battle against Albert of Brandenburg. Albert, refusing to be included in the Treaty of Passau, levied a body of troops, and ravaged Germany like a freebooter—secretly encouraged by the emperor. The princes determined to take up arms against him. On the 9th of July he was thoroughly beaten, and his army fled in confusion. But in the very moment of victory a random shot laid Maurice low. He was lamented by both Protestants and Catholics as "an able and faithful guardian of the laws and constitution of his country." He was but in his thirty-second year.

Almost at the same time as the welcome news of the death of Maurice of Saxony reached the emperor, that of Edward VI. of England, on the 6th of July, was announced to him. It at once inspired him with the ambitious hope of uniting that country to his other possessions, by the marriage of Philip with the Princess Mary—England thus compensating him for the loss of Germany. Edward had left his crown to Lady Jane Grey, granddaughter of Mary, the Duchess-queen of France. But the English were not disposed to accept her as their sovereign, Mary, the elder sister of Edward, being preferred — even by the Protestants — notwithstanding her religion. The suppression of some obnoxious taxes, with some promised concessions in religious matters, sufficed to obtain their support, and Mary, having assumed the title of queen, entered London without opposition.

With a promptitude that pleased Mary, a numerous embassy, splendidly equipped, arrived in London from the Spanish king to congratulate her on her accession. The ambassador was also the bearer of a missive offering her marriage from Charles on behalf of his son. The emperor, it is said, had at first intended making proposals on his own account to the lady he had been betrothed to thirty-three years before — undeterred by his age and now great infirmities — his idea being that Philip would probably not be willing to marry a princess eleven years older than himself, and whose crown was her sole attraction. Charles was then in the Netherlands; Philip was in Spain. But on being consulted respecting this marriage the young widower offered no objection to it, and Charles was released from the painful obligation he would have imposed on himself in order to make England a dependency of Spain. France, of course, sent an embassy also; but had the mortification of having no eligible French prince to offer as a rival to Philip.

Mary eagerly accepted the husband offered her, and henceforth was greatly influenced by the emperor's counsels, both in political and religious matters. In the former she is said to have sometimes hesitated to adopt the rigourous measures he urged on her (probably because she thought them too lenient). In the latter she was completely ruled by him. The persecution he could no longer continue in Germany was thus transferred to England; where, in "Mary of sanguinary renown," he found an accomplice after his own heart. The signing of her marriage convention with the gloomy bigot, Philip of Spain — a union most repugnant to the nation — took place on January the 12th, 1554, and was worthily celebrated by the death of Lady Jane Grey and her husband on the scaffold, that same day.

Many restrictions were imposed on Philip. He was permitted to assume the title of king, but could exercise no power as such. Mary, too, was prohibited from disposing of the crown by will, should she die childless; and the united efforts of Charles, and Philip, and Mary to get this prohibition cancelled were unsuccessful. The marriage did not take place till July. On the 19th, Philip, attended by several grandees of Spain and a numerous and brilliant retinue, landed at Southampton; on the 25th the nuptial ceremony was performed. Charles on this occasion, to the mortification of Henri, and even more so of François de Guise, made the kingdom of Naples and the duchy of Milan, in full sovereignty, a marriage present to his son.

Whilst Charles was arranging Philip's marriage and conquering a kingdom, as he hoped, without striking a blow, Henri, who saw in this marriage a renewal of that league which had been so disastrous to Francis I., was making great efforts to raise and equip a powerful army. Yet Mary's marriage contract guaranteed the maintenance of peace between France and England, and the offer of her mediation was made to the emperor and Henri II. This was a mere formality, an inveterate personal dislike, deepened by recent events, existing between Charles and Henri. The latter was also desirous, before listening to proposals of peace, of taking his revenge for the ravages committed by the emperor on his territory in the preceding year. Mary's proffered good offices were, therefore, not in requisition.

But Mary's own affairs demanded all her attention. She had on her hands the undoing of the work of her brother's reign, and the bringing of England again under the yoke of Rome; persecuting, burning, hanging, beheading, tearing the dead from their graves, with other atrocities which even the persecuting bigots, Charles and Philip, felt compelled to check, and which gained her the revolting epithet still attached to her name. Elizabeth would have been sent to the scaffold,

Queen Mary of England.
Photo-etching from an old print.

had not both the emperor and his son forbade it —not from humane motives, certainly, but because of the advantage which politically would accrue to France by Mary Stuart, the betrothed bride of the dauphin, becoming heiress-presumptive to the English throne.

The "great English marriage," as it was called, excited much jealousy at the Court of France, as well as dread of the possible results of such an alliance. But Mary's health and fretful, gloomy temper gave so little promise of length of life that in 1555, less than a year after his marriage, Philip confided to Cardinal de Fresneda, his confessor, that, in the event of Mary's death—which heaven avert!—he had thoughts of marrying Elizabeth;" * which explains his opposition to her being declared illegitimate. It is remarked by the editor † of a "Collection of Ancient Letters," that, having examined the point and studied her letters with great care, it appears to him that she who is so generally execrated as "the bloody Queen Mary" was naturally rather an amiable person until she married at the age of thirty-nine.

The gradual change which then, he admits, "took place in her conduct and feelings may be traced," he says, "to her devoted attachment to Philip and his cold neglect of her, which could not fail to tell on a kind and ardent heart. For blighted hope,"

* State papers addressed to the Venetian Seigniory.
† Mr. Patrick Fraser Tytler.

says Mr. Tytler, "and unrequited love will change the best dispositions, and she whose youthful years had undoubtedly given good promise, became disgusted with the world, suspicious, gloomy, and resentful. The subsequent cruelties of her reign were deplorable," he allows, yet he thinks it "but fair to ascribe much of them to her ministers rather than to herself." This seems but a poor apology for the horrors of the reign of Mary of execrable memory.

The English treasury appears to have been rather empty when Edward died, as Charles V., whose coffers were never overflowing, is said to have been much crippled in his resources from the large sums he sent to England,* and thus was unable adequately to resist the overwhelming force which Henri had found the means of equipping, and with which he took the field in spring. Again towns were invested, the country ravaged, the inhabitants pillaged, taken prisoners, or put to the sword.

But Charles at last got together an army, though Germany would render him no assistance. A battle took place near Renti, a frontier town of Artois, which the French had besieged. The imperialists were driven in disorder on their camp, where Charles, confined to his litter, gave his orders and received news of the progress of the battle. This

* For Philip's use, probably—as he was then in England assisting Mary to carry out her great designs.

achievement was due to the impetuous charge of the infantry commanded by Gaspard de Coligny, and that of the cavalry by the Seigneur de Tavannes. But François de Guise, who commanded that wing of the army, and had displayed great valour, in his eagerness to reap all the laurels of the battle-field, attributed to himself alone the honour of the great success obtained by the exploit of Coligny and Tavannes. "A very sharp altercation took place, in consequence, between the duke and Coligny, in the presence of the king — the rivalry between these two famous commanders being then first openly displayed."

But victory, whether declaring for king or emperor, seems never to have led to anything decisive. The disasters of one campaign were avenged in the next, and strife and warfare thus indefinitely prolonged. Rarely were the victors able, if willing, to follow up the advantage gained. On the present occasion Henri had made vast preparations and incurred enormous expense, his own camp rivalling in luxury and splendour that of some Eastern despot, while his generals and officers of his retinue vied with him in the costliness of their arms and accoutrements, and the equipment of their followers. But the sole achievement of this grand army, which in order to raise and equip the king had drained France of her resources, was the plundering, laying waste and burning of two or three Belgian towns. Even Renti was not taken; for provisions falling short, and an epidemic appearing amongst the troops, the siege was raised and the French decamped, Henri then disbanding a large part of his army.

There was war also in Italy, where fortune favoured the imperialists. Its chief and most deeply interesting incident is the siege of Siena — the last of the great Italian republics. The details of this event are vividly related in the memoirs of the Governor-General Montluc, who commanded the garrison and was entrusted with the defence of the town — the Sienese having sought the protection of France. The precautions taken by Montluc against surprises; his measures for preventing as long as possible the failure of provisions; his exhortations to his soldiers, whom he animated by his own example of moderation and endurance; his encouragement to perseverance; his counsels to the inhabitants, and their enthusiastic resolve to submit to any privations rather than become the slaves of Cosmo de' Medici or the despotic emperor; the heroic patience and self-denial of the ladies of Siena — are all narrated by Montluc with a force and eloquence that awaken sympathy in the reader.

For nearly ten months the garrison and the citizens held out. Not a morsel of bread or other food then remained to them. Famine and sickness began to thin the population, and Montluc, despairing of relief from De Brissac, thought it right to offer to capitulate, but required honourable terms. Twice De Brissac sent an earnest request to the king for orders to march to the assistance of Siena. But De Montmorency prevailed on Henri — who never presumed to enforce his own views — to refuse to do so. He was jealous of De Brissac's ability and popularity, and made a point of discountenancing all suggestions which, if carried out, seemed likely to thwart or vex the emperor.

That Siena was starved into surrender was well known; but Montluc and his soldiers were allowed to march out with the honours of war — drums beating, colours flying. Several thousands of the inhabitants accompanied them, and the imperialists took possession of an almost deserted city. These spirited republicans preferred to abandon their country rather than lose their liberty. They put no faith in the promises of either Cosmo or Charles V., and the event justified their distrust. Many hardships were endured, but they contrived to establish themselves at Monte Alcino, where many Sienese families of rank afterwards joined the first emigrants, and a government was organised after the model of that of the former free city of Siena.

CHAPTER XVII.

Sumptuary Laws Disregarded. — Extravagance at Court. — Changes of Fashion in Dress. — Too Little Marital Vigilance. — A Severe Critic. — Fontainebleau in 1555. — Reading the Stars. — Mingled Emotions. — The Arrogant Paul IV. — De Montmorency Overruled. — Death of Joanna of Aragon. — Abdication of Charles V. — An Oversight of Early Years. — The Spains Resigned. — A Five-Years' Truce. — The Truce Is Broken. — The Soldier-Cardinal. — The Consecrated Sword. — A Pontiff of the Olden Time. — Philip's Pious Scruples. — Asking the Holy Father's Pardon. — A Humiliating Ceremony.

NOTWITHSTANDING desolating wars, and the ever-recurring necessity for fresh expedients to obtain supplies of money, the French Court, under Henri II.'s reign, had at this time gone far beyond that of Francis I. in extravagance in dress and lavish expenditure on the luxury of the table. The sumptuary laws issued at the beginning of his reign had long been disregarded by all classes, wholly set at defiance, and no attempt made to renew them. Never had any Queen of France — except, perhaps, Queen Eleanor — and her court been arrayed in brocades so costly, or bedecked with gems more precious than Cather-

-ine de' Medici and her ladies — though the crown jewels were worn by Madame Diane.*

Never had the *chefs-d'œuvre* of Italian cookery been served at any state banquets on gold and silver plate in greater profusion or of more artistic workmanship, or the table ornamented with such magnificent productions of the glass manufactories of Venice, or Venetian establishments in France, as now at the royal repasts at Des Tournelles and other French palaces. Carriages sufficiently capacious, luxuriously furnished, and "ornamented with thousands of gilt nails," now took the place of the litter for travelling — the gentlemen, when not aged or gouty, still preferring horses.

"The nobility," says Michel Suriano, "who generally are not rich, ruin themselves at court with the numerous retinue of servants, horses of high breed, expensive liveries, sumptuous clothing, grand banquets, and the rest of the magnificence now indispensable there." For the excellent reason that they were unable long to continue this extravagant manner of living, and yet were unwilling wholly to withdraw from the court, it was arranged among the courtiers to attend quarterly, each one taking his three months' turn of service. The rest

---

* At least they were transferred to her when the reign of Madame d'Étampes ended. Diane wore pearls only — black and white — which harmonised with her mourning dress. She may, however, have sometimes condescended to wear the crown diamonds — though they were not of great value.

of the year they could spend at their châteaux on their own domains. There the habits of life were simple and superfluities not needed; thus, by a sort of exile and strict economy, they could make up for expenses which attendance at court imposed on them.

Jeromio Lippomano, writing to the Senate, says: "The novelties or changes in the fashion of dress succeed each other from day to day — I might almost say from hour to hour. The French spend without measure on their wardrobes and their table. As the profession of the French noble is that of arms, he wears a short coat. But it would be difficult to send you a model, so often is it varied in colour and form. To-day the brim of his hat will extend beyond his shoulders; to-morrow his hat or cap will scarce cover the top of his head. His mantle sometimes reaches to his ankles; at others no lower than his loins. His shoes are either in the Greek fashion or that of Savoy — so wide and so high that they reach the middle of the leg, or so short and so narrow that they resemble tubes. If," continues the ambassador, "the form of the garments is frequently changed, no less so is the ridiculous manner of wearing them — as buttoning one sleeve and leaving the other open. When on horseback, these young warriors carry the sword in the hand, and gallop through the city as if in pursuit of an enemy, after the manner of the Polish cavaliers."

This continual change of fashion, with the state they were required to keep up at court, was thought a heavy burden by the more needy courtiers. Twenty-five to thirty dresses of different form, and all elaborately embroidered, with an ample stock of fine laces, feathers, and jewels, scarcely sufficed to make a decent appearance at this extravagant and luxurious court. The ladies cared not to bestow their smiles on a cavalier who proclaimed his poverty by the scantiness of his wardrobe. The ladies, generally, the Venetian critic thought, had too much liberty; their husbands exercising too little vigilance over them, entrusting them not only with the management of their households, but frequently submitting to be governed by them themselves. He had little faith in the sincerity of their devotion, though on the grand ecclesiastical *fêtes* they would spend half the day in the churches, and attend high mass, vespers, and sermons. On other occasions, however long they remained out, no inquiry as to where they had been was made by their liege lords on their return.

But he is careful to observe that the ladies who enjoyed so much freedom were the married ones only. The unmarried were under more strict supervision; nevertheless the daughters of the nobility were permitted to walk out, accompanied only by a man servant or female attendant. The daughters of the upper *bourgeoisie* were more vigilantly chaperoned, being "invariably preceded by their mothers, when taking their walks, and followed by servants, male or female." On the whole, this severe critic of French fashions and manners, while considering the ladies of the court blamable for their exceeding extravagance, pronounces them very pleasing in manners and conversation, graceful and elegant, but "all more or less having at least one and the same fault — avarice." In this they did but follow the example of the Duchesse de Valentinois, who, having to provide for daughters, sons-in-law, granddaughters, and grandsons, could have left but few pensions, places, or lucrative posts of chanoinesse, etc., to satisfy the avarice of ladies no less ambitious, though less influential than herself.

With all the splendour of the Court of France, then considered the most brilliant in Europe, comfort and cleanliness were almost unknown. When at Fontainebleau in 1555, the court were compelled to shorten their stay because of the offensively dirty condition of the palace. Even those who were habituated to the noisome odours of Des Tournelles found this abode of the *chefs-d' œuvre* of painting and sculpture intolerable. It seems, however, to have been the usual condition of the royal residences of the period. Hampton Court was no less miserably dirty. The removal of the English Court to Oaklands in 1555 being announced to the Venetian Senate, the ambassador gave as a reason for it the further information that "Hampton Court was in so filthy a state that cleansing was absolutely necessary. There was no ventilation, and clay floors and rushes were not conducive to health or cleanliness."

The health of Queen Mary at this time may have made the cleansing of the palace an affair of greater urgency. An heir to the English throne was expected; an event which created some anxiety at the French Court with reference to the pretensions of the young Queen of Scotland to be Mary's presumptive heir. No less anxiously did Charles V. await the auspicious event that was to bind England more closely to Spain. Business of state appears to have been interrupted by Mary's entire seclusion and the religious processions that paraded the streets praying for the queen's safe accouchement. But it is evident, from the tone in which these particulars are related, that the feeling very generally prevailed that no necessity existed for the queen's strict retirement on the grounds supposed.

Letters, nevertheless, were prepared — date wanting, but believed to have been ready in May — announcing the birth of a prince to Mary of England. That there might be no delay in communicating the news of the birth of the expected prince to the emperor, the King of France, the King of the Romans, and King of Bohemia, the passport, signed by Philip and Mary, for Sir Henry

Sydney's special embassy was in readiness to be despatched to him at a moment's notice.* Some astrologers, who from curiosity had ventured to calculate the nativities of Philip, Mary, and Elizabeth, with a result unfavourable to the queen's expectations, were denounced by an accomplice, apprehended, and severely punished. The astrologers, for once at least, had read the stars aright.

While Mary repined at this blow to her hopes, Philip bore it like a philosopher. The emperor bowed meekly under the stroke of fate, and France rejoiced as at some triumph. War, of course, was looming, and "King Philip" would have had Mary declare against France; but the English preferred to remain neutral, and to let Charles V. and Henri II. fight their own battles. An attempt, however, was made to arrange terms of peace, and on the 23d of May a conference was opened at Marcq, a village between Ardres and Gravelines, being British territory. Plenipotentiaries were sent by the emperor and the king; Cardinal Pole and the Bishop of Winchester representing Queen Mary, the mediatress, to smooth away difficulties if possible. But no arrangement was come to, as neither potentate would abate an iota of his demands, and these were so extravagant that evidently no sincere desire for an adjustment of differences then existed.

On the same day as the conference opened, one

* "Calendar of State Papers."

of the haughtiest, most arrogant, and terribly orthodox of prelates, Cardinal Caraffa, was elected to the papal throne, and took the name of Paul IV. He was eighty years of age, the oldest of the College of Cardinals. But old as he was, his elevation seems to have wrought an entire change in his character; for none suspected the contemner of ecclesiastical dignities, the founder of the strict monastic Order of the Theatines, on whom the cardinal's hat had been thrust against his will by Paul III., was about to develop into another Julian II., as determined to turn the Spaniards out of Italy as his prototype to free it from the presence of the "barbarians." He who had passed years in the convent of the order he had founded, subjecting himself to all its austerities, was crowned with unusual pomp; and when the major-domo of the papal palace inquired what arrangements he would wish to be made respecting his table and household generally, he replied, haughtily: "Such as are suited to a great prince."

The emperor was much annoyed at Paul's election, and thought the cardinals who favoured the imperial interests had not done their duty. Their opposition to his election had, however, been sufficiently earnest to excite the new pontiff's deep resentment, and to add to his distrust of the emperor and hatred of him. Incited by his nephews, who, like all the nephews of Popes, sought duchies and principalities which Charles

V. was not willing to cede to them, he secretly proposed to Henri II. an alliance offensive and defensive. He allured him by the project of an attack on Tuscany and the kingdom of Naples, by the united French and papal armies, and promised the investiture of a certain portion of the Neapolitan territory to one of the king's sons. The part reserved was designed for his own nephews.

Henri inherited his father's earnest desire for conquest in Italy. He, therefore, gave a willing ear to Paul's proposals, though firmly opposed by De Montmorency. The Guises, however, saw in the papal alliance a possibility of the realisation of their own views in Italy, and as the Cardinal de Lorraine, who had hopes of succeeding the aged Paul, was still a worshipper at the feet of Diane, her voice in favour of the scheme, and support of the Guises, overruled all De Montmorency's arguments against it. The cardinal immediately left Blois for Rome, armed with full powers to negotiate with his holiness.

The object of this alliance appeared likely to be defeated by a resolve on the part of the emperor — long meditated, it is said, but now first openly announced to astonished Europe — to resign his hereditary dominions to his son, and withdraw from all participation in the affairs of the world. It was but very recently he had been free to do so; his mother, Joanna of Aragon, having died at Tordesillas only in the early part of 1555. She had been nearly fifty years in confinement, with very rare lucid intervals, or power to divest her mind of that extreme melancholy and despondency which, from the time of her husband's death, had overwhelmed reason and incapacitated her from transacting business of state. But only conjointly with her, and in her name, which preceded his in all state documents, was Charles allowed by the Spaniards to assume the title and functions of king.

The nation, it was thought, from the great respect in which they held their afflicted queen, would not have accepted Philip as King of Spain if Charles had abdicated before her death, unless associated with Joanna and with her sanction. Philip was in England—very wretched, it seems, with his amiable English wife. Yet they should have been a happy pair. Their tastes were similar; both solicitous for the glory of God and anxious to promote it after the same ardent fashion. But Mary was peevish, we are told, fretful and jealous; and as the English people were not in love with their new king, if Mary was, and would not let him manage their affairs, Philip was well pleased to be summoned by the emperor to Brussels.

There, in the great hall of the palace, on the 25th of October, with much pomp and many formalities, the sovereignty of the Netherlands was transferred to him in the presence of the assembled states. On the left of the emperor's throne, or chair of state, sat the Queen of Hungary, who for twenty-five years had governed the Low Countries, under her brother's direction, and was now to resign her office. On the emperor's right hand sat Philip. Surrounding these royal personages stood the princes of the empire and a numerous retinue of Spanish grandees in full court costume. The president of the council having read the Act of Abdication, Charles then rose, and, as he was suffering acutely from the gout, leaned for support on the shoulder of the Prince of Orange, while he read to the assembled states a long address. Its tone was that of one who felt that he had been a father to his people, had ever sought their welfare, spiritual and temporal, and the prosperity of their country, instead of that of a cruel despot, who had oppressed and mercilessly punished them, depopulated and laid waste their towns — a very scourge of humanity.

"His health was now broken," he told them, "the vigour of his constitution gone, through the wearing, racking pains of an incurable distemper. He, therefore, gave them a successor, in the prime of life and vigour of manhood, and possessing, besides, the sagacity of maturer years"— his worthy son Philip, whom they he addressed held in aversion, strong as that he had inspired in the German princes. Philip then fell on his knees, and an affecting scene ensued — one of those dramatic situations that will sometimes bring a ready tear to the eye, though they touch no chord in the heart.

Before deciding on this step Charles once more urged his brother Ferdinand to renounce his claim to the imperial crown in favour of Philip. It was a severe blow to him that by the oversight of an act of generosity to his brother in early years, "he was compelled to leave Philip in a rank inferior to that he himself had held among the princes of Europe. Deprived of the imperial crown, which, though but elective, and its jurisdiction little more than ideal, Philip, in Charles's eyes, was disinherited, as it were, of a portion of the possessions he was now about to resign. The Spains, the Netherlands, Italy, Mexico, and Peru, and possibly England, were not enough to pass under the sway of that gloomy, persecuting fanatic. He must wear the imperial diadem, also. Without Germany, so fertile in heretics, his territories might not be wide enough to supply victims for his *autos-da-fé*, and the carrying out in orthodox manner his father's injunction to "maintain inviolably the Catholic faith in its purity, and to extirpate heresy." But Ferdinand was firm. He would not yield to his brother's unreasonable demand. Some few weeks after Charles V.'s resignation of the sovereignty of the Netherlands, the more important abdication took place of the crowns of Aragon and Castile, and their European dependencies, with those of

Mexico and Peru. This was a great event, and a grand and inspiring solemnity. But what a misfortune that such vast dominions should pass into the unworthy hands of one whose execrable deeds gained him the appellation of the "Demon of the South!" Charles did not immediately set out for Spain. He remained some months at Brussels, and during that time negotiation with France was again proposed. He wished, before entering the retreat he had built for himself, adjoining the Monastery of Sant-Yuste (Saint Justus), at Plasencia, in Estremadura, in order to prepare for another world, to leave this one in the enjoyment of that peace and tranquillity which he for so many years had sought every occasion of banishing from it.

But no satisfactory basis could be established on which to conclude a treaty. Henri was hampered by his secret alliance with the Pope. De Montmorency suggested a truce, and succeeded — the Cardinal de Lorraine being absent — in bringing Henri to consent to it. It was a long truce of five years, and very advantageous to France. The Pope, though no time was given to consult him, was included in it by Henri's express desire, with the hope of soothing the anger it was foreseen the exasperated pontiff would give way to when the unwelcome arrangement was made known to him. The truce was signed at the Abbey of Vaucelles on the 6th of February, by Admiral de Coligny on the part of the King of France, and afterwards ratified at Brussels by the emperor and his son, the latter being designated in it merely King of England and Naples. It has been noticed also as remarkable that all the stipulations were in the emperor's name, though Charles had resigned his dominions to Philip some weeks before.

But however readily Charles may have acceded to the proposed French truce, Philip, it appears, was not satisfied with it. His manner of showing his feeling towards the French greatly shocked the sensibilities of that polite nation. He received the French embassy at the Palace of Brussels in an apartment hung with tapestry representing the battle of Pavia, the taking of Francis prisoner, and the various incidents of his captivity. He would have opposed the truce; but it was represented to him that so ungracious an act, at the moment of his father's resignation of his dominions in his favour, must necessarily draw much censure on him.

But before the year was out the truce was broken, and instead of five years it had scarcely five months' duration.* When Paul IV. heard that a truce was signed, his disappointment and rage were excessive; for he had begun hostilities

* Charles, who thought, or at least hoped, that he had secured some years of peace, had not left his native Netherlands for his retreat in Plasencia when hostilities were renewed. He embarked at Zuitburg in Zealand on the 18th of September, and arrived at Sant-Yuste the 3d of February, 1557.

by banishing the Colonnas — friends of the emperor — and seizing their fiefs, transferred them to his nephews. Paul and his nephews were believed by the cardinals to be in a position of considerable danger. The alliance with France was no longer a secret, and Philip, much incensed, was sending troops, under the command of the Duke of Alba, to the frontiers of the Papal States. But the wily old pontiff was an adept in intrigue. He dissembled his anger, declared his full approval of the truce, and, as "the common father of the monarchs of France and Spain," offered his mediation, with the hope, as he said, "of converting the truce into a lasting peace."

Cardinal Rebiba, his nuncio, was despatched to Philip II., then at Brussels, with a strict injunction not to fatigue himself by undue haste on his journey. Cardinal Caraffa, the Pope's nephew — a rough soldier of whom Paul had made a cardinal — was sent off post-haste to the French Court, with public instructions similar to those of Rebiba, strongly urging peace in the interests of Christendom. But Caraffa had also private instructions, and was the bearer of a sword blessed by the Pope. The Cardinal de Lorraine had preceded the Pope's legate to smooth the way before him. The military cardinal was attended by a numerous retinue of red hats and helmets, the extraordinary pomp of his entry into Paris creating immense sensation. The kneeling people eagerly sought his blessing, and he, much amused, is said to have murmured in irony some very profane words, denoting the soldier rather than the ecclesiastic.

He was received by the king and court in great state — the queen and the Duchesse de Valentinois attending to witness the presentation of the consecrated sword. The legate being seated, the king advanced, and, falling on his knees, reverently received the sacred weapon, which he was exhorted "to employ in defence of a parent in distress." The real object of the mission was then entered into. The Pope solicited the king to renounce the truce, and to renew his engagement with God's vicegerent. Paul had desired his legate to leave no means untried likely to obtain his object. Diane was gained (Caraffa was unstinted in the amount of his bribes). Catherine also gave her voice for the Pope, stimulated chiefly, perhaps, by family hatred of that branch of the Medici then adverse to Paul. The private views of François de Guise and the cardinal, his brother, of course made them Paul's eager supporters. De Montmorency and Coligny, who signed the treaty, were in favour of maintaining the truce. The king himself, but for his scruples respecting his oath, inclined towards the papal alliance. But the remedy for setting these scruples at rest was at hand. The legate produced his powers to absolve the king of all such obligations. This was conclusive. A new league was signed, a large remittance was made to the Pope, and the command of the army of Italy given to Duc François de Guise (July 31st).

Paul, much elated, recalled Cardinal Rebiba ere he had reached the Court of Brussels, and, entirely throwing off the mask of the mediator, began to hurl his menaces on all sides — to excommunicate, to confiscate, to arrest, and imprison. The representative of Spain in Rome was seized and sent to the Castle of St. Angelo, and the celebration of divine service was strictly prohibited throughout the Spanish territory. The emperor and the kings of Spain and of Rome were cited to appear before this terrible Pope as rebellious vassals, his direst vengeance awaiting them should they dare to disobey. The peace of Passau and the "Recess" of Augsburg which had recently confirmed it, granting liberty of conscience to the Protestants, Paul denounced as "impious, illegal, and void."

Thus, while awaiting the arrival of the French army, he continued to launch forth extravagant decrees with all the arrogance of a pontiff of the eleventh or twelfth century, whose fulminations might then have shaken thrones and struck terror into the hearts of vassal monarchs. Such was not the case in the middle of the sixteenth century, Charles V. had defied more powerful Popes than the aged Paul IV., and although Philip II., brought up by Spanish monks, profoundly venerated the Holy See, he yet felt compelled to defend himself against the Pope's attacks on him. An army under the Duke of Alba invaded the Campagna, and advanced even to the gates of Rome. But the duke did not enter the Holy City. Philip's scruples restrained him. He feared that he had already gone too far, and was inquiring of learned and pious theologians whether it were not sacrilege to carry on war against the Holy Father.

Meanwhile, the French were advancing. Towards the end of January, 1557, François de Guise arrived in Italy at the head of a small detachment of 11,000 men. He was accompanied by a corps of volunteers composed of the young nobility, who took several places and entered Milan. But the papal troops were not in readiness to aid the French. After some successes in the Milanais, he turned his arms towards Naples, which was held by the Duke of Alba. Reinforcements had been promised Guise to enable him to wrest it from him; but when demanded they were not forthcoming — the Pope's nephews, it was believed, having sold themselves to Spain. This failure, together with the conflicting interests of the Guises respecting Naples with those of France, brought the Italian expedition to a speedy and fruitless end.

François de Guise having waited a month in Rome to please the Pope, on the chance of being reinforced, was recalled in all haste to France. Paul would still have detained him in Rome; for whatever his nephews may have been, he was inexorable towards Spain. But the duke pleaded the peremptoriness of his orders. Finding that he could not prevail on him to attend to his wishes and disregard the orders he had received, he became exceedingly irritated.

"Go then," he said. "You have done but little service for your king, less still for the Church, and nothing at all for your honour."

Paul now listened to the proposals for peace which Philip more than once had very humbly preferred to the Holy Father without avail. The Duke of Alba was his plenipotentiary, and though he was himself little inclined to yield so entirely to the Pope's arrogant pretensions, he was compelled, such being his royal master's will, to subscribe to the terms that Paul dictated. All places that had been taken from the Holy See were restored. One concession only was made. Paul consented to renounce the alliance with France; but in return he exacted, and Philip assented, that the Duke of Alba should personally repair to Rome and ask pardon in his own and Philip's name for having invaded the patrimony of the Church.

On the same day that the Duc de Guise left Rome (recalled so urgently to avenge, if possible, the battle of St. Quentin) this humiliating ceremony took place. The duke, in the posture of a humble suppliant, kissed the pontiff's feet and implored the forgiveness of him whom, by his arms, ne had just reduced to the last extremity. Forgiveness and absolution were then haughtily vouchsafed by the tyrannical Paul.* This degrading act of submission to papal authority, while it gratified the Pope, was a great trial to the proud Duke of Alba. He is reported to have said : " If I had been the King of Spain, Cardinal Caraffa should have gone to Brussels to implore at the feet of Philip II. the pardon I have just now asked at the feet of Paul IV." The emperor is also said to have been greatly enraged when he heard of this debasing condition of peace. Naturally Charles's thoughts were more occupied with what was passing in the outside world than with the penances of the Cenobite's cell.

* Robertson's " Life of Charles V."

CHAPTER XVIII.

Fortune's Favourites. — The Battle of St. Quentin. — Mary Declares War. — Philip's Transports of Joy. — Consternation in Paris. — Averting the Wrath of Heaven. — "Is my Son in Paris?" — The Guises Rule France. — Besieging Calais. — Surrender of Calais. — Hearty Enthusiasm. — "The Chief Jewell of the Realme." — The Recovered Country. — Opposition Silenced. — The Scotch Refuse to Aid Henri. — Scotland given to France. — Another Jewel in the Crown. — Mary's Regret for Calais. — The Great Scotch Marriage. — Interest on the Two Millions. — The Young Queen of Scotland.

WHETHER victory or defeat attended the French arms, fortune had always some advantage resulting from it to bestow on her favourites, the Guises — either elevating them in rank or adding to their already great influence in the state. François de Guise was now returning from Italy, mortified exceedingly at the inglorious part he had, chiefly through his own fault, found himself compelled to play there. Paul had plainly told him, and truly, too — though the reproach did not come well from him — that he had "done little for the king, and less for the Church;" but that which the duke felt most keenly was that "he had done nothing at all for his own honour." Yet his return was awaited with the utmost anxiety. Another disaster to France was to raise him to a yet higher pinnacle of glory. The king had sent courier after courier to hasten his journey homeward — his arrival being looked forward to as that of the only man who could avenge the blow the French had received in the crushing defeat of the battle of St. Quentin;* a battle then threatening more fatal results — even the existence of France — than the nation had experienced since the ancient defeats of Crécy and Agincourt.

English troops had taken part in it; Philip having crossed over to England to urge Mary to aid him with a part of her army, threatening never to visit her again if she did not comply with his request. This terrible menace induced Mary to brave the remonstrances of her ministers and people, to send a herald to declare war against Henri II., and at the same time to despatch a contingent of 10,000 men to increase Philip's army of Spaniards, Swiss, Germans, Italians, and Flemings, already 60,000 strong. The commander-in-chief

* The Spaniards called it the battle of St. Laurence, from having been fought on that saint's *fête* day. In gratitude for the victory vouchsafed him, Philip vowed to erect a building which should be church, monastery, and palace, in one. It was to serve as an atonement for having borne arms against the Holy See, as well as to celebrate the victory obtained under the auspices of the martyr of the gridiron. That implement of his martyrdom was to be the model for the ground plan of the building, which was begun that year, and named the Escurial.

was Philibert Emanuel, Duke of Savoy, son of Duke Charles, whom Charles V. and Francis I. had dispossessed of nearly the whole of his duchy. Mary also contrived to raise a large sum of money for Philip's use, with which he took leave of her, and returned, not to his army, then investing St. Quentin, but to Brussels. The desperate battle that ensued was fought in his absence.

It was but a small force the French could oppose to the powerful one of the enemy — less than half their number; but the mistakes of De Montmorency — who commanded in chief, his nephews De Coligny and D'Andelot serving under him — are said to have facilitated the defeat. Great valour was displayed by the troops and their commanders, but with no avail. The slaughter was terrific — a savage massacre. Two of the Bourbon princes were killed, and three hundred of the nobility and corps of gentlemen. De Montmorency was taken prisoner, with Saint André, another of Henri's favourites. But notwithstanding the annihilation of the army, De Coligny, who was Governor of St. Quentin, resolved not to surrender the citadel, but with the handful of troops he had with him to hold out to the last extremity. He could scarcely hope that this would save Paris, or allow time for the return of Guise and his army; for the Duke of Savoy proposed to improve his victory by marching on the capital, leaving St. Quentin behind him.

Philip had been three weeks in Flanders when the news of this victory was brought him. In great haste he set off for the camp, where he was received with the military pomp of one who came as a victor. Philip was not ambitious of acquiring military fame; but the triumph of his arms at the very outset of his reign appeared to him of such happy augury, so signal a mark of the favour of heaven, that the haughty, severe, gloomy, discourteous Philip gave way to such transports of joy as temporarily changed his very nature. The Duke of Savoy was in the act of kneeling to kiss this gracious monarch's hands, when he, who exacted almost divine homage, clasped the duke in his arms and embraced him with fervour. "You have gained me," he said, "a glorious and almost bloodless victory" (bloodless comparatively, perhaps, as regarded his own army), "and it is I who should kiss your hands to express my appreciation of your services."

But Philip was opposed to his able commander's intention of marching on the capital, until the citadel was taken. Ill-fortified, the garrison small and dispirited, and scantily supplied with provisions, yet the gallant example of De Coligny succeeded in animating his troops with similar ardour, and for seventeen days the citadel was assaulted in vain. It was then taken, and De Coligny, after a valourous resistance, was made prisoner, fighting in the breach. Meanwhile consternation prevailed in Paris. Many of the inhabitants, in their terror of the barbarous hordes they expected to be let loose on the capital, fled with their families and all they could carry with them; others prepared to offer the most desperate resistance, however unavailing.

Catherine de' Medici displayed much courage. Hastening to the Hotel de Ville, she harangued the people, and bade them calm their fears. The authorities were summoned to assemble, and Catherine, with great firmness, clearness, and decision, spoke of the need of an immediate levy of troops, requiring them to furnish her with a grant of 100,000 crowns for that purpose, which very readily they gave her. Other cities followed the example of Paris, and Henri actually employed the sum so raised for the object for which it was given.

Henri, who was at Compiègne, returned to Paris, and ordered public processions, and the shrine of Sainte Geneviève to be carried through the city, to avert the wrath of heaven. The infidel Turk was, however, appealed to for the assistance of his fleet and a subsidy. But Henri seems not to have neglected other measures for the protection of the city while De Coligny was detaining Philip's army — displaying, it is said, "firmness and activity in this hour of danger, guided and sustained by the Cardinal Charles de Lorraine." Some support or guide he seems always to have needed; and all were so alarmed at this time for their personal safety, as well as for the safety of the kingdom, that under its influence intrigue and dishonesty were, for the time being, laid aside.

Philip having taken St. Quentin (which, from being the chief emporium of the commerce between France and the Netherlands, afforded much booty to his marauding army) and the small fortresses of Ham and Catelet, forbade any further advance into the enemy's country. He remembered his father's expedition to Provence, and said France was a kingdom of great resources. Towards the middle of October, having given orders for fortifying and provisioning St. Quentin, he returned to Flanders to celebrate his triumph, and not long after issued orders for the disbandment of the greater part of his army.

This paltry result of so formidable an invasion, and the most decisive and brilliant victory of the century, was keenly mortifying to the recluse of Sant-Yuste. He had eagerly inquired when the news reached him, and in a tone that seemed to anticipate but one answer, "Is my son in Paris?" A sort of dismay seized him when he learned that not only he was not in Paris, but had not even been present at the battle, and had hastily visited the camp only to prevent the march of the Duke of Savoy on the French capital. Charles is said to have acted as his son's first minister and counsellor, and as far as Philip's influence extended, to have directed the affairs of Europe in his retreat at Plasencia, though often greatly chagrined at finding how far from obediently his son followed the advice he sought from him.

France had partly recovered from her panic when Guise landed at Marseilles. In every town he passed through on his triumphal progress, he was received with enthusiasm, which reached the height of extravagance in Paris. He was welcomed at St. Germain with every demonstration of favour; and a few days after royal letters conferred on him the appointment of the king's lieutenant-general — the representative of majesty throughout the kingdom, with unlimited powers, even to receiving and despatching ambassadors in the king's name. The ambition of the Guises, one might suppose, was now fully satisfied. All power was in their hands. Their rival, De Montmorency, being a captive, there was no check on their authority; and Cardinal Charles and Duc François reigned over France under the name of Henri II. Their schemes in Italy had failed, but fortune was preparing elsewhere the culminating point of their greatness and glory.

Henri was unhappy under the rule of François de Guise, whom he feared rather than loved. He sighed for the relief of his "good gossip," De Montmorency, and lest in his captivity this favourite should suppose that his conduct at St. Quentin had lowered him in his sovereign's good graces, means were found to assure him that constraint, not increase of favour, had led him to confer such high honours on his rival. He could not, in fact, do without him. The nation looked to him alone to retrieve its military honour, so great was the public confidence in him, inspired by his martial skill, his almost unfailing success and great humanity after victory; and it must be acknowledged that he was ever anxious to justify the high opinion his countrymen had formed of his character and abilities.

He had now in his mind a great enterprise by which he hoped to revive the dimmed glory of the French arms, and to do an immense service to the nation. He proposed to the king to besiege Calais. The king approved. Those who would deprive François de Guise of some portion of the glory of this conquest assert that it was the king who suggested the expedition and commanded Guise to undertake it. At all events, he accomplished it with vigour and success. In the course of two hundred and ten years it is more than probable that the project had entered many heads, at least as desirable; but it is surprising that none had before attempted to drive the English from this gate of France, by which a passage, easy and secure, was always open to them into the French dominions.

The depth of winter, though favourable for Guise's views on Calais, was a time of the year so unusual for putting troops in motion, that when one of the divisions of the army which Guise had assembled began, as a feint, to march on Luxembourg, Philip trembled for the safety of his new possessions, over the taking of which he had rejoiced so immoderately. But Calais was already invested (1st of January, 1558). The siege was pressed forward with so much energy and rapidity that on the 8th the town surrendered. The governor, Lord Wentworth, and fifty of the principal English officials or residents were made prisoners. The rest of the garrison and the inhabitants were permitted to retire either to England or Flanders. The conquest was not sullied by slaughter.

A very considerable booty rewarded the exertions of the officers and victorious troops, Guise declining any portion for himself. This was his usual course. Though so eager to secure wealth and honours at court, he was always disinterested and magnanimous in the camp. Guines surrendered on the 21st, after the example of Calais; and the troops in the Castle of Hames marched out ere the conquering enemy approached them, and there remained not a foot of territory in France belonging to the English. The people, so recently terror-stricken, trembling for the very existence of their country, now gave way to joy so excessive that it might well be termed frenzy. They ran wildly through the city exclaiming,

"Calais is taken!" "Guise has taken Calais!" For all classes, the king, the court, and the nation generally, the event was certainly a very legitimate one for much rejoicing, and never, perhaps, was triumphal entry celebrated with so much real and hearty enthusiasm as that of Henri II. into his "good city of Calais," accompanied by the victorious general and his staff, amongst whom were De Coligny's brother, D' Andelot, and the gallant Gascon commander, Blaise de Montluc.

But while the fame of François de Guise resounded not only through France but throughout Europe, as that of the greatest general of the age, the English vented their indignation on the head of their Spanish king. He had brought this humiliation, this disgrace upon them by urging their queen to a declaration of war, contrary to the wishes of the nation. Calais, that had long been much neglected — an attack upon it having never been dreamed of — was now pronounced to be one of "the most precious gems of the English crown, the most important of England's possessions.

Philip, on passing through Calais on his return to Flanders in the spring, is said to have noticed that the garrison, not more than 500 men, was insufficient for its defence, and proposed to Mary to send a detachment of his army to strengthen it. But the ministers in council rejected his proposal, believing that it concealed some views of his own on Calais. Its investment by the French was not known early enough in England to send troops to its relief, though as soon as the startling news arrived, an order signed by the queen was issued to "the special gentlemen in every shire," urging them immediately to raise men for the succour of Calais, "the chief jewell of the Realme," and "not to spare any liberties or franchises, nor any lord, gentleman, nor other men's tenants"— the men to be "clothed in white coats with red crosses." *

That the deed was to be so speedily done was not anticipated; but before the "special gentlemen" could receive the queen's commands Calais was no longer English. Some vessels were sent off at once to the relief of the town, but Calais had surrendered before they arrived. They served, however, to take away those inhabitants and soldiers of the garrison who preferred to return to England rather than be sent to Flanders. It was, doubtless, a terrible blow to Mary; already odious to her people from her bigoted, persecuting spirit and sanguinary decrees against the reformers, they now execrated her as the willing slave of her Spanish husband, to further whose schemes she had declared war, humiliated the nation, and sacrificed the interests of England.

Thus gloom and sadness filled the English Court,

* "Calendar of State Papers," 1558.

and murmuring and repining prevailed through the length and breadth of the land, while songs of triumph and sounds of mirth and gaiety alone were heard on the other side of the Channel. The placing of strong garrisons in Calais and Guines followed these rapturous rejoicings, and, to induce French families to reside there, many privileges were bestowed on the "good city," which, with Guines and its neighbourhood, was named "the recovered country." The rest of the army was then disbanded, with orders to re-assemble early in the spring to resume the war with vigour. The king, the court, and the splendid military escort then returned to Paris to resume festivities and to celebrate a royal marriage.

The taking of Calais had also greatly served the king in a matter of finance he had much at heart. This was the raising of a large loan, which would have been far less willingly granted had that event not occurred, and the news of it happened to arrive at the very moment when the Cardinal de Lorraine was explaining to the judicial body "his majesty's desire to borrow three millions of gold crowns from the richest of his subjects." "A list had been sent in," he said, "of the names of a thousand ecclesiastics promising each a thousand gold crowns without interest, besides the year's tithes" — the clergy considering that they could not sufficiently repay the orthodoxy of which royalty had set an example since the appearance of the great heresy. The "good towns," he continued, "must furnish the remaining two millions, on which interest at the rate of twelve per cent. would be paid."

"Guise has besieged and taken Calais!" "Calais is taken!" "Guise has taken Calais!" is the startling cry that meets the ear, again and again reiterated by a joyous throng parading the streets, eagerly proclaiming the wonderful achievement of François de Guise to astonished and — until further confirmed — incredulous Paris.

Voices about to be raised in opposition to this loan or gift — for such no doubt it was — were immediately silenced, and all obstacles swept away in the patriotic enthusiasm the glorious news excited. This unexpected readiness to supply the king's needs doubtless relieved him of some anxiety, and enabled him with a lighter heart and more triumphant spirit to take possession of "the recovered country."*

While seeking, at the instance of the Guises, the consent of the Scotch Parliament to the celebration of the marriage of their young queen to her betrothed husband, the dauphin Francis, Henri had also asked the aid of the Scotch on the renewal

---

* Henri did, however, acknowledge the liberality of his "good towns" by abolishing certain imposts prejudicial to commerce — his edict beginning with a sort of profession of faith in political economy, and declaring freedom of trade and of barter ("*liberté du commerce et des échanges*") to be the principal means for enriching nations. — Recueil d' Isambert.

of hostilities with England. Though pressed by the French ambassador and the queen-regent, in her brothers' interests, the Scotch were firm in their refusal to take any part in the quarrel between France and England. No objection, however, was raised to the celebration of the marriage — Scotland being represented at the ceremony by eight Scottish noblemen, empowered to sign such deeds as might be necessary to ensure its full liberty and independence. The aim of the French was to secure the crown of Scotland for the dauphin, in the event of Mary's death preceding his.

But the Scotch were not willing that their country should become a French province. The Guises therefore determined to secure it by a secret treaty, signed by Mary Stuart ten or twelve days before her marriage, making a donation of her kingdom to France. A second treaty resigned the usufruct of Scotland to Henri II., until the crown of France was indemnified to the extent of a million crowns, for the expenses incurred in affording aid to Scotland. The Guises are said to have wished "to give Scotland to France in order to increase their influence and secure a stronger claim to rule the destinies of their country." On this account they were so urgent for the early celebration of the marriage. Catherine de' Medici was greatly opposed to it, and pressed the king to consider the youth and ill health of the dauphin.

Madame Diane supported her objections, but rather to thwart the Guises than from any real interest she took in Catherine's views or in the children who were to be married.

The duke and the cardinal were both much indebted to Diane for their first elevation at court; for Henri never really liked them, and but that they were her *protégés* would probably have followed his father's injunction "to beware of them." Their greater force of character and despotism of will oppressed him, and if he could have shaken them off he would. Diane had lost none of her influence with Henri. But the Guises no longer paid homage to her; believing from the position they had gained, and their power in the state, they were too strong to need her support, or, except for form's sake, that of Henri himself.

To marry their niece to the dauphin was still beyond their power, unsanctioned by the king. Catherine had pleaded for at least a year's delay, and Henri, thinking, perhaps, that such delay was desirable, seemed likely to consent. But that finished courtier, the Cardinal Charles de Lorraine, with his accustomed foresight, had begun to transfer to the queen the servile homage with which until latterly he had flattered Diane. Catherine was little accustomed to have so devoted a slave at her feet. Doubtless, she knew what was of advantage to the state as well as the cardinal; yet he prevailed on her to withdraw her opposition to an event which, "deferred, might deprive France of the opportunity of placing another jewel in her crown." This jewel was not the cairngorm; that was secured, or supposed to be, by the secret treaties — the unfortunate Mary's initiation into a career of intrigue and falsehood, for which her bringing up at the French Court had so thoroughly trained her.

It was reported that Mary of England was in a languid state of health; not merely pining for the neglectful Philip's society, but lamenting the loss of Calais, which she had taken so much to heart that she believed the name of this so valued but lost possession would be found engraven on it after her death. Mary of Scotland was the heiress of her crown — so said the French. The daughter of Anne Boleyn — an excommunicated heretic, a faithless mistress (they would not allow her the name of wife), who had come to an ignominious end on the scaffold — would she ever sit on the English throne? Forbid it, heaven! Let right prevail! And there was every hope (if not every chance) that prevail it would; and Scotland's queen — the daughter-in-law of the powerful King of France, with his armies, if needful, to support her cause — would doubtless have her own.

It was not merely a new jewel, then, but a jewelled crown, that was to be the prize of the heir of France. The happy dauphin, though he would probably never wear the tiara, might yet wear a triple crown as King of England, France and Scotland. But there must be no delay. "Mary, the execrated," was ill, and the partisans of the disinherited heretic Elizabeth on the alert to seize the throne.

"The great Scotch marriage"— the marriage of the dauphin Francis, then fourteen, and the young Scottish queen, who was fifteen years and a half — was appointed to take place on the 24th of April, when each made oath, according to the terms of the marriage treaty, to preserve the laws, the independence, and the liberties of Scotland, Mary having already ceded her kingdom to France. The celebration of the marriage brought the princes and the nobility to Paris from far and near. The King and Queen of Navarre attended, and several gentlemen of their court; forming a colony of heretics in the midst of the fold of the faithful. This gave rise to much tumult in Paris from the boldness with which the presence of these heretics of high rank inspired those of humbler station. They assembled in the open spaces of the city, and sang, with religious fervour and enthusiasm, the Psalms of Marot, which lately had been set to more appropriate music. Many arrests were made, but as secretly and quietly as possible, that these proceedings might not transpire inopportunely, and interrupt the series of brilliant *fêtes* with which the marriage was celebrated.

They served, however, to make known how

greatly reform had lately progressed in France, and to reveal the unsuspected fact that many persons, even of the king's household, were tainted with this abominable heresy. Strong measures and unflinching firmness in applying them, it was felt, would be necessary to effectually crush the hydra-headed monster called Reform. But soon the heretical guests would disperse; meanwhile, come what may, let the passing hour be enjoyed, for, surely, never did France behold *fêtes* so magnificent as those which made happy the good people of Paris and all the good towns of the kingdom, when the boy-dauphin was married to Mary Stuart and proclaimed King of Scotland.* All, too, had the satisfaction, or otherwise, of having contributed towards these national rejoicings — the loan of three millions of gold crowns, to be employed in equipping an army for the renewal of the war with England and Spain in the spring, and the strengthening of the frontier towns, being nearly exhausted by the reckless extravagance of the six weeks' festivity.

Nothing equalling the gaiety and brilliancy of these marriage *fêtes* was probably ever again witnessed by the unfortunate Queen of Scotland, whose after life was so piteously disastrous. To the sad calamity of her bringing up in the de-

---

* The Scotch people were opposed to the dauphin's assumption of the title; but the influence of the queen-regent prevailed with the Scottish Parliament to confirm it.

praved, intriguing French Court, under the direction of Catherine de' Medici, who so well trained her own daughters, doubtless much that was reprehensible in her conduct must be attributed. At the time of this marriage she is described as a charming, graceful, light-hearted girl, not yet in the full bloom of her beauty, but gracious in manner, and accomplished, after the custom of the time; singing simple ditties to the accompaniment of the lute; dancing like a fairy; writing pretty rhymes, and perhaps, as it was the fashion, mastering a little Latin.

Often, probably, in the sadness of later years, and in the dreary hours of her captivity, memories would arise of those happy days of her youth spent in (as she wrote when leaving France, a girl-widow) —

> "*Le plaisant pays de France,*
> *Qui a nourri mon jeune enfance.*"

CHAPTER XIX.

Ready Again to Take the Field. — Sighing for His "Good Gossip." — Amicable Relations Renewed. — Unexpected Aid. — Contemplating Each Other. — A Terrible State of Things. — Not Quite Sound in the Faith. — Exceedingly Perplexed. — The King and the Heretic. — A Mutual Desire for Peace. — In Bondage to the Guises. — De Montmorency on Parole. — A Death-bed Reproach. — A Lamentable Ending. — Death of Mary of England. — Calais Must Be Given Up. — Mary Stuart Queen of England. — A Too Hasty Offer of Marriage. — Sparing England's Feelings. — The Unfortunate Peace. — Two Royal Marriages.

THE marriage festivities were scarcely ended ere François de Guise, eager to gather fresh laurels, was again at the head of his army, ready to take the field. The government of the kingdom was now pretty equally shared between him and his brother. The duke ruled the camp, the cardinal the court; the latter being also, to their mutual advantage, the head of the financial department. Henri and Diane, under this despotism, exercised but a secondary influence on affairs of state — she, much to her amazement as well as her indignation; he, to his great chagrin.

De Montmorency's absence was becoming intolerable to him. His ransom was fixed at 200,000 crowns, and he was wealthy enough to have paid it. But the king would have paid twice that sum for the release of his "good gossip," whose return to court he so sighed for, that he might at least have a change of masters. But he had not that sum at command. The greater part of the three millions had been frittered away, and the duke had taken what remained for the needs of his army. Before the fatal battle of St. Quentin, while François de Guise was in Italy, Diane — who had induced Henri to favour that expedition, then so much desired by both duke and cardinal — began to perceive the falling off in the homage the latter so long had paid her.

"They were growing too powerful, those ambitious scions of the House of Lorraine. She had protected them until they fancied they could do without her." She therefore determined to be revenged on them, and to renew her old friendship with De Montmorency. A coldness had long subsisted between these rivals in favour and influence. But that mattered not; the constable knew that Diane was a valuable ally, who could often bring the king over to some settled views when he was powerless to do so. To her first friendly overtures he, therefore, very readily responded, and the renewal of amicable relations between them — like the treaties of peace between royal personages — was to be cemented by a marriage. Diane proposed that De Montmorency's second son should marry one of her granddaughters, to which he cordially assented. Before the needful arrangements could be completed the constable was called away to the battle-field, and became the victorious general's captive.

Yet De Montmorency had unswervingly endeavoured to keep France in submissive alliance with the emperor, and was no less desirous that peace should be maintained on any terms with the emperor's son; so that, although a prisoner of war, he could scarcely be considered to have fallen into an enemy's hands. His capture, indeed, served to smooth the way for peace, numerous as were the obstacles opposed to it. Some reverses experienced by the French arms on the opening of the new campaign seemed also likely to lead to an attempt to a settlement of differences. Fortune, however, had not forsaken François de Guise. Wherever he appeared, victory followed. But his exceeding avidity for military glory; his desire to reap all the laurels for himself; to be the hero of every great achievement of the army, led to a sad disaster.

Detained before the fortress of Thionville longer than he expected, he was unable to join, as appointed, the detachment commanded by Marshal de Termes, Governor of Calais, who had been very successful in Flanders, taking Dunkirk and other towns; but encountering at Gravelines the more numerous army of the Governor of Flanders, he was defeated, his troops massacred, and he and his officers taken prisoners. A fleet of ten English vessels of war, that chanced to be cruising off the coast, attracted by the noise of the artillery, ascended the river Aa, and cannonaded the French on their right wing; the consequence of this unexpected aid to the Flemish governor being the signal defeat of the French. It proved a complete check to Guise's schemes of conquest, and compelled him to hasten with all speed to Picardy to protect the exposed frontier.*

The two armies soon after assembled their forces, in number about equal — 50,000 strong. The French encamped at Amiens; the Spanish army a few leagues distant. Henri and Philip arriving to command in person, the soldiers expected a speedy and decisive battle. They, however, remained contemplating each other in this position for some time, without engaging in any hostile encounter.

Some two or three months previously the Duchesse de Lorraine, whom the French had

* To compensate for the loss of Calais, the English at this time made an attempt to take Brest with a fleet of more, it is said, than a hundred English and Dutch ships — many of large tonnage. Fires were lighted on all the hills, and the people called to arms — the attack ending in the discomfiture of the men who landed. The survivors fled to their ships, and the fleet departed.

deprived of the regency of the duchy, begged that the king would allow her to see her son, who was being brought up at the Court of France, destined by and by to marry the Princesse Claude, Henri's daughter. The cardinal accompanied the young duke to Marcoing. Granvelle, Bishop of Arras, the emperor's former chief minister, and now the minister of Philip II., attended the duchess, who was a niece of Charles V. The two diplomatic ecclesiastics availed themselves of this meeting to confer together on the desirableness of peace, and the terms on which it might possibly be acceptably proposed. Moderate concessions, the cardinal said, would be made by France. But the pretensions of Spain, as he gathered from Granvelle, appeared to be too immoderate to be entertained for a moment.

From discussing temporal affairs they naturally turned to spiritual ones, and lamented over the spread of the pestilent doctrine of heresy, which was stifling the Christian spirit in men's hearts and threatening the destruction of the world. Torture and the stake, aiding the pious efforts of the Holy Inquisition, scarcely sufficed to repress it in Spain. The zeal of the queen and the vigilance of her clergy with difficulty kept it down in England. In the Netherlands the people had actually begun to rescue the criminals condemned to the stake from the hands of the executioner; while "in France," he said, "as the cardinal must be aware, it was increasing from day to day; and what had been done in Germany might soon be looked for in those countries." The cardinal was doubtless as deeply pained by this terrible state of things in the religious world as was the diplomatic bishop. But with reference to France, he replied that "the French people, he considered, were naturally averse to heresy, and that it was owing to that sentiment the nation had always been so valiant in defence of the Holy See."

The bishop, however, pointed out to him that the heretical sentiment threatened to become the sign of a political party in France, almost openly protected by his and his brother's rivals. There were the Calvinistic Bourbon princes, irritated at not being called upon to take part in the government; also the De Châtillons, the constable's nephews, who were very far from holding the orthodox principles of their uncle. De Coligny, the admiral, was then a prisoner. "A letter," Granvelle said, "from his brother D'Andelot had been intercepted. In it he spoke of the sacrifice of the mass with great irreverence, and promised the admiral that he would find means of passing into his prison some books from Geneva."

"How much more to the interest then," said Granvelle, "of the two courts and the men whose influence is greatest in them, to come to terms and unite their efforts against their common enemy — this inveterate heresy — than to exhaust their strength in a fruitless and apparently endless contest." The cardinal laid these things to heart, but was not then sure that peace with Spain would suit his or his brother's views; for François de Guise, with vast ideas of glory and conquest, was then about to open the new campaign. One item of information he, however, turned at once to account. He denounced D'Andelot to the king, who had already received some hints that he was not quite sound in the faith, but had allowed them to pass unnoticed. This shows that D'Andelot must have stood very high in the favour of the narrow-minded, bigoted Henri.

On this second intimation he was exceedingly perplexed what course to take; for D'Andelot was a very brave officer, besides being the nephew of his "good gossip," of whose orthodoxy there could be no doubt, and who would doubtless bring this erring nephew to his senses when he had obtained his liberty. He had fought valiantly at St. Quentin, and his dauntless courage at the siege of Calais had gained him high commendation from the king himself. This had displeased Guise, who felt his own glory dimmed by a ray of it having rested on D'Andelot and other commanders who took part in that successful exploit. The magnanimity with which François de Guise is credited was surely greatly at fault when, following up his brother's denunciation, he told the king that "he had but little hope of a prosperous campaign if 'that heretic' maintained his command of the French infantry."

The king immediately sent for D'Andelot, charging his brother, the Cardinal de Châtillon (himself suspected of heterodox views), to warn him to reply, when questioned by him respecting the mass, in a proper and suitable manner, for that by so doing he would afford him much pleasure. D'Andelot arrives. The king immediately inquires "whether he considers the mass an abomination." As fearless before the king as before his enemies, he will not deny his faith. Taking no heed to the warning given him, he replies, "There is but one sacrifice once made, full, perfect, and sufficient for the sins of the whole world — that of our Lord Jesus Christ; to make the mass a sacrifice for the sins of the living and the dead is a detestable and abominable thing."

The king, in a furious passion, snatched up a plate (they appear to have been dining together) and threw it at D'Andelot's head. He missed his aim, and struck the poor, puny, sickly dauphin. He then hastily drew his sword as if to kill the heretic, but let it fall again in its scabbard. The guard was summoned to arrest him, and he was sent to the fortress of Mélun. No proceedings were taken against D'Andelot; but he was deprived of his command, which was given by Guise to Montluc. A brave soldier and thoroughly orthodox, yet he did not enable Guise to carry out the plan of his campaign with that prosperity he professed to expect on the displacement of the heretic.*

As the two armies continued so long inactive almost in sight of each other, it began to be whispered about that both monarchs were more desirous of a peace than a battle. Philip's army, too, was wanted elsewhere. The Turks were retaking their African possessions and ravaging the coasts of Italy. He was himself very anxious to return to Spain. An invasion, as it was termed, of Protestant doctrines had occurred in some of the Spanish towns, especially in Valladolid and Seville, among the upper and educated classes. The Inquisition had much work on its hands, and *autos-da-fé* on a grand scale were preparing. Henri desired peace, that he might be freed from the tyranny of the Guises, and, while solacing himself in the more congenial society of the constable, concert with him some effectual means for stemming the overwhelming tide of reform, which in Paris and other large towns of France threatened to become formidable even to the true Church.

* When, some months after, De Montmorency obtained his liberty, D'Andelot was offered his, on condition that he would hear a mass. No verbal abjuration was required of him. He refused for some time, but afterwards, overcome by the entreaties of his wife and his brother the cardinal, who had a more accommodating conscience, he consented. He soon repented of this concession, and reproached himself ever after with having committed an act of idolatry.

Diane, no less zealous for the faith of Rome, and very anxious for the success of her intrigue to displace the Guises, was of opinion that the constable was the fittest person to make proposals for peace. Henri, as he had ever done, adopted her views. He had kept up a regular correspondence with Philip's important prisoner. His helpless writhings to free himself from the bondage of the arrogant men who then ruled France in his name were, therefore, no secret in the enemy's camp; and Philip and his wily minister, Granvelle, were fully prepared to take every advantage of Henri's weakness and the constable's ascendency over him.

Hints were thrown out, but supposed to be on no official authority, that peace would be acceptable to France, and some concessions made to secure it. They were well received in the Spanish camp. Leave of absence on parole was granted to De Montmorency, with the promise of the remission of half (some writers of the time, more correctly, probably, say the whole) of the sum fixed for his ransom. He immediately visited the king in his camp at Amiens, and was welcomed with open arms, as though he had regained the province lost by his obstinacy and his errors. That singular honour and sign of highest royal favour, as it was considered at that period, the invitation to share the monarch's couch, was conferred on him. After two or three private conferences with the king, who could scarce consent so soon to part with his long-absent friend, De Montmorency repaired to Beauvais, where the marriage of his son with Diane's granddaughter was then celebrated — Queen Catherine, the young Queen of Scots, and ladies and gentlemen of the court attending; all delighted at the presence of the constable. There, too, of course, Henri's instructions to him concerning a truce or a peace were submitted to the beautiful sexagenarian duchess, and were revised and ratified by her.

On returning to the Spanish camp a truce of fifteen days was signed. De Montmorency, assisted at Henri's request by Saint André — another favourite and prisoner of war sighing for his release — then met the Spanish king's commissioners at the abbey of Cercamp, to settle, if possible, the conditions on which to conclude a treaty. A prolongation of the truce, however, became necessary — news arriving, before any decision could be come to, of the death, on the 21st of September, of the modern Charlemagne, the Emperor Charles V., at his retreat in the grounds of the monastery of Sant-Yuste.

Charles had not so entirely withdrawn from public life as to make his death an affair of no moment in the arrangements now proceeding. The cenobite never ceased to be the emperor, or to take interest in the affairs of this world while preparing for another. His opinion and advice were sought on all questions of public importance; though Philip, while affecting much filial docility, really preferred the counsels of the Bishop of Arras. Charles's fanaticism and intolerance appear to have become actually ferocious in his last days. He had heard that Protestantism had found its way into Spain. It drove him frantic, and probably hastened his death. The gout, which for a time had left him, returned with increased intensity of agony, while mind and body were fevered by the task he had set himself of urging on his son (by no means undutiful in this case) the vigourous extinction of the heretical sentiment in Spain by horrible tortures and the burning of whole families together in one monstrous *auto-da-fé*.

The only thing this fanatical emperor could find to reproach himself with on his death-bed was (referring to the German princes) that "he had kept his word with heretics." He might, however, have eased his conscience by remembering that he had done so because he could not help it—the heretics had compelled him. "Tradition," writes the historian, H. Martin, "has surrounded Philip II. with a certain sinister grandeur. He, however, was great only in obstinacy and inhumanity." The same may surely be said of Charles V. He was always at war, certainly, slaying his thousands and tens of thousands, ravaging his neighbours' territories, and, as far as his power extended, filling the world with misery and wretchedness. Even by his wars he gained no permanent advantages. What was taken in one campaign was lost in the next. However, his greatness — if such scourges of humanity must be called great men — had a lamentable ending; his glory setting in clouds and darkness.*

Peace was so pressing a necessity for Philip II. that the discussion of the preliminaries was soon after resumed, and resulted in the appointment of plenipotentiaries, who assembled at Cercamp towards the end of October. De Montmorency and Saint André being again charged with the interests of France, together with the Duc de Guise, the Cardinal de Lorraine, Marvilliers, Bishop of

---

* The accounts which some biographers of Charles V. have given of the penances and privations he inflicted on himself at Sant-Yuste appear to be greatly exaggerated. M. Mignet, who took considerable pains to ascertain their truth or falsehood, has entirely disproved the statement that the emperor lived with the monks. On the contrary, he had built a very charming residence in the grounds of the monastery, and so far from reducing himself to the nakedness of a cell and the rigours of monastic life, his abode was wanting in none of the domestic conveniences and even elegancies with which princes at that epoch had already begun to surround themselves. The walls of his own apartments were hung with silk tapestry from Flanders, with velvet door hangings or portières. His bedroom was furnished luxuriously. The curtains and coverlet of the bed were of rich embroidered silk. His table was well supplied. He had sixteen long velvet dresses, bordered with ermine and lined with *plume de l'Inde;* and a sufficient number of couches and easy invalid chairs. His attendants alsowere numerous. — Mignet.

Orléans, and Claude de l' Aubespine, Secretary of State. Granvelle, Bishop of Arras, was, of course, Philip's principal representative, with the Prince of Orange and two of Philip's Spanish ministers. The Duke of Savoy was also represented, but Henri allowed his cousins, the King and Queen of Navarre, to be sacrificed to Spain. Not being requested to send a plenipotentiary, no demand for the restitution of the portion of their dominions seized by Charles V. was made. Scarcely had the conferences begun than they were interrupted by another death — that of Mary of England, on the 17th of November.

Philip had demanded, on her behalf, the restitution of Calais. Every other point in dispute seemed settled; but in the most disadvantageous manner for France — De Montmorency being willing to show his gratitude to Philip for the remission of his ransom by consenting to Granvelle's every demand. These large concessions were strongly opposed by the Guises, who showed far more patriotism during these conferences than the mighty constable. "Calais must be given up," Granvelle declared. "Spain could not separate the interests of England from her own." The constable seemed on the point of yielding; but the cardinal and the duke so strenuously contended against it that Philip's plenipotentiaries advised that the "veteran constable" should again be sent to France to consult with his sovereign, in order that he might realise his good-intentions, and thwart the views of those ambitious, "inexperienced young men."

It was supposed then that Henri, at the constable's bidding, would actually have given up Calais. He would not, surely, have dared to do so. He was not, however, put to the test. Mary's death greatly modified the situation of affairs, and suspended the conferences until its results in England were ascertained. But De Montmorency, meanwhile, was free, and returned triumphantly to Paris to pay his *devoirs* to the no less triumphant Diane, and with her again to take the helm of the state, which the Guises readily yielded to them. To contend with their rivals was no part of their policy; they stepped aside, and awaited the next turn of fortune's wheel.

Meanwhile, their importance was temporarily increased by their niece becoming Queen of England — so far as the title of king and queen, together with the royal arms, being assumed by the dauphin and Mary Stuart, at the solicitation of the princes of Lorraine, with Henri's full approval. None among his advisers was found to dissuade the king from this impolitic act, though he was not prepared to support by force of arms the pretensions thus put forth on behalf of the young Queen of Scotland, against the claims of the daughter of Henry VIII. and Anne Boleyn, Mary Stuart being only that monarch's great niece. It was exceedingly offensive to Elizabeth, whose legitimacy was not contested, and who ascended the throne amidst the joyous acclamations of the people — delighted to be freed from the oppressive rule of her sanguinary half-sister and her Spanish husband.

The plenipotentiaries appointed by Mary received fresh powers from Elizabeth to treat at the conference about to re-assemble at Câteau, Cambresis, and to act as before, in strict association with Spain. Philip thought this favourable to his matrimonial views, and lost no time in assuring her of his devotion to her interests. At the same time he made his offer of marriage, for which he undertook to secure the Pope's dispensation. The wary Elizabeth — now in her twenty-fifth year — did not reply in a tone that forbade all hope. She had peremptorily demanded the restitution of Calais, that being almost the only point that concerned England in the pending negotiations, and Philip's aid was needed to support this claim. But Philip, warm in her cause at first, became exceedingly lukewarm when from the tenor of her first acts relating to religious worship he found that he must wholly renounce all hopes of a second English marriage — Elizabeth was a hopeless heretic! He perceived that what she had most at heart was to succeed where her father had failed — to found a Protestant England, and to unite Scotland to it.

Henri made great professions of friendship to Elizabeth, and was anxious to secure her alliance, notwithstanding the resentment he had provoked by his sanction of the affront offered her at the instance of the Guises. He urged on her the advisability of separating her interests from those of Spain, and concluding a separate peace with him. An arrangement was at last arrived at, "considerately intended to spare the feelings of the English and their queen at the loss, so severely felt, of Calais and its dependencies." They were to be retained provisionally for eight years, and then restored to the queen. In case of delay or refusal the crown of France was to forfeit a million and a half of *francs*, and still be under the obligation, at some undefined period, to give up this valued possession to England. Any breach of the treaty or hostile act of the queen towards the King of France, the King or Queen of Scotland (included in the treaty), would, however, absolve the crown from its engagement.

The fulfilment of this treaty was never intended, it appears, and probably was never expected. But as Elizabeth was informed by Philip's plenipotentiaries that Calais could not be retaken in less than seven or eight campaigns, and perhaps not at all, the treaty was signed on the 2d of April, and Calais was lost to England forever. Nor was that any misfortune, as it had served during the two hundred and ten years it had remained a British possession only to draw the nation into ruinous continental wars. The treaty between

France, Spain, and Savoy was signed on the following day — a farewell polite attention on the part of Philip towards Elizabeth having caused the signing of her treaty with France to have the precedence of his own with France and Savoy.

The peace of Câteau-Cambresis was called by France "*La paix malheureuse*" — all the military men, the statesmen, and the nation generally, regarding it as most humiliating and degrading. Whatever his enemies demanded the king granted, and, heedless of the sentiments of his people, and the remonstrances addressed to the congress by his allies and his relatives, he ratified the treaty. The Duc de Guise and the cardinal opposed it to the last. "Sire," exclaimed the duke, "you sacrifice in one day more than thirty years of reverses would deprive you of." But what of that? his "good gossip" was now really free, released from his parole; his companion in captivity, Saint André, also — the liberation of these two favourites having cost France more than two kings' ransoms.

"Thus ended the struggle between the Valois and the House of Austria. France was conquered, not by the sword, but by diplomacy. The dynasty that imposed such a treaty on France signed its own downfall, and was never to rise again in the esteem of the people" (H. Martin).

There were, as usual, many promises between the contracting Powers of perpetual friendship and alliance, sealed, of course, by two royal marriages.

Henri II.
Photo-etching from painting by Biozot.

HENRY II.
LVIIIe Roy de France,
Mort a Paris, le 9 Juillet 1559.
Apres 12 ans de règne.

As Philip could not have Elizabeth of England for his third wife, Elisabeth of France, Henri's eldest daughter, who had been betrothed to his son, Don Carlos, and was then but in her thirteenth year, was sacrificed to the "Demon of the South." A more mature bride was found for the Duke of Savoy — his cousin Marguerite of France, sister of Henri II., then about thirty-five years of age.

CHAPTER XX.

Secret Reasons for the Peace. — A Crime to Be Punished. — Heresy in the Parliament. — Reprimanding the President. — More Heterodox Than Orthodox. — A Great and Worthy Act. — A Strong Temptation. — D'Andelot Again a Prisoner. — The Counsellor Anne du Bourg. — The Counsellor Du Faur. — Arrest of Du Bourg and Du Faur. — Courtly Festivities. — Marriage of Madame Elisabeth. — Tilts and Tournaments. — The King's Promised Pleasure. — Yet One More Lance Must Be Broken. — A Mournful Wedding. — The Arm of the Lord. — Faithful unto Death.

THE reason secretly assigned by De Montmorency for concluding a treaty so entirely contrary to the interests of France that the nation regarded it as an indelible stain on its glory, was the necessity for putting a stop to the progress of the hero of Metz and Calais. His ambition led France, he said, into dangerous wars, and placed the alliance of Spain and Austria, so necessary to her, in continual jeopardy. In other words, it was for the gratification of the constable's feelings of envy and enmity towards François de Guise. But Henri had a higher motive for his concessions. "Freed from the anxiety of foreign warfare, he would be able to devote his whole attention and to bend the full force of his government to extirpating heresy in France. With that view he had entered into a pact with his Catholic brother of Spain — determined, like himself," he said, "to pursue their common enemy with unrelenting rigour" — the consecration of this pact being his daughter's nuptials.

When the Spanish army was expected, after the battle of St. Quentin, to march on Paris, and Henri, to avert the calamity, ordered the shrine of Sainte Geneviève to be carried in procession through the city, the reformers publicly ridiculed this mode of providing for the safety of the capital from the ravages of an invading army. So great was the confusion occasioned by the terror of the people, that the moment was unfavourable for duly punishing those irreverent heretics. But it was not intended that such offenders should escape with impunity. Soon after the tide of fortune turned, and Calais was taken. Before setting out to make his entry into the "re-conquered country," the king issued an order to the Parliament of Paris requiring the president to register the Bull of Paul IV., establishing the Inquisition in France, at the king's request, in 1557, which they had then failed to do — protesting against it.

The Parliament replied, renewing more earnestly the remonstrance they had made in 1557, to the effect that hitherto no good purpose had been served by the punishments daily inflicted on unfortunate people because of their religion. That instead of fire and sword for the correction of error, it would be advisable to try other methods — pure doctrine, for instance, and good example in the priesthood. The king closed his ears and heart to this appeal. It was too evident to him that heresy had found its way into the judicature. Several of its members openly supported the cause of the Reformation, and announced, in full assembly, the same opinions as many persons had suffered for at the stake — sentenced, with some few changes, by that same Parliament. The sentence was, undoubtedly, often extorted under heavy pressure.

Now, however, the Parliament represents the true feeling of France — the king and the fanatics of the ultramontane faction excepted. The nation is weary of burning and putting its fellow creatures to horrible tortures for the vague crime called heresy or reform. But the cry for leniency and mercy only enrages the persecutors, and at the Parliament, whence that cry emanates, a heavy blow is to be aimed.

The salaries of the assembly of judges and counsellors were two years in arrear. The president, Séguier, was deputed to request that the king would order their payment. The Cardinal de Lorraine, who controlled the finance department, availed himself of this opportunity of severely reprimanding the president, in the presence of the king, for the laxity of the Parliament in carrying out the royal edicts against the reformers, and substituting banishment for the required sentence of death. This course had been latterly adopted when deterred by the danger menacing themselves from pronouncing an acquittal. Madame Diane — always present to look after his majesty's interests — also took upon herself to utter reproaches and invectives against the president and his offending colleagues; the king listening in silent approval to the vituperative eloquence of the cardinal and the lady.

The provincial Parliaments had but partially followed the example of the judicial chamber of Paris. But that they might not further err in that direction, the cardinal forcibly impressed on the president that "uniformity in the administration of the laws must be re-established among the Parliaments of the kingdom; also the strict execution of the king's edicts." The chief members of the parliamentary chambers, generally, were accustomed to meet quarterly in Paris at what was termed the "Mercuriale." Any question in the interval having arisen concerning the laws and customs regulating the magisterial office was then introduced for private discussion.

The cardinal's reprimand for failure of duty with respect to the reformers, and his injunction to unite with other Parliaments in passing sentence on the accused brought before them, were considered questions of so much importance that the meeting which took place a few days after the president's interview with the cardinal was numerously attended. The members were severally requested by the procurator of the assembly to give a free and full opinion on the matter before them, and to vote for toleration or otherwise, as seemed to them right. The discussion occupied some days, and many who took part in it were men of learning and eloquence or distinguished jurisconsults. On the whole, the opinions expressed appear to have been more heretical than orthodox, and the discussion would have resulted, by a large majority of voices, in a declaration of tolerance, which many Protestants of rank and influence, were prepared to follow up by a demand for liberty of religious worship.

There were, however, traitors in the camp — the Presidents Le Maistre and Minard — who informed the Cardinal de Lorraine of the tone the discussion had taken, and to what it was surely tending. It immediately occurred to him that to obtain its prolongation by means of his servile spies, that the king might surprise those abominable heretics in the very act of expounding their pestilent doctrines, and thus with a sure hand bring down vengeance on them, would be a great and worthy act. The king, notwithstanding his fanaticism, had so much sense of honour left as to hesitate, though not enough firmly to refuse, when it was first proposed to him to intrude on a private conference. It was an infringement of one of the privileges of the Parliament, and for the despicable object of surprising and taking advantage of a confession of sentiments on the part of men who, as it proved, were too honourable and too fearless to deny them before him, had he sought to know them in a manner less humiliating and degrading to himself.

The cardinal is said to have employed all the arts of a courtier, in which he was so well skilled, to recover his lost favour with Diane. He had done his part, as a minister of God, by "denunciations of divine wrath following the king's neglect of this opportunity of inflicting condign punishment on heretical judges, until Henri trembled for his soul's salvation."* He now needed the elderly favourite's aid to remove from the weak monarch's mind any yet lingering scruples or sense of shame. To tempt her to a reconciliation he held out hopes of large confiscations — for these were not needy men whom the arm of the king was to strike. Together with the names of those judges suspected of heresy, the value of the offices they held, and the amount of their private incomes had been supplied to the cardinal. True, an edict had been issued to the effect that all fines and confiscations should be employed in works of piety, and that, otherwise disposed of, the gift

* "*Mémoires de Vieilleville.*"

would be annulled and restitution required. But this regulation would not, probably, affect Madame Diane's share.

The cardinal appears to have succeeded. France undoubtedly had arrived at a great crisis in her history; for at that very moment there were deputies assembled in Paris, sent by the Protestants of various towns of France, to propose a confession of faith and rules of ecclesiastical discipline. "A great resolution was needed," Diane told the king; "some decisive act on his part." This was true, but in a contrary sense to that she recommended. The cardinal continued his exhortations to let the Catholic King of Spain have a convincing proof that his most Christian majesty of France was no less firm in the faith than he.

The constable remained neuter, annoyed by the prominent part the cardinal was taking in this matter, conjointly, too, with the fickle Diane. His nephew, D' Andelot, was again a prisoner; De Coligny and De Châtillon were suspected heretics; but, although the blow aimed at the Parliament was to rebound on them, the constable would neither raise hand nor voice to save them. Catherine seems to have taken no part whatever in this affair. She was occupied, probably, in preparing for her oldest daughter's marriage, which was to be celebrated with exceeding pomp. The Palais de Justice, where the deliberations of the Parliament took place, was given up for balls and banquets; their sittings being held, meanwhile, in the convent of the Grands Augustins.

Thither, on the 10th of June, Henri repaired, accompanied by the cardinal and his brother, François de Guise, De Montmorency, Saint André, the two younger Bourbon princes, who had separated from the elder Protestant branch, and several other of his courtiers, officers of the household, etc. Thus numerously attended, he arrived at the convent, and was admitted. No doors, probably, might be closed against the king, and there was no objection to admit him, though such intrusion was almost without a precedent. The proceedings were briefly interrupted; but the king desired the discussion to be continued.

"The judges who had not yet spoken or given their votes did so in the presence of the king with as much unreserve as those who, in the privacy of the assembly, had preceded them. The counsellor Anne du Bourg, "an eloquent and learned man," began his address by "thanking God for having brought the king thither to be present at the decision of such a cause — the cause of our Lord Jesus Christ." " The condemnation of those who, in the midst of the flames, invoke the name of Jesus Christ is not," he said, "a matter of small importance. Shall crimes," he continued, "worthy of death — blasphemies, adulteries, horrible profligacy, perjury — be daily committed in the face of heaven with impunity, and new tortures, new horrors, be every day invented against the men whose sole crime is to have discovered by the light of the Holy Scriptures the turpitude of Rome, and to have demanded a salutary reformation.

The counsellor Du Faur, after a very animated discourse on the abuses of the Church of Rome, concluded with : " Let it be well understood who they are that trouble the peace of the Church, lest perchance it should be said, in the words of Elijah to King Ahab, ' It is thou who troublest Israel ! ' "

These words, said to be levelled at the Cardinal de Lorraine, were immediately applied to the king, who with difficulty restrained his wrath while another speaker — the traitor Le Maistre — endeavoured to refute the charges Du Faur had brought against the Church of Rome, and to give his vote for continuing to treat heresy with unabated rigour. As examples of holy zeal worthy of imitation, he recommended to the consideration of the assembly the crusades against the ancient Albigenses, and the extermination of the modern Vaudois.

The votes should then have been counted. But the king, after consulting with those members of his council who had accompanied him to this conference, ordered the registrar to hand him the report of the whole proceedings, which was not returned.* He then, addressing the assembly, said : " It displeases us greatly to discover that

* " For this reason it is not to be found in the French archives, having probably been destroyed " (H. Martin).

there are persons in our court who have strayed from the true faith. Those who are loyal and true we will ever support; the rest we will punish, as is our duty, to serve as a warning to others." Becoming excited, he turned to the constable and desired him to seize with his own hand the counsellors Du Bourg and Du Faur on their magisterial benches. With much alacrity he executed his sovereign's degrading mandate. A captain of the Scotch guards (Montgomery) then conducted them to the Bastille. The arrest of five other magistrates was ordered that same day; two of whom, Paul de Foix and Du Ferrier, as legists, were among the most eminent men of the sixteenth century.

Some few days after the scene at Les Augustins, royal letters were despatched to all the provincial tribunals, requiring the magistrates to be zealous and active in the destruction of heresy. His majesty deigned to inform them that "having made peace with the King of Spain, the extermination of the heretics, under whatever name— Lutherans, Calvinists, or Reformers—was that which of all things he now had most at heart." Warnings, terribly menacing, bidding them beware of incurring the king's displeasure by any weak yielding to pity or clemency, concluded this royal message.

On the 17th of June the Duke of Alba arrived in Paris, accompanied by several grandees of Spain, and attended by a numerous and splendid retinue, as the representative of Philip II., to espouse Madame Elisabeth of France. The assistance which the two crowns, now in close bonds of amity united, were mutually to render each other, if needful, in the holy war of extermination they with pious zeal were about to engage in, was then discussed and satisfactorily settled by Alba and the constable. The court then began its round of bridal festivities, and there, at least, all was mirth and gladness.

Brilliant balls, where the courtiers and grandees vied with the ladies in the splendour of their costumes, alternate with *fêtes-champêtres* in the grounds of Catherine's Château de Monceaux. The delicate looking child-bride seemed gay and happy, oppressed by no forebodings of the sad future; but her enjoyment of the revelry of the passing hour was somewhat marred by the novel restraints and etiquette of her now important position, her jewels, and her cumbersome finery. Perhaps no fairer vision of youth and gaiety there met the eye than the young Queen of Scotland with her boy-husband at her side, entranced, as he always appeared to be, in the contemplation of her grace and beauty.

On the 20th of June Madame Elisabeth was married at Notre Dame by the Archbishop of Paris. Such a procession of the priesthood, Spanish and French, from the highest dignitaries (conspicuous amongst whom was the Grand Inquisitor) to the lower grades, as attended the nuptials of the gloomy bigot Philip II. with his son's betrothed bride, was probably never before or since seen at any royal wedding. The king and queen, the bride, the bridegroom's representative, followed in capacious and elaborately ornamented carriages; the ladies of the court on their *haquenées* or in litters; the Spanish grandees and French nobles on splendidly caparisoned horses, escorted by a detachment of French and Spanish soldiers, made up a very effective bridal pageant. Yet it attracted little attention; created no enthusiasm among the usually sight-loving people of Paris.

In the midst of these courtly pleasures what was termed the trial of the counsellors Du Bourg and Du Faur was proceeding, and all France was in a state of feverish excitement, agitation, and terror. It was one of the privileges of the Parliament that its members, when any accusation was brought against them, should be judged only by the Chamber of Counsellors in full assembly. But Henri having violated one of their privileges, now set at naught another, and nominated a special commission for that purpose — two or three bishops, the Inquisitor De Mouchy — or Démochurès, as he preferred to be called — the President Saint André, and two counsellors, all sworn to extirpate heresy and condemn the accused.

The festivities of the Spanish marriage being concluded, on the 27th the marriage contract of the Duke of Savoy and Madame Marguerite was signed. The duke, at the beginning of the war a soldier of fortune, with little more than his sword to depend on, having recovered the larger part of his ancestral dominions, with a vague promise of the rest, was now able to appear at the Court of France with a retinue of some importance. Balls, banquets, and masquerades were now to give place to tilts and tournaments. Preparations were made in the large open space in front of the Palais des Tournelles, at the end of the Rue St. Antoine, just under the prison where the offending magistrates were confined.

A tournament invariably put Henri into high spirits; on the present occasion he was unusually elated, the news having been brought him that Du Bourg and Du Faur were sentenced to have their tongues cut out and to be burnt alive. Their boldness of speech in his presence and daring allusions to the profligacy of the court had so thoroughly irritated him that he vowed he would give himself the pleasure of seeing these audacious heretics burnt.

On the 28th the lists were opened, the king and the Duc de Guise holding them against all comers. The Queens of France, Spain, and Scotland, with their ladies, were present in their pavilion. In another sat Diane, still fairest of the fair, though surrounded by daughters and granddaughters, none of whom appear to have inherited her beauty in any striking degree. On the 28th, and again on the 29th, king, princes, and courtiers had displayed their prowess in the presence of the ladies, who distributed the prizes. Henri, as usual, wore Diane's colours, black and white, and greatly distinguished himself in the mock combat. The passage-of-arms was drawing to a close; but before retiring from the lists he was desirous of breaking yet another lance. On the morrow he promised himself a pleasure of a different kind, and the lists would on that day be closed.

Catherine's astrologer, Luigi Guario, in whose predictions she placed great confidence, had some few years back, at her request, "cast Henri's nativity," and given, as the result of his study of the stars, that the king would receive his death-wound in a duel when he had attained his fortieth year. Guario was told that royalty was exempt from the hazards of a duel.* Catherine, remembering the prophecy, and perceiving that the king had invited Montgomery — the captain of the Scotch guards, who had conducted the magistrates to the Bastille — to break a lance with him "*pour l'amour des dames*," sent one of her attendants with a pressing entreaty, to which he gave no heed, that he would continue the pastime no longer. Montgomery in vain endeavoured to excuse himself, by reminding the king that he had already had his turn in the combat; but a second command compelled him to obey.

* Varillas, "*Histoire de Henri II.*"

"He entered the lists and took a lance. The two combatants came violently into collision, and broke their lances with great dexterity; but Montgomery omitted to throw away, as was the custom, the portion of the lance remaining in the hand. He carried it lowered, and in running it came with great force in contact with the king's helmet, and raised his visor. A fragment of the wood entered his eye, and he fell forward on his horse, clinging to his neck, and was carried by the frightened animal to the end of the course. The grooms having assisted the king to dismount, he was carried to the palace, and the most skilful surgeons in France attended, but vainly endeavoured to extract the splinters of wood from his brain. A courier was despatched with all haste to Brussels by the Duke of Alba to bring the famous anatomist Vesale (surgeon to Philip II.) to Paris. He was not, however, more successful than the surgeons who had preceded him" (Vieilleville).

The greatest confusion and terror reigned in the palace and throughout the capital. The king was in a high fever and delirious. On the fourth day he became calm, and the fever left him, when he sent for the queen and desired her to hasten his sister's nuptials. They were celebrated in the dying king's bedchamber on the 9th of July. "It was more like a funeral than a wedding," continues Vieilleville's editor; "for instead of hautbois, violins, and other rejoicings, there were only tears, sobs, sadness, and regrets. The king had already lost the power of speech, and knew no one." On the following day he died, in the forty-first year of his age and twelfth of his reign.

In the blow that had struck down the persecuting monarch in the midst of his courtly revelry, Protestant Europe beheld the arm of the Lord. Many who had wavered between their desire to join the reformers and their dread of persecution, seeing, as they fancied, in the catastrophe that had befallen the king a sign of Heaven's displeasure at the cruel course he had pursued, and his impious compact with the fanatical ruler of Spain, at once embraced the "new doctrines." But his death brought no remission of their sentence to the counsellors Du Bourg and Du Faur. The urgent entreaties of their friends to induce them to retract the opinions they had expressed in favour of mercy and the abolition of persecution, proved unavailing, and, although Henri was not permitted to gloat over the agony of these righteous men's death, the sentence, with all its accompanying horrors, was fully carried out.

"But the race of Valois was condemned; their days numbered; though destined yet for thirty years to struggle at random through the tempests of religious warfare, and finally to disappear in a sea of blood."

THE END.

INDEX

Accoutrements, I., 67.
Adrian VI. (Pope), I., 226 et seq., 232, burning of Lutherans, 233, death of, 238, note.
Alba, Duke of, II., 355 et seq., 360.
Albret, Henri d', King of Navarre, I., 198, 218, 285, 291, m. Madame d'Alençon, 324; II., 16, 84, 111, 113, 140, 171, 324.
Albret, Jeanne d', II., 16, 17, 112, m. Guillaume de la Marck, Duc de Clèves, 115, 213, m. Antoine de Bourbon, Duc de Vendôme, 214 et seq.
Alcazar of Madrid, The, I., 302.
Alençon, Duc d', I., 66, 81, 133, 220, 294, death, 301.
Alençon, Marguerite, Duchesse d', I., 45, 69, 74, 82, 136, 179, 190, 301, 305 et seq., 319 et seq., m. Henri d'Albret, 324; II., Queen of Navarre, 4 et seq., 12, 15, 103, 110, 112, 140, 216 et seq., 324.
Amboise, Cardinal Georges d', I., 24, 34, 110.
Amyot, Jacques, II., 35.
Andelot, D', II., 315 et seq., 322 et seq., 334, 352.
Angoulême, Comte d' (*vide* Francis I).
Angoulême, Duc d', II., 56, Duc d' Orléans, 75, 132, death of, 158.
Angoulême, Duchesse d' (*vide* Savoy, Louise of).
Anjou, Duchess of (*vide* Savoy, Louise of).
Anjou, Princes of (*vide* Guise).
Annebaut, Admiral d', II., 143, 149, 155, 159, 169.
Anne of Brittany, Queen of France, I., funeral of, 1 et seq. (*vide* St. Denis), 10 et seq., life and virtues, 13-17, 160; II., 210.
Arches, Triumphal, first use of, II., 208.
Aumale, Duc d' (*vide* Guise, François de, and Guise, Claude de).
Austria, Margaret of, La Paix des Dames, I., 20, 356; II., 264, 265, 275, 312.

Balafré, Le (*vide* Guise, François de).
Bastille, I., 135.
Béda, II., 13, 15.
Bellay, Guillaume Du, II., 246.
Blois, Castle of, I., 97, 137, 235, 278; II., 1, 32, 104, 139.
Brandenburg, George of, II., 262.
Briandos, Court Fool, II., 161 et seq.
Briçonnet, Bishop of Meaux, I., 319.
Brion, Admiral Chabot de, II., 48 et seq., 89, 96, death, 97 (note).
Brissac, Duc de, II., 245 et seq., 286 et seq.
Brittany, Duchy of, I., 6 (note).
Boissy, Artus de Gouffier, I., 54, 89.
Boissy, Bonnivet, Admiral of France, I., 58, 81, 126, 129 et seq., 161, 188, 201, 247, campaign in Italy, 268 et seq., 276 et seq., death in Battle of Pavia, 286.
Boleyn, Anne, I., 325 et seq.; m. Henry VIII., II., 23, 76, 341.
Bordeaux, II., 206 et seq.
Bourbon, Duc Charles de, I., 30, constable of France, 57, 67, 69 et seq., 81, 82, 87, 88, 114 et seq., 133, 135, 187, 216 et seq., 219-220, 241, conspiracy against the estate of, 242 et seq., leaves France for Spain, 257, lieutenant-general of Imperial Army, 272, 282, 286, 290, campaign in Italy and death in the assault on Rome, 330 et seq.
Bourg, Anne du, II., 353, 357 et seq., executed for heresy, 358.
Boyer, Antoine, II., 273.
Brandon, Charles (*vide* Suffolk, Duke of).
Budé, Guillaume, I., 66, 145.
Calais, I., 139; II., 315 et seq.
Calvin, II., 14.
Cambray, Treaty of, I., 356; II., 10.
Carloix, Vincent, II., 160.
Carriages, Use of, II., 6, 7, 9.
Cellini, Benvenuto, II., 118 et seq., 127.
Chambord, Château de, II., 104 et seq.
Charles VIII. of France, I., 1, 6, 11, 16, 39, 160.
Charles V. of Spain, I., 18, 20, 26, 61, 86, 89 et seq., 104, betrothal to Louise, 105, 125, m. Isabella of Portugal, 126, 143 et seq., 161 et seq., Emperor of Germany, 165, 175 et seq., in England, 178, 193, 195 et seq., Diet of Worms, 206,

207, 217, war with France, 219 et seq., 252 et seq., 274, 281, 289, 292, imprisonment of Francis, 294 et seq., 301, 302 et seq., 335, 346, 347 et seq., 356, 359; II., 18, 20, 49 et seq., 58, 59, 60, war with France, 63 et seq., 85, 87, truce, 89, Aigues-Mortes, 90 et seq., 98 et seq., through France to Ghent, 100 et seq., 110, subjugation of Ghent, 114, campaign in Algiers, 128 et seq., 139, invasion of France, 148 et seq., treat of Crépy, 150, 159, 189, 202 et seq., 240, 248 et seq., war with German Princes, 253 et seq., treaty of Public Peace, 265, siege of Metz, 266 et seq., 277, destruction of Terouenne, 278, 280 et seq., abdication, 297, 313, 314, death, 337.

Châteaubriand, Comtesse de (*vide* Foix, Françoise de).
Château de Blois, I., 1 et seq., 14 et seq., 32, 81.
Châtillon, Cardinal de, II., 171, 330, 331, 334, 352.
Châtillon, Général de, I., 221.
Chaumont, I., 13.
Chenonceaux, Duchesse de (*vide* Poitiers, Diane de).
Chevalier Bayard, I., 25, 30, 72, 75, 222, death, 269, 270, character, 271.
Claude, daughter of Anne of Brittany, I., 18, m. Dauphin Francis, 22 et seq., Duchess of Brittany and Comtesse d'Angoulême, 23, 28, Queen of France, 36, 44, 66, 73, 82, 84, "Sainte Claude," 85, coronation of, 106 et seq., 172, 179, 183, 190, 193, 241, death, 277.
Clement VII. (Pope) (*vide* Medici, Cardinal Giulio).
Clermont, Comte de, I., 116, christening at Moulins, 119, death, 123 (note).
Coligny, Gaspard de, II., 241, 285, Admiral, 300, 310, 311, 332, 352.
Colonna, Prospero, I., 226, 267.
Concordat, The, I., 97–103.
Condé, Prince de, II., 221.
Costumes; of the Nobility, I., 43 et seq., 185 et seq., 193; II., 215 et seq., 232, 290; of the *bourgeoisie*, II., 101 et seq., 227, 233.
Cranmer, Archbishop of Canterbury, II., 23.
Crossing the Alps, I., 70 et seq.
Danés, Pierre, I., 147.
Diane, Madame (*vide* Poitiers, Diane de).

Dolet, Étienne, II., 162 et seq., execution of, 163 et seq.
Dorea, Andrea, I., 352 et seq.; II., 68, 128 et seq.
Dorset, Marquis of, I., 185.
Duel, Judicial, II., 192 et seq.
Duprat, Antoine (Chancellor), I., 56, 60, 80, 97, 98 et seq., Cardinal, 100, 133, 220, 229, 238, 243, 322, Archbishop of Sens, 349; death, II., 42–45.
Edward VI. of England, II., 168, 225, betrothed to daughter of Henry II., 242, death, 279.
Eleanor of Austria, I., 20, 24, 253, 308, m. Francis I., 358; II., 2, 3, coronation of, 4 et seq., 8, 50, 73, 83, 87 et seq., 91, 139, 177.
Elisabeth, daughter of Henri II., m. to Philip of Spain, II., 345, 356 et seq.
Elizabeth, Queen of England, II., 341 et seq., treaty of Calais, 343.
Ely, Bishop of, I., 41, 131, 133 et seq.
Enghien, François de Bourbon, Comte d', campaign against Spain, II., 141 et seq., battle of Cerisola, 144, death, 146 (note).
Erasmus, I., 146, 149, 322, 323.
Este, Anna of, II., betrothed to Duc d'Aumale, 214 et seq., 221.
Este, Herculano d', Duke of Ferrara, m. Renée, daughter of Louis XII., I., 348 et seq.
Étampes, Comtesse de (*vide* Anne of Brittany).
Étampes, Duchesse d' (*vide* Pisseleu, Anne de).
Faith, Defender of the (*vide* Henry VIII.).
Farnese, Ottavio, II., 247 et seq.
Ferdinand of Spain, I., 19, 26, 62, 64 et seq., death, 85.
Ferdinand of Spain, II., 4, 130, 300.
Ferrara, Duke of, I., 142.
Field of the Cloth of Gold, I., 185–192.
Fleuranges, I., 23, 49, 75, 81, 192, 285; death, II., 73.
Foix, Françoise de, Comtesse de Châteaubriand, I., 59, 83, 84 et seq., 88, 115, 198, *maîtresse-en-titre*, 278, 312, 315 et seq.
Foix, Gaston de, I., death, 21.
Foix, Lesparre de, I., 198 et seq., death, 200.

INDEX

Foix, Lutrec, Maréchal de, I., 59, 70, 75, 81, 83, 88, 223 et seq., 228, 241, 309, 341, 352, death, 353.
Fontainebleau, I., 13; II., 16, 56, 106, 120, 126, 150, 169.
Fra-Giocondo, I., 15.
France, Diane of, m. Horatio Farnese, II., 276 et seq.
Francis I., Comte D'Angoulême, m. Princesse Claude, I., 23 et seq., Duke of Brittany, 30 et seq., King of France, 36, 37 et seq., entry into Paris, 42 et seq., 45 et seq., 53, 54 et seq., 58 et seq., invasion of Italy, 67 et seq., 75, 76 et seq., return to France, 81 et seq., Paris, 93 et seq., 97 et seq., conflict with Parliament, 101 et seq., licentiousness of court, 106 et seq., 116 et seq., 126, 132 et seq., 138 et seq., 143, Father of Letters, 146, 148 et seq., 161 et seq., 170, 172, 175 et seq., Guines, 183 et seq., 195 et seq., 203, 204, 205, 217, war with Charles, 219 et seq., Milan lost, 227, war with England, 232, 238, conspiracy against Charles de Bourbon, 243 et seq., legitimacy of Francis, 248, 259 et seq., campaign in Italy, 276 et seq., Pavia, 282 et seq., capture by Lannoy, 286, 287 et seq., imprisonment, 296, 302 et seq., treaty of Madrid, 307, 309, 315, 318, 320, 327, 345, 350, 352, La Paix des Dames, 356, 357 et seq., m. Eleanor of Portugal, 358; II., 2, 3, coronation of Eleanor, 4 et seq., 10 et seq., 14, 19 et seq., 34 et seq., 49 et seq., 57, war with Charles, 63 et seq., alliance with Turkey, 82 et seq., 87, truce, 89, Aigues-Morte, 90 et seq., 98, 103 et seq., 110, 117 et seq., war against Spain and England, 131 et seq., Rochelle, 134 et seq., Crépy, 150, 154, first naval campaign, 158-160, 166 et seq., death, 169, burial, 179 et seq.
Francis, Dauphin, birth of and betrothal to Mary of England, I., 124, 127, 129, hostage in Spain, 309, 311, ransomed, 356 et seq.; death, II., 69.
Francis, Dauphin, II., 186, 225.
Fregosa, Ottavio, I., 66.
French Parliament (*vide* Francis I.).
Freundsberg, Georges, I., 283, 331.
Gabelle et Gabeleurs (*vide* Taxation).
Garde, Baron de la, II., 156, 198 et seq.
Ghent, II., 110 et seq.
Goujon, Jean, I., 114.

Granvelle, Bishop of Arras, II., 331 et seq., 340.
Greenwich, I., 126, betrothal ceremonies, 127 et seq., 180.
Grève, Place de, I., 321; II., 33, 227, 237, 331, 334, 347 et seq.
Grey, Lady Jane, II., 279.
Guario, Luigi, II., 359.
Guasto, Del, II., 141 et seq.
Guinegate, Battle of, I., 25.
Guines, meeting of Henry and Francis, I., 185 et seq.
Guise, Charles de, Archbishop of Rheims, II., 171 et seq., 190 et seq., 203, 238, Cardinal de Lorraine, 244, 296, 302, 312, 320, 322, 327, 331 et seq., 341, 348, 349 et seq.
Guise, Claude de, Marquis de Mayenne, II., 172, 177, Duc d'Aumale, 244.
Guise, François de, II., 133, 146 et seq., 169, 171 et seq., 189 et seq., 203, Duc d'Aumale, 210, betrothed to Anna d'Este, 214 et seq., Prince of Anjou, 222, Le Balafré, 223, Duc de Guise, 244, 245 et seq., Metz, 266 et seq., 282, 285, 303 et seq., lieutenant-general for the king, 314, 315, capture of Calais, 316 et seq., 327 et seq., 333 et seq., 339, 341, 344, 346, 353, 358.
Guise, Mary of, m. James V. of Scotland, II., 80, 225.
Havre, founded, I., 139; II., 155.
Henri II., I., hostage in Spain for Francis, 309, 311, ransomed, 356 et seq., Duc d'Orleans; II., 23, m. Catherine de' Medici, 25, 50 et seq., 62, 72, dauphin, 75, 86, 146, Henri II., 170 et seq., character, 173, 193 et seq., 198, coronation, 203 et seq., 213 et seq., 220 225, Paris, 227, 229, 230 et seq., 237 et seq., Boulogne, 241-248, union with Protestant princes against Charles, 254 et seq., occupancy of Metz, Toul and Verdun, 258 et seq., 281 et seq., 288, alliance with Pope Paul IV., 296, five years' truce, 300, St. Quentin, 310, war with England, 309 et seq., 312, 314, capture of Calais, 315-316, 317 et seq., 321 et seq., 336 et seq., 341, 343, *La paix Malheureuse* 344, 347 et seq., death from accident in tournament, 359-361.
Henry VIII., I., 8, 24, 26 et seq., 41, 42, 48, 86, 124, 126, 127 et seq., 136, 138 et seq., 144, 162 et seq., 172, 175 et seq., Guines, 183, 185 et seq., Defender of the Faith, 215, war with France, 219 et seq., 232-273, 325 et seq., divorce from

Katharine, 343, 347; II., 10, 18, 21 et seq., m. Anne Boleyn, 23, 76, 79, 132, 139, 146, 149, 166, death, 167.
Heretics, persecution of, I., 319, 320 et seq., II., 94, 133, 137, Vaudois, 150, 163 et seq., 199, 227, *chambre ardente*, 238, 246, interim, 251, 252 et seq., 331, 334, 335, 338, 347 et seq., 361.
Honneur, Filles d' and Dames de Des— I., 40.
Hunting, I., 13; II., 86, 103, 118, 139.
Infanta of Spain, II., 115.
Isabella of Portugal, m. Charles V., I., 126, 308.
James V. of Scotland, II., 77, m. Princesse Madeleine of France, 79, m. Mary of Guise, 80, 84, death of, 132 (note).
Jarnac, Chabot de, II., 192 et seq.
Jeanne de France, I., 6.
Joanna of Aragon (The Demented Queen of Spain), I., 86; II., death of, 296.
Julian II. (Pope), I., 8, 326.
Julian III. (Pope), II., 240, 247 et seq.
Katharine of Aragon, Queen of England, I., 124, 128 et seq., 177, 180, Guines, 185 et seq., 325; II., 22.
La Fayette, M. de, I., 131.
Lannoy, I., 279 et seq., Pavia, 286, 308, 327.
Leo X., Pope, I., 9, 25, 64, 75 et seq., 87, 98, 108, 112, 140 et seq., 149-151, 157, 164, 170, 177 et seq., 180, 194 et seq., death, 226.
Leonardo da Vinci, I., 109 et seq., death, 111.
Leyva, Antonio da, I., 280 et seq.
Longueville, Duc de, Louis d' Orleans, I., 25 et seq., 44.
Lorraine, Cardinal de (*vide* Guise, Charles de).
Lorraine, Cardinal Jean de, II., 171, death, 244.
Lorraine, Duc de, II., 331.
Lorraine, Duchesse de, II., 330.
Louis XI., I., 6.
Louis XII., I., 2, 6, 8, 9, 14, 16, 19 et seq., 24, 26, m. **Mary of England**, 27 et seq., death, 32, character and reforms of, 33 et seq.
Louise, Madame (*vide* Savoy, Louise of).
Louise, d. Francis and Claude, II., 89, betrothal to Charles V., 105, death, 125.
Loyola, Ignatius, II., 39, Society of Jesus founded, 40, 41.

Luther, Martin, I., 149, 151 et seq., 154, 158, 170, 201, Papal bull burned, 202, 206 et seq., 212 et seq., doctrine, 319, 320; II., 94, 153, death, 154.
Lyons, II., 70 et seq., 81.
Madeleine, d. Francis I., m. to James V., and death, II., 79, 80.
Marguerite, d. Henri II., m. Duke of Savoy, II., 345, 357.
Marignan, Battle of, I., 73 et seq., 138; II., 144.
Marot, Clement, I., 145, Psalms of; II., 138, death, 139 (note).
Mary of England, Queen of France, I., 26 et seq., 30 et seq., Queen Dowager, 42, 45 et seq., m. Charles Brandon, Duke of Suffolk, 49 et seq., The Duchess-queen, 51, death, 25, 128 et seq.
Mary of England, d. of Henry VIII., and Katharine of Aragon, betrothed to the Dauphin Francis I., 124, betrothed to Philip of Spain, 126, 127 et seq., 182, betrothed to Charles V., 219, 311; II., 279 et seq., Queen of England, 219, m. Philip of Spain, 281, 282, Bloody Mary, 283, 293 et seq., 297, 317 et seq., 323, death, 340.
Mary, Queen of Scotland (*vide* Stuart, Mary).
Maximilian of Germany, I., 86 et seq., 92, 143, 144, et seq., 152, death, 157, 159, 160.
Mayenne, Marquis de (*vide* Guise, Claude de).
Medici, Cardinal Giulio, I., 226, Pope Clement VII., 274, 284, 328, 333, sack of Rome, 335 et seq., 351, 359, 360; II., 21 et seq., 24, 28 et seq., death 30.
Medici, Catherine de', II., 23, m. Henry d'Orléans, 25, 71, 178, 184 et seq., 204, 219, 225, 235, 253 et seq., 269, 272, 273 et seq., 288, 303, 312, 321 et seq., 326, 352, 356, 359.
Medici, Cosmo de', II., 262, 286.
Mendoza, II., 181 et seq.
Metz, II., 261, siege of, 266 et seq.
Michael Angelo, I., 110, 360.
Montausier, Duc de, I., 16.
Montgomery, Captain Scottish Guards, II., 353, causes death of Henri II., 359 et seq.
Montluc, Blaise de, II., 141 et seq., 286 et seq., 315, 334.
Montmorency, Anne de, Constable of France, I., 357 et seq.; II., 13, 15, 32, 65, 73, 86, et seq., 93, 94 et seq., 111, 146, 169 et seq., 189, 207, Bordeaux, 209 et seq., 214, 237, 245, 248, 251

et seq., 260, 278, 296, 300, St. Quentin, 310, 314, 327 et seq., 336 et seq., 341, 344, 346, 352.
Most Christian King (*vide* Henry VIII. and Francis I., I., 8).
Moulins Châteade, I., 116, et seq.; II., 214 et seq.
Music, I., 43.
Nantes, Cathedral of, I., 10.
Navarre, King of (*vide* Albret, Henri d').
Navarre, Queen of (*vide* Alençon, Duchesse d').
Navarro, Pedro, I., 64, 70, 71 et seq., 81.
Navy, II., 154 et seq.
Notre-Dame de Paris, Cathedral of, I., 3, 134.
Notre-Dames des Champs, Church of, I., 2.
One hundred and one grievances, I., 207.
Oppède, Baron d', II., 198 et seq.
Orléans, Duc Charles d', II., 110, 112.
Palice, M. de la, I., 221, 276.
Pallisy, Bernard, II., 271.
Papal Court (Leo X.), I., 76 et seq., 108, 150.
Paré, Ambroise, II., 224.
Paris, I., 1, 2, 38, 42 et seq., 93 et seq., 97 et seq., 106.
Paul III. (Pope), II., 37, 60 et seq., 85, 88, 200, death, 240.
Paul IV. (Pope), II., 295, 301 et seq., 347.
Pavia, Battle of, I., 282 et seq.
Philip of Spain, II., 113, Duke of Milan, 115, m. Mary of England, 281, King of England and Spain, Emperor of Germany, 297 et seq., 302, St. Quentin, 310, war with France, 311 et seq., 316, 319, 335 et seq., Câteau-Cambresis, 344, m. Elisabeth of France, 345, 356 et seq.
Pisseleu, Anne de (M'selle d'Heilly), Duchesse d'Étampes, I., 313, 314 et seq., *maîtresse-en-titre*, 317, 344, 351; II., 9, 12, 15, 51, 52, 76, 83, 89, 91 et seq., 110 et seq., 124, 148 et seq., 155, 159, 163, 177, banished from court, 188, 192.
Poitiers, Diane de, I., 262, 266; II., 51, 76, 97, 169, 171 et seq., *maîtresse-en-titre*, 175, 178, 184 et seq., 202, 215, 219, 229, 238, 244, 253, 269 et seq., Duchesse de Chenonceaux, 273, 289, 292, 296, 303, 322, 349, 351, 358.
Poitiers, Jean de, I., 262 et seq.
Pragmatic Sanction, Repeal of, I., 97, 98 et seq.
Quintana, I., 24.

Rabelais, II., 165 et seq.
Raphael, I., 112 et seq.
Ravenna, I., 21, 64.
Reines blanches, I., 6.
Renée, Princess of France, I., 39, 61, 89, 181, 241, m. Herculano d' Este, Duke of Ferrara, 348 et seq.
Rheims, Archbishop of (*vide* Guise, Charles de).
Rheims, I., 40.
Robertet, Florimond, I., 54.
Rochelle, II., 134 et seq.
Rome, Sack of, I., 230 et seq.
Royal banquets, I., 13, 16, 37, 46, 120 et seq., 134, 136, 137, 350; II., 100 et seq., 358.
Saint André, II., 161, 163, 171, 177.
Saint Denis, Abbey of, I., 1, 3, 29, 40 et seq., 107.
Saint Germain, I., 13, 106; II., 167, 170, 193, 197.
Saint John's, Prior of, I., 131, 133 et seq.
Saint Remi, Cathedral of, I., 41.
St. Angelo, Castle of, I., 336, 338; II., 304.
Savoy, Louise of, Regent-mother, I., 17, 31, 36, Duchesse d'Angoulême and d'Anjou, 53, 56, 66, 74, 82, 84, 88, 95, "Mère Sotte," 96, 99, 114, 115 et seq., 122, 169, 179, 190, 194, 195, 203, 216, 220, 221, avarice of, 229, 230, 241, revenge on Charles de Bourbon, 242 et seq., 272, 294 et seq., 312 et seq., persecution of Lutheranism, 320 et seq., La Paix des Dames, 356, death, 359.
Savoy, Philibert Emanuel, Duke of, II., 89, 93, 310, 340, m. Marguerite of France, 345, 357.
Saxony, Frederick, Elector of, I., 152, 155, 157, 164.
Saxony, Maurice, Elector of, II., 250 et seq., 256 et seq., public peace, 265, death, 279.
Selim I., I., 140, 141.
Semblançay, I., 225 et seq., 229, death, 230.
Sforza, Duke of Milan, II., 46 et seq.
Sion, Cardinal, I., 63, 72.
Soderini, Cardinal, I., 226.
Solyman, Sultan, I., 287, 310; II., 19, 38, 57, 82 et seq., 130, 251.
Somerset, Duke of, II., 168.
Sorbonne, The, II., 181 et seq.

INDEX

Spurs, Battle of the, I., 25 (*vide* Guinegate).
States General, I., 21, 103.
Ste. Chapelle, I., 105 et seq.
Stuart, Mary, Queen of Scotland, birth of, II., 132, 204, betrothed to Dauphin Francis, carried off to France, 225, 321 et seq., m. Francis, 324 et seq., 340, 356.
Suffolk, Charles Brandon, Duke of, I., 27, 28, 30, 32, 41, 45 et seq., m. Dowager-queen Mary, 49 et seq., 185.
Sumptuary Laws, II., 234.
Tavannes, Seigneur de, II., 254, 255, 285.
Taxation in France, I., 171 et seq., national debt founded, 239; The *Gabelle*, II., 134, Bordeaux Gabeleurs, 206 et seq., 215, 230, 319, 320.
Terouenne, destruction of, II., 278.
Toul, II., 261.
Tournay, I., 27, 138, 174, 219, 221.
Tournelles, Palais des, I., 14, 16, 29, 32, 93, 96, 110, 132, 240; II., 9, 89, 108, 271, 289.
Tournon, Cardinal de, II., 164, 198.
Trémouille, M. de la, I., 221, 276.
Trivulzio, Marshall, I., 223, death, 224.
Utrecht, Cardinal d' (*vide* Adrian VI., Pope).
Valentinois, Duchesse de, II., 178 (*vide* Poitiers, Diane de).
Vaux, Sir Nicholas, I., 131, 133 et seq.
Vendôme, Antoine de Bourbon, Duc de., II., m. to Jeanne d' Albret, 214 et seq.
Verdun, II., 261.
Vesale, II., 360.
Vincennes, I., 13.
Vinci, Leonardo da, II., 122.
Vio, Cardinal da, I., 152 et seq.
Wolsey, Cardinal, I., 26 et seq., 48, 50, 126, 139, 174, 176 et seq., 181, 185 et seq., 217, 226, 274.
Worcester, Earl of, I., 131, 133 et seq.
Worms, Trial of Martin Luther, I., 209 et seq.
Xativa, Fortress of, I., 302.
Ximenes, Cardinal, Archbishop of Toledo, I., 86, 90.

www.ingramcontent.com/pod-product-compliance
Lightning Source LLC
Chambersburg PA
CBHW030214170426
43201CB00006B/79